web publishing

with Adobe PageMill 2

web publishing

with Adobe PageMill 2

The Ultimate Guide to Designing
Professional Web Pages

Daniel Gray

VENTANA

Web Publishing With Adobe PageMill 2
Copyright ©1997 by Daniel Gray

Library of Congress Cataloging-in-Publication Data
Gray, Daniel, 1961-
    Web Publishing With Adobe PageMill 2 / Daniel Gray. —1st ed.
        p.   cm.
    Includes index.
    IBSN 1-56604-458-8
    1. HTML (Document markup language) 2. World Wide Web (Information retrieval system) 3. Adobe PageMill. 4. Electronic publishing.
I. Title.
QA76.76.H94G734 1996
005.75—dc20   96-19509
                                                          CIP

First Edition 9 8 7 6 5 4 3 2 1

Printed in the United States of America

Ventana Communications Group, Inc.
P.O. Box 13964
Research Triangle Park, NC 27709-3964
919.544.9404
FAX 919.544.9472
http://www.vmedia.com

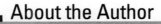

About the Author

Daniel Gray manages the editorial content of *PrePRESS Main Street* and writes for a number of graphics and Web-related publications. His books about the computer and graphic arts fields include *Looking Good Online* and *The Comprehensive Guide to CorelWEB Graphics Studio* (both published by Ventana), and the best-selling *Inside CorelDRAW!* (New Riders).

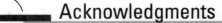

Acknowledgments

This book would not have been possible without the hard work and dedication of the entire staff at Ventana. In particular, I would like to offer my thanks to: Judy Wilson, my project editor, for her wisdom and patience as we steered this project through a long and circuitous path; Neweleen Trebnik for signing and sticking with me as the road got twisty; JJ Hohn, Patrick Bragg, and all the good folks responsible for helping to pull together the CD-ROM; Brian Little for his astute technical editing; Susan Klopfer for helping me stay on track; and Judy Flynn for her excellent copy editing.

To the wonderful folks at Adobe who allowed this book to happen—Kevin Wandryk, Kelly Davis, Rebecca Michals, and all the PageMill developers, tech support folks, and Q&A crew—a big thank you! It's been an honor to have been able to write about such an insanely great product.

To Jaime Levy and David Yip for their insight, observations, and good humor. To Steve Guttman at Fractal Design; Jane Chuey at Macromedia; Ellen Elias at O'Reilly; and Mike Fairbarn at RM Classic (for the use of the wonderful auto photographs), many thanks for your kindness. May your ways be paved with light.

To my comrades at PrePRESS, with whom I live and breathe the Web every day, I've never had the pleasure of working with a better team. Thank you Bob, Mike S., Joe, Allyson, Rob, and Mike P., king of all scanners.

And of course, to my family, my loving wife and those two howling wolverines whom I've ignored and neglected through the course of this book…one day Daddy won't be chained to the computers anymore.

Contents

Introduction

Page creation for the World Wide Web (WWW) was once the exclusive province of the UNIX gurus. If you aren't familiar with UNIX, it is a powerful operating system (or set of instructions for computers) with an arcane and difficult-to-use interface. Thankfully, times have changed. No longer does the chore of building Web pages fall into the exclusive realm of our friends, the pocket protector-wearing techie-nerds. No longer can Web page design be considered a tedious coding chore, best left for the techno few.

Adobe Systems, Inc.—the company that revolutionized the print-publishing world with such products as PostScript, Illustrator, and Photoshop—has moved its magic to the electronic publishing world, bringing Web publishing to regular-type folks, not just UNIX gurus. Adobe's PageMill, the first application to make Web page construction easy, operates in a completely painless What You See Is What You Get (WYSIWYG—pronounced "whiz-ee-wig") environment, using a drag-and-drop interface. PageMill is so easy to use you won't have to understand or use difficult coding procedures to create your Web pages. With a WYSIWYG environment, you always know what your Web pages will look like, without having to preview them in a browser. This saves time and eliminates nasty surprises. Drag-and-drop editing lets you quickly move objects—whether they're images, blocks of text, or hyperlinks—from place to place and page to page. Just click on the object you want to move and drag it to where you want to place it.

 ## A Little PageMill History

PageMill made its first showing at Macworld Boston, in early August 1995. The Macintosh community immediately embraced the product, with none other than Apple Fellow (and perennial pundit) Guy Kawasaki heralding it as "the PageMaker of the Internet." The tiny booth of PageMill's original developer, Ceneca Communications, was constantly packed five and six deep with enthusiastic show goers.

The attention was well deserved. At long last, there was a product that allowed mere mortals to build classy pages for the World Wide Web. Kawasaki and other Mac mavens were, no doubt, ecstatic that such an application had arrived first on the Macintosh platform. For if 1967 is best remembered for its Summer of Love, some might remember 1995 best for its Summer of Windows 95 Hype. The Macintosh needed a "killer app" and PageMill happened at just the right time.

Adobe Systems was quick to react. The company moved to acquire Ceneca just a month or so after PageMill's triumphant debut. Adobe rushed PageMill to market, releasing it on October 31, 1995. The program was first released for sale for delivery over the Internet, with packaged software following soon afterward. In its first month of release, Adobe reportedly shipped a hefty 30,000 copies, ensuring a rapid return on its wise investment.

The software engineers that originally wrote PageMill—Bill Kraus, John Peterson, Robert Seidl, and Roger Spreen—formed Ceneca as a start-up operation. When Ceneca first showed PageMill at Macworld Boston, the company had been in existence for only a short time. Some industry watchers speculate the deal was easily worth eight figures.

While some might say that the American Dream is dead—only to have been replaced by the State Lottery—it is clearly still alive and kicking in the software industry.

Why PageMill Is So Cool

The best way to understand why PageMill is such a beautiful thing is to take a quick look under the hood of an everyday Web page. Just as only a serious gearhead can fully appreciate the workings of a high-performance engine, only a serious codehead can fully appreciate the underpinnings of a cool Web page.

For instance, check out the snappy little Web page illustrated in Figure I-1. You're looking at a page created for RM Classic Cars, a purveyor of fine antique automobiles, as it appears when viewed with the Netscape Navigator browser. The 1934 Duesenberg SJ LaGrande Dual Phaeton looks so nice, one might consider placing a call to the bank.

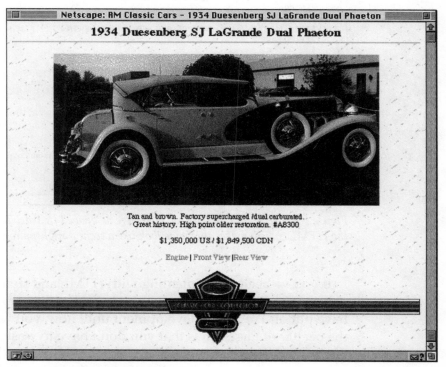

Figure I-1: Get out the checkbook!

On the other hand, Figure I-2 doesn't look quite as inviting (an understatement). This figure shows how the very same Web page looks in a text editor (in this case, Apple's SimpleText). What's all that nasty-looking gobbledygook, you ask? Any grizzled, veteran Web page builder (or savvy 12-year-old) will tell you that it's HTML (HyperText Markup Language) code. But to the uninitiated, it seems more like HTML-hell.

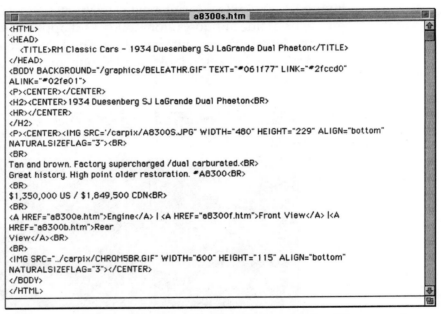

Figure I-2: The 1934 Duesenberg Web page as viewed in TeachText—note how the HTML coding makes this page look like a techno-nightmare!!

If you've been experimenting with HTML and trying to develop a good page, or if you've shuddered at the very thought and have put off Web page development until now, you will soon find the beauty of PageMill is that you don't have to waste half your life just trying to create your first page. In short, you don't have to memorize and then apply a list of commands that makes the periodic table seem like the Yankees' lineup on opening day. You can forget the codes and concentrate on your design, instead.

PageMill hides all that scary HTML coding and allows you to build pages in a WYSIWYG environment. Figure I-3 illustrates how the very same Web page looks within PageMill; compare it to the two figures that preceded it. Look Ma, no codes! The Web page appears in PageMill in a form that closely emulates a "real" Web browser. The program is so slick that you should be able to build your first Web page within 15 minutes...without knowing a lick of HTML coding.

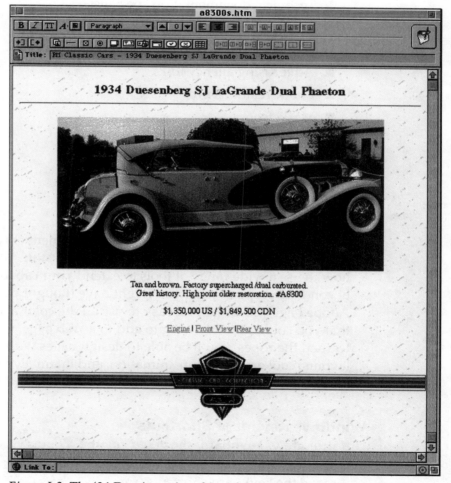

Figure I-3: The '34 Duesie as viewed in Adobe PageMill 2. Compare this figure to Figure I-2 and you'll quickly see how much easier it is to use PageMill than to write HTML code.

Who Needs This Book?

Web Publishing With Adobe PageMill 2 is intended for the beginning-to-intermediate PageMill user who is not a techie; it has been designed to get you up and running in nothing flat. The potential audience for this book is huge and surely includes:

- Graphic designers
- Multimedia developers
- Technical documentation specialists
- Teachers and students
- Business owners
- Advertising agency folks
- Public relations pros
- Marketeers
- Webmasters (fledgling and otherwise)
- And even Hobbyists

What's Inside?

This book starts off with the most basic of maneuvers and works its way into some very cool and sophisticated stuff. You'll learn how to use a wide range of tools to extend your capabilities far beyond the scope of what you might have thought possible. Adobe PageMill 2 makes it easy to use all the color and images that you could possibly want to add to a Web page. Once you've learned the ropes, you'll be able to design pages with intricate layouts, cool graphics, fun animation, and interactive forms.

Windows Keyboard Shortcuts

Unfortunately, keyboard shortcuts for the Windows version of PageMill were not yet available at press time. However, you can download the keyboard shortcuts from this book's Online Updates (http://www.vmedia.com/updates).

How This Book Is Organized

Web Publishing With Adobe PageMill 2 is arranged in five sections:

- Part 1: "PageMill Basics" shows you how to become productive right out of the gate. You'll learn how to work with text, graphics, forms, tables, and frames.

- Part 2: "Good Design" helps you get your message across in style. You'll begin by focusing on the needs of your audience, then move on to design issues, problems, and solutions.

- Part 3: "Pumping Up PageMill" provides the lowdown on how to handle things that PageMill doesn't do, such as moving files, keeping track of your visitors, and linking to databases. You'll also learn the basics of Web site management.

- Part 4: "Resources for Web Page Builders" delivers a host of sources and product reviews to make you a more productive Web page architect. It includes a rundown on text conversion tools, cool typefaces, powerful graphics programs, and Web page animation.

- Part 5: "Appendices" guides you through this book's CD-ROM and walks you through installing PageMill 2.

Online Updates

As we all know, the Internet is constantly changing. As hard as we've tried to make our information current, the truth is that new sites will come online as soon as this book goes to press (and continually thereafter). Ventana provides an excellent way to tackle this problem and to keep the information in the book up-to-date: the *Web Publishing With Adobe PageMill 2* Online Updates. You can access this valuable resource via Ventana's World Wide Web site at http://www.vmedia.com/updates.html. Once there, you'll find updated material relevant to *Web Publishing With Adobe PageMill 2*, as well as the Windows keyboard shortcuts.

Hardware & Software Requirements

You don't need a killer Mac or PC to create Web pages with Adobe PageMill. Version 2 asks for a minimum of a 68020 processor-equipped color Mac running System 7 or later, along with 4MB of RAM available to PageMill. Adobe recommends a 60840 or better with 6MB available to the program, along with System 7.5. In addition, you'll need 3.5MB of space free on your hard drive, and Adobe recommends installing QuickTime 2.1 or later.

On the PC side, you'll need a modestly equipped Windows 95 machine. (As we went to press, final Windows 95 hardware requirements were not yet available.)

It's even possible to create pages on a machine without an Internet connection. There's no inherent need to be hooked up to a corporate network or even an Internet Service Provider (ISP) while creating pages. Road warriors can create Web pages while on the go, whether they are at a remote site or at cruising altitude. Once your pages are lookin' good, you can plug in, log on to the Net, and beam 'em up.

And while this book doesn't provide a copy of PageMill, it does include just about everything else you will need to create exciting, effective Web pages.

 ## Fire Up the Mill!

Since its introduction in 1995, PageMill has represented the best Web page creation application for novices and professionals alike. PageMill 2 has upped the ante. Together with a copy of the program, this book will help you to create awesome, effective Web pages in record time. By the time you finish Chapter 1, you'll be tagging text and hyperlinking like a pro! Without further ado, let's get down to business.

PageMill Basics

Getting Started With Text

PageMill 2 makes Web page creation a breeze by hiding the arduous task of HTML (HyperText Markup Language) coding. This benevolent approach is at the core of the program's continued success. Like it or not, HTML coding lies beneath every Web page, and it's never a treat to create. Writing HTML code by hand is akin to crafting a little program. The beauty of PageMill is that you never have to deal with HTML code if you really don't want to. Rest assured, you can still tinker with the code if you're so inclined. While the first version of the program hid the HTML source code entirely, version 2 allows you to "hack itx out by hand" with its integrated ASCII text editor.

What This Chapter Covers

This chapter will help you learn how to produce text pages with PageMill. Before long, you'll be churning out Web pages like a pro—pages that include such basic text features as heading and body styles, alignment, type sizes, and linking (advanced text features, such as tables, forms, and frames are covered in Chapter 3). As this chapter progresses, you'll learn a bit about the HTML code that underlies every Web page.

Why get into the code? Your effectiveness in building Web pages will be limited if you can't deal with some raw HTML once in a while. It's strong medicine, but it's inherently palatable—once you've acquired a taste for it. To this end, we're sneaking in a touch of code, so that you learn through doing (and possibly through osmosis). We'll begin with an overview of the PageMill environment, then cover a bit of HTML gobbledegook before finishing up the chapter with a quick little exercise. The second half of the chapter is devoted to creating your own text-based page, in a step-by-step exercise.

Working in the PageMill Environment

The PageMill environment is uncluttered and free from "featuritis." The program allows you to have many Web page windows open at one time, and in fact, this multiple document interface is key to its operation. With more than one Web page open, it's easy to drag and drop images, text, and links between pages. Although (for some) the act of dragging and dropping can take a bit of adjustment, it ultimately saves time and keystrokes.

If you've grown weary of bloated word processing programs with bewildering interfaces, you're in for a treat. PageMill's streamlined interface consists of a toggling main window along with three floating palettes. (There's also an "out-of-place" image editing window, but we'll delve into that in the next chapter.)

The Main Window

PageMill's main window has two personalities. Clicking on the large button at the top right-hand corner toggles the window between *Edit* and *Preview* modes. (The pen and paper icon denotes Edit mode; the world icon represents Preview mode.) You'll spend most of your time in edit mode while developing Web pages. Figure 1-1 offers a summary view of the Edit window and its features, by listing the title of each button. PageMill is a very polite program. If you forget the function of a button, there's no need to dig out the manuals. As the cursor passes over each button, a definition will conveniently pop up. The first few chapters of this book will explain each section of the Edit window in detail.

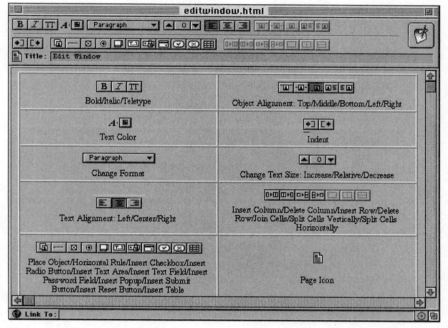

Figure 1-1: The PageMill Window in Edit Mode (as shown by the pen and paper icon). Clicking on the big button at the top right switches to Preview Mode (denoted by the world icon).

The Preview mode mimics how a Web page looks when viewed in a Web browser, such as Netscape Navigator or Microsoft Internet Explorer. Preview mode is quite handy; it even allows you to click on (and check) links before pages are published to your Web server. A Web page will look very much the same when viewed in either Preview mode or Edit mode. The difference is akin to turning a pair of trousers inside out. In edit mode, you can see some of the seams (such as table marquees) that hold the page together.

The Attributes Inspector

The Attributes Inspector is a context-sensitive floating palette, which is summoned from the Window menu, or by the command-; keyboard shortcut. Its four-tabbed appearance changes depending on what's selected in the main window. The first three tabs display the attributes of any currently selected frame, page, or form, respectively. The fourth tab is variable; it displays object attributes for images, tables, or media (such as Java applets, Acrobat PDFs, or sounds). When starting on a new Web page, the first tab chosen in the Attributes Inspector is likely to be the Page tab (see Figure 1-2). This is where the base font size, base target, color, and background image attributes are assigned.

What Is...

Acrobat PDF—Adobe's Acrobat Portable Document Format files are platform independent. They look almost exactly like a printed document and can be viewed on any computer equipped with the Adobe Acrobat Viewer.

Java applet—a little downloadable program, written in Sun's Java language. Java applets run the gamut from cute animations to full-blown programs.

Sounds—recordings in AU, WAV, and other formats.

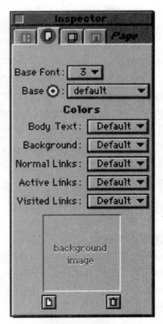

Figure 1-2: The Page tab in the Attributes Inspector.

PageMill delivers total control over color, by both a page and a character basis. This allows you to assign a basic color scheme that can be overridden in special circumstances. The Attributes Inspector provides the means to set the global color characteristics for:

- Body text.
- Background.
- Normal links (places the visitor hasn't been).
- Active links (the color that flashes as someone clicks on a link).
- Visited links (places the visitor has been).

Changing the color of a page attribute can be done by one of two methods. While HTML specifies color in cryptic codes like "ffd303," PageMill eliminates the need to mess with hex. Instead, colors are defined by selection from the system's visual color picker. Selecting Custom from the pop-up menu next to each item will summon the color picker. From there, it's a point-and-shoot procedure. Colors can also be dragged and dropped from the color panel directly onto a pop-up menu to make an instant color assignment.

The large square well at the bottom of the Attributes Inspector provides a preview of the background image (if any). Background images override background color. GIF and JPEG image files can be dragged and dropped from the desktop onto the background image well. Background images can also be assigned, via a dialog box, by clicking on the page icon at the lower left of the Attributes Inspector window. Clicking the little trashcan icon (at the lower right of the window) removes the background image from the page. We'll cover the topic of background files in depth in Chapters 2 and 5.

PageMill's page attributes can be preset via the Preferences I Page dialog box. The controls include color settings for body text, background, normal links, active links, and visited links as well as background image. If you use one set of standard colors in your Web pages, presetting the page attributes will save you the trouble of resetting them each time you sit down to create a new page.

The Color Panel

It's a kindergarten flashback! PageMill's convenient Color Panel (as shown in Figure 1-3) looks just like your very first watercolor palette and is capable of holding 16 different colors. Colors can be dragged and dropped from the Color Panel onto selected text, as well as onto page attributes. To alter a color on the Color Panel, double-click on it and make adjustments in the Color Picker. PageMill allows only one persistent Color Panel at a time. The last group of colors used in a PageMill session will be the colors loaded the next time you launch the program. The Color Panel is accessed via the Window menu, or by the command-' keyboard shortcut.

Figure 1-3: The Color Panel provides quick access to 16 user-defined colors.

Using Multiple Color Panels & Pasteboards

It's possible to save and use multiple Color Panels and Pasteboards through a sneaky workaround. After setting up a custom Color Panel and Pasteboard for a particular Web site, quit PageMill and copy the PageMill Preferences folder from the System folder into that site's folder. Later on, when you want to use that custom Color Panel and Pasteboard, just copy it back to the System folder.

Color selection can be a thorny issue. The colors chosen in the system's Color Picker may not accurately convert to non-dithered (or pure) browser colors. The surest method is to choose colors by using a third-party utility such as PANTONE's ColorWeb, which provides a familiar swatch book approach for color selection. ColorWeb adds an "Internet-safe" color palette of non-dithered colors. You'll find more information on color palettes and dithering in Chapter 5.

The Pasteboard

The Pasteboard is a handy little holding area that uses a notebook metaphor (see Figure 1-4). Text and graphics can be dragged and dropped to and from the Pasteboard. The Pasteboard's five pages are extremely useful as a holding area for repetitive graphics, such as site navigation bars, ID graphics, icons, buttons, and horizontal bars, as well as anchors, links, and other recurrent objects. The Pasteboard is accessed from the Windows menu, or via the command-/ keyboard shortcut.

Roll 'Em Up!
The Attributes Inspector, Color Panel, and Pasteboard are all *roll up palettes.* This handy feature allows you to temporarily hide (or roll up) each palette to cut down on screen clutter. It's especially handy when using a computer with a smaller monitor.

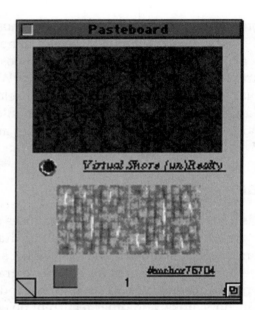

Figure 1-4: The Pasteboard provides a convenient holding tank for text, links, and images.

Here are a few hints for working with the Pasteboard:

- To copy objects from the Pasteboard, hold down the Option key while dragging.
- To flip between pages, click on the curled edge of the page at the lower-left corner of the Pasteboard.
- To resize the Pasteboard, click and drag on the lower-right corner.

The Sad Truth About HTML Text

If you've had experience working with page layout packages such as QuarkXPress or Adobe PageMaker, you're accustomed to some rather extensive control over text. The current crop of word processors do quite an impressive job, as well. Most of these programs provide a high level of control over typeface selection, type size, letter spacing, and line spacing.

The sad truth about working with Web page text is that you have practically no control over how your text will be viewed. Almost everything is browser dependent. The HTML spec allows the browser to set individual preferences for typeface and size on a style-by-style basis. When you specify text on the Web pages that you create, you're taking a leap of faith. What looks right and works well on your screen will appear totally different when it reaches your audience. That having been said, HTML *does* provide a sufficient range of text styles for most situations.

Paragraph Formats vs. Character Styles

HTML uses both *paragraph formats* and *character styles*. The difference between the two is that a character style will affect selected characters only. A paragraph format, on the other hand, affects an entire paragraph. Character styles are used within a paragraph to bring emphasis to a particular word or phrase, as when the title of a book, such as Web Publishing With Adobe PageMill 2, is set in italics.

There are three basic types of paragraph formats:

- *Heading* formats
- *Body text* formats
- *List* formats

A properly structured Web page should make efficient use of the various formats. Let's take it from the top (of the page).

Heading Formats

HTML provides six logical heading formats. PageMill allows you to assign each format with a keyboard shortcut, from the Change Format pop-up menu, or from the Format | Heading menu. Figure 1-5 illustrates the half dozen heading style choices, while Table 1-1 shows the HTML equivalents and keyboard shortcuts.

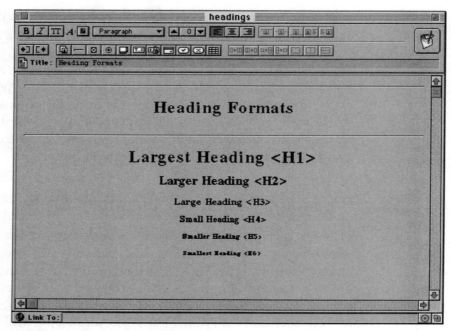

Figure 1-5: Heading formats on parade.

PageMill	Mac Shortcut	HTML Code
Largest	Cmd-Opt-1	<H1>...</H1>
Larger	Cmd-Opt-2	<H2>...</H2>
Large	Cmd-Opt-3	<H3>...</H3>
Small	Cmd-Opt-4	<H4>...</H4>
Smaller	Cmd-Opt-5	<H5>...</H5>
Smallest	Cmd-Opt-6	<H6>...</H6>

Table 1-1: Heading formats and their equivalents.

Since heading commands are paragraph formats, they affect everything in a text block, from one paragraph return until the next. This being so, a heading style cannot be assigned to selected words within a paragraph. When assigning a heading format, all you need to do is have the cursor flashing somewhere within the text block. When the style is chosen, it will be assigned to the whole enchilada.

Try typing a few lines of text now, separating the lines with a return. Then, go ahead and assign different heading styles to the text. Did you notice that headings 5 and 6 are actually smaller than the body text style? Although this may seem odd, there are places where you can use these tiny heading styles to great effect—we'll get into that in Chapter 5.

Paragraph Formats

HTML's default paragraph format uses non-indented text, set in a plain Roman font. In practice, you'll use the paragraph format for most of the text on your Web pages, although you may apply different character styles and type sizes. In addition to the default paragraph style, there are two special types of body text.

The preformatted text format is handy for displaying large blocks of text in a monospaced typewriter typeface. It's often used to create crude tabular text without using the table commands. The address text format is used to denote "mailto" address lines— for the purpose of soliciting visitor feedback via an e-mail link— which usually appear in an italic typeface. Paragraph formats can be assigned with a keyboard shortcut, from the Change Format pop-up menu (on the button bar), or from the Format | Heading menu. Figure 1-6 displays the three different paragraph formats. Table 1-2 shows the HTML equivalents and keyboard shortcuts.

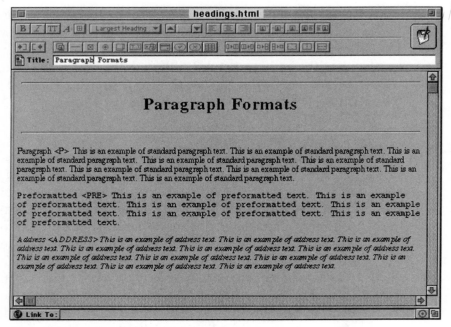

Figure 1-6: Paragraph formats on parade.

PageMill	Mac Shortcut	HTML Code
Paragraph	Cmd-Opt-P	<P>...</P>
Preformatted	Cmd-Opt-F	<PRE>...</PRE>
Address	Cmd-Opt-A	<ADDRESS>...</ADDRESS >

Table 1-2: Paragraph formats and their equivalents.

List Formats

There are a number of list formats for use in various situations, as shown by Figure 1-7. Table 1-3 contains the HTML equivalents and keyboard shortcuts.

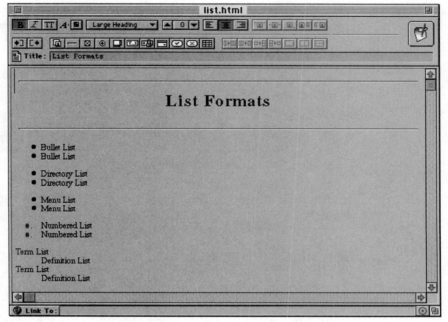

Figure 1-7: List formats on parade.

The formats include:

- Bullet—indented and bulleted.

- Directory—indented and bulleted.

- Menu—indented and bulleted.

- Numbered—indented and numbered. (Numbers only appear in the browser. PageMill displays the # sign.)

- Term—used together with the definition format. Set on the left margin.

- Definition—indented text, used together with the term format.

While the first three formats appear to be identical, the difference between them has to do with the theoretical structure of the document. In practice, however, it's likely that you'll just use the bulleted list format.

PageMill	Mac shortcut	HTML
Bullet	Cmd-Opt-B	<UL><LI>...</UL>
Directory	Cmd-Opt-D	<DIR><LI>...</DIR>
Menu	Cmd-Opt-M	<MENU>...</MENU>
Numbered	Cmd-Opt-N	<OL><LI>...</OL>
Definition	Cmd-Opt-E	<DL><DD>...</DL>
Term	Cmd-Opt-T	<DL><DT>...</DL>

Table 1-3: List formats and their equivalents.

To create nested outlines, use the indent left and right commands.

Physical Character Styles vs. Logical Character Styles

Character styles can be either *physical* or *logical*. A physical style tags specific words with specific font attributes, such as bold or italic. Logical styles tell the browser what the intent of the text is rather than defining a particular type style. Physical styles appear in the browser as the Web page designer intends for them to appear. If you assign a bold style to a chunk of text, you can rest assured that it will be bold. In contrast, text assigned a logical style can vary in appearance from browser to browser, depending on how the browser's preferences are set.

If you're confused by all this, you're not alone. Suffice it to say, you can play it safe by assigning physical styles, rather than logical styles. If you want something to appear in bold, make sure that you use the bold style. Don't leave your typographical decisions to the whims of the browser.

Physical Character Styles

There are four physical character styles. They can be assigned with a keyboard shortcut, from the button bar, or from the Style menu. Applying the plain paragraph style clears all the other paragraph formatting. Table 1-4 lists the physical character styles and their HTML equivalents.

PageMill	Mac Shortcut	HTML
Plain	Cmd-Shift-P	<P>...</P>
Bold	Cmd-B	<B>...</B>
Italic	Cmd-I	<I>...</I>
Teletype	Cmd-Shift- TT	<TT>...</TT>

Table 1-4: Physical character styles and their equivalents.

Teletype is an interesting style. It uses a monospaced (as opposed to proportionally spaced) font, such as Courier. Every character in a monospaced font takes up the same width, as opposed to a proportionally spaced font, where the "I" is much thinner than the "W," and so on. This characteristic makes it possible to create quick and dirty tables—as if on an old typewriter—simply by using the space bar to line up columns.

Logical Character Styles

There are a number of logical character styles. Note that there's a fair amount of overkill with regard to the limited set of typefaces. Figure 1-8 displays the seven logical character styles and Table 1-5 lists them with their HTML equivalents.

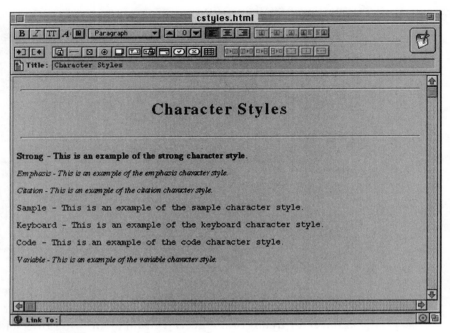

Figure 1-8: Character styles on parade.

Some of the character styles share the same kind of typeface:

- Strong—usually a bold typeface.
- Emphasis—usually an italic typeface.
- Citation—usually an italic typeface.
- Sample—usually a typewriter typeface.
- Keyboard—usually a typewriter typeface.
- Code—usually a typewriter typeface.
- Variable—usually an italic typeface.

PageMill	Mac Shortcut	HTML
Strong	Cmd-Shift-S	<STRONG>...</STRONG>
Emphasis	Cmd-Shift-E	<EM>...</EM>
Citation	Cmd-Shift-C	<CITE>...</CITE>
Sample	Cmd-Shift-A	<SAMP>...</SAMP>
Keyboard	Cmd-Shift-K	<KBD>...</KBD>
Code	Cmd-Shift-O	<CODE>...</CODE>
Variable	Cmd-Shift-V	<VAR>...</VAR>

Table 1-5: Physical character styles and their equivalents.

Additional Text Controls

A highly designed Web page calls for enhanced control over text attributes. PageMill provides the means to manipulate a variety of text attributes other than those managed via the paragraph formats and character styles. These additional text controls allow you to more precisely define your Web page designs. They include:

- Text alignment
- Text indent
- Text size
- Text color

Text Alignment

Web page text can be left aligned, right aligned, or centered (HTML does not support full justification). Text is set left aligned by default. To center a block of text, all you have to do is highlight it and click the Center Align button. To set the text back to a left alignment, just click the Left Align button. Follow the same procedure to right align text. PageMill also provides control over text alignment as it relates to inline graphics as well as text wrapping (where text appears to flow around a graphic). These controls are used in the exercise in Chapter 2. Text alignment controls are implemented in the HTML paragraph and heading commands, as ALIGN=CENTER or ALIGN=RIGHT.

Indents

Text indents are implemented through a very basic interface. The left and right indent buttons move the indents in and out, respectively. The indents push the text around by predetermined increments, as shown by Figure 1-9. Unfortunately, there are no controls over the amount of indent provided by each click of the indent button. When you use the indents to alter any list with bullets, you will notice that the bullets change. Normal bullets are solid black. First indents get an open circle bullet, while second indents and beyond get open square bullets.

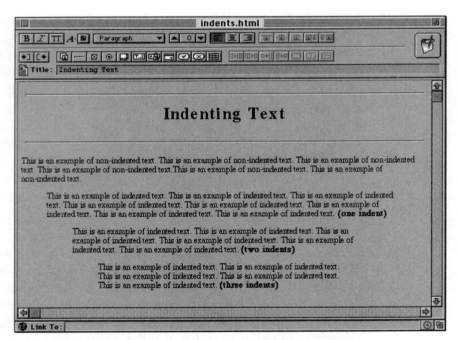

Figure 1-9: Indenting sets off passages of text.

Text Size

It's not necessary to assign a heading style if all you want to do is change the type size of a selected block of text (and especially if you don't want the text to be bold). PageMill's button bar affords a convenient way to change the relative font size. Relative to what, you ask? Text size choices are relative to the base font set in the Attributes Inspector. HTML allows only seven type sizes. As such, the higher the base font is set, the fewer the choices will be when you go to increase the size of a chunk of text. PageMill uses HTML's <FONT SIZE=X>...</FONT> command to control the text size.

Clicking on the up arrow increases the font size, while clicking on the down arrow decreases the font size. Font size can also be set by choosing a specific size or via keyboard shortcuts, which are shown in Table 1-6.

PageMill	Mac Shortcut
Increase	Cmd-Shift->
Decrease	Cmd-Shift-<

Table 1-6: Change Font Size keyboard shortcuts.

Assigning a larger type size to a block of text within a paragraph will alter the line spacing (or leading) on the lines on which the text appears. This results in a noticeably uneven look, as shown in Figure 1-10.

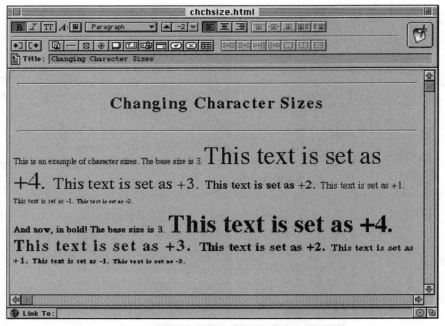

Figure 1-10: Changing the type size affects line spacing as well.

Text Color

While the Attributes Inspector provides full control over text color attributes on a per-page basis, it's easy to assign colors to specific text as well. To change the color of a selected block of text, you can either drag and drop a color from the floating color panel or summon the color picker by clicking the Text Color button (on the button bar) and selecting Custom.

Hyperlinks

Hyperlinks (or more simply, *links*) are at the core of the World Wide Web's allure. Some may even say that it's the medium's entire reason for being. Links are what allow folks to jump from one spot to the next—be it from page to page or from server to server—in a single mouse click. There are three basic types of links, *internal,* *external,* and *anchored.* Links within your Web site's directories are known as internal links. From a strictly navigational standpoint, they are what ties a Web site together. When a visitor to your site clicks on an internal link, they jump to a different spot on one of your pages. External (or outbound) links, conversely, are what tie your Web site to the World Wide Web. When a visitor to your site clicks on an external link, they leave your server behind, as they go off in search of the new page (and Web site). Anchored links are links that refer to an exact position within a page, and can be either internal or external (though most commonly the former).

Links can be attached to text or to graphics. In the following pages, you'll learn how to create text links between your pages, as well as to other Web sites. Graphic links and image maps are covered in the next chapter.

Creating Links

Like most things "PageMillian," hyperlinks can be accomplished with drag-and-drop ease or through direct text entry. Take a look at the little page icon at the top of the main PageMill window (just below the indent buttons near the top left corner, and to the left of the Title line). The page icon is a crucial part of the program's integral drag-and-drop page-linking scheme. To review, there are three basic types of hyperlinks:

- *Internal* links are hyperlinks to other Web pages within your Web site.

- *External* links are hyperlinks to other Web sites.

- *Anchored* links are hyperlinks to specific places on a Web page and are often used to link to different locations within a page.

Creating Internal Links

To link two internal pages via drag and drop, start by opening both pages. Highlight the linking text, then drag and drop the document page icon (from the page you want to link to) onto the highlighted text. Bingo! The pages are linked. You can also drag and drop existing links from page to page. In practice, it can be a bit tricky to position both pages on your monitor if you have a small screen or are running at a low resolution (such as 640 X 480). Chapter 5 includes a number of hints for creating an optimum working environment.

To link internal pages via direct text entry, begin by highlighting the linking text (the text you want to link from). Then, click in the Link To bar at the bottom left of the PageMill window, type in the URL (address) of the page you want to link to and press the Enter key. Alternatively, you can cut and paste the URL from the browser window or from the Pasteboard.

Creating External Links

External links are most commonly entered in the Link To bar. The Link To bar uses a very cool "assisted URL entry" feature to help speed the tedious process of typing URLs from scratch. As you type the first letter of the protocol—most typically the *H* in HTTP— PageMill will fill in the rest if you simply press the Right arrow key. Type the first *W* in WWW, press the Right arrow key again, and PageMill will fill out the second and third *W*s. Type the domain name (followed by a period), press the Right arrow key again, and PageMill will cycle through domain type (such as .com or .net).

First Position "Link To" Shortcuts

Don't worry, you don't have to know what all of these cryptic acronyms stand for! Most often, all you'll need to use are h, ft, and m. The first position "Link To" shortcuts are:

```
h  = http://
f  = file://
ft = ftp://
g  = gopher://
m  = mailto:
n  = news:
r  = rlogin://
s  = shttp://
t  = telnet://
w  = wais://
```

PageMill also allows you to drag and drop links out of Web pages that have been opened in Netscape Navigator or from Navigator's Bookmarks folder. These links can be dropped either on the selected text or in the Link To bar. If you drop the link onto the Link To bar, be sure to press the Enter key afterward to implement the link.

Domain Types

There are half a dozen common domain types in the United States. Domains in other countries typically end with abbreviations of the name of the country.

.com—commercial

.edu—educational

.gov—government

.mil—military

.net—network

.org—organization

Dropping Anchors

HTML provides the means to link to specific places within a Web page by using *anchors.* These handy devices can be thought of as akin to nailing up house numbers. Once the anchors have been dropped in the proper places, your links can deliver visitors to the exact doorstep (i.e., location within a Web page). Anchors are placed via the Edit I Insert Invisible menu. They are only visible in PageMill's Edit mode. When an anchor is placed, PageMill assigns an arbitrary anchor name, such as "anchor245189." Clicking on a placed anchor enables you to specify a meaningful anchor name on the Attributes Inspector's Object tab.

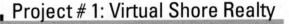

Project # 1: Virtual Shore Realty

Our first hands-on project will be a text-only page for Virtual Shore Realty, a mythical real estate company on Long Beach Island. Virtual Shore caters to well-heeled beach lovers. Their first tentative foray into Internet advertising is a single page affair, sans graphics. Even though the page will not feature any images, it will have a distinctive look through the judicious use of text and background colors.

As you work through the exercise, you will notice that it's a bit iterative of the basics covered earlier in the chapter.

Bringing Text Into PageMill

To begin the exercise, you will need to have PageMill running on your PC or Macintosh. Open the ASCII text file lbi.txt in the CHAP-1 directory on this book's CD-ROM. You can use either of the following methods to bring text files into PageMill:

- Open the file with any text editor, then copy and paste into PageMill.
- Open the file with a text editor that supports drag and drop, then drag and drop the text into PageMill.

Selecting Text

PageMill follows conventional text selection procedures. The program allows text to be chosen via these methods:

- Clicking once selects an insertion point.
- Double-clicking selects a word.
- Triple-clicking selects an entire paragraph.
- Clicking and dragging selects a range of text.

Deleting Extra Line Spaces

PageMill goes to work the instant the text is brought into the program by inserting HTML coding. If you opened up the file in a text editor, you'll notice that the text seems spaced out in PageMill (as shown in Figure 1-11). This is due to PageMill's automatic placement of <P>...</P> paragraph commands around each paragraph return encountered. Since the paragraph command includes an extra line space, it will be necessary to go in and delete the extra line spaces that were placed in the text file.

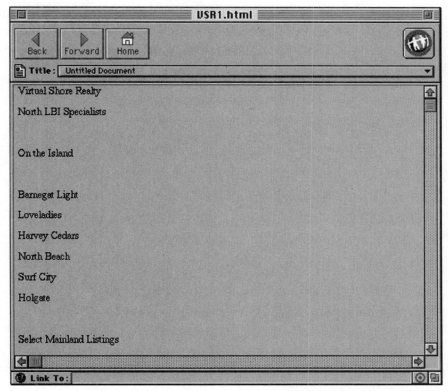

Figure 1-11: It's spaced out! PageMill opens up imported text by inserting paragraph commands.

When you first open a file, PageMill presents it in Preview mode. Before you start editing the file, PageMill must be in Edit mode (the pen and paper icon). Change modes by clicking on the large button at the top right of the window. Then, begin editing the text by deleting the extra line spaces, as you would in any word processing program. Move the cursor to the line you want to delete—using either the cursor keys or the mouse—and press the Delete key. Once the extra line spaces have been deleted, the paragraphs will still appear to be separated by a line space. Don't fret: this is the normal interparagraph spacing. Once the extra line spaces have been removed, the file should appear as in Figure 1-12.

Please note that the figures in this section show PageMill in Preview mode. It's a good idea to get into the habit of previewing each major change, before saving the file. Frequently saving your work is always a wise move, no matter which program you use. When you save a file for the first time, select File | Save File As. After it's been saved once, you can quickly save the revised page with the command-S keyboard shortcut.

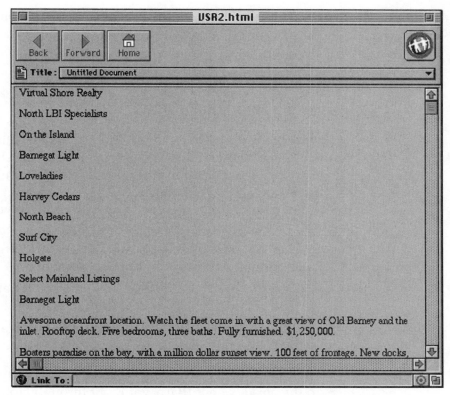

Figure 1-12: With the blank lines removed, more text fits in the window.

What's the Difference Between a Hard & Soft Return?

When you press a Return, you create a *hard return*, which commonly includes an extra line space after the line ending. Pressing a Shift-Return creates a *soft return*, which does not add any extra line space. The soft return uses a <BR> command to "hold the line."

Assigning Heading Formats

Now that the text is cleaned up, it's time to assign some heading formats. Since heading formats work on a paragraph basis, it's not necessary to have the entire block of text selected. You only need to click somewhere within the block. Let's try that out on the first three lines of text. You'll use the Paragraph drop-down menu (in the top row of the button bar) to assign styles:

1. Click on "Virtual Shore Realty," and select Largest Heading from the Paragraph drop-down menu.

2. Click on "North LBI Specialists," and select Larger Heading from the Paragraph drop-down menu.

3. Click on "On the Island," and select Large Heading from the Paragraph drop-down menu.

4. Save the file.

Skip the next six lines (Barnegat Light through Holgate) right now. You'll come back to them in a moment. Go through the rest of the text, and assign Large Heading to "Select Mainland Listings" and each of the subsequent town names (the first town name, Barnegat Light, is shown in Figure 1-13).

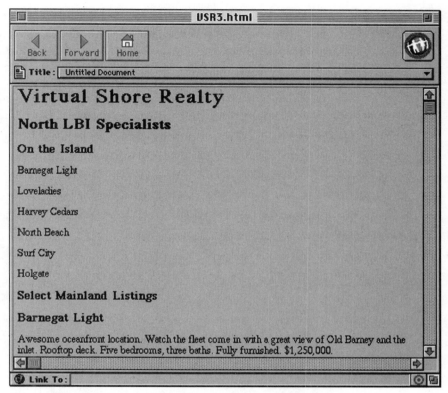

Figure 1-13: Heading styles help define a text hierarchy.

Assigning a List Format

The six town names between "On the Island" and "Select Mainland Listings" will form a bulleted internal jumplist for the page. The Bullet List is undoubtedly the most popular of HTML's six list formats. In fact, the Bullet List, the Directory List, and the Menu List all look pretty much the same.

The method used to assign a list format differs a bit from the method you used to assign the heading styles in the last section. When assigning a list style, you'll want to select all the lines of text in the list (instead of just clicking an insertion point). This is done by clicking and dragging over the block of text. Let's give it a whirl.

Click and drag from the *B* in Barnegat Light (under "On the Island") through the *e* in Holgate. Select Directory List from the Paragraph drop-down menu. The text should appear as it does in Figure 1-14. When it looks right, save the file. Try experimenting with the different lists to see if there's any difference in appearance. You'll definitely be able to see a difference once you've completed the next section. And further on, you'll turn this bullet list into a jumplist by assigning links.

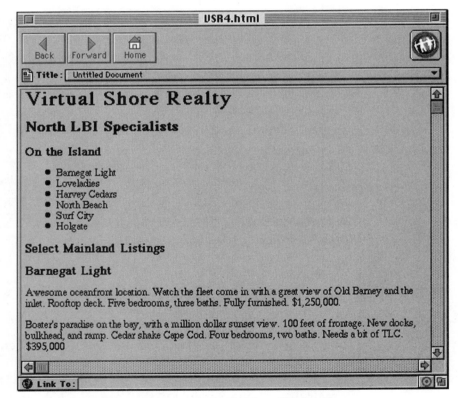

Figure 1-14: Bullets are a great way to tie a jumplist together.

Assigning Indents

PageMill provides basic control over indents through the progressive use of HTML's <BLOCKQUOTE> command. Each time you click on the Indent Right button, text and other objects are indented equally on both margins. Clicking on the Indent Left button pushes the text back out towards the full margin. It's not complicated, but it's effective.

Let's indent the jumplist to give it the appearance of being centered on the page. Click and drag from the B in the first "Barnegat Light" through the e in "Holgate." Click the right indent four times. Watch how the level of indent affects the bullet style. The list should appear as in Figure 1-15. If it looks OK, save the file.

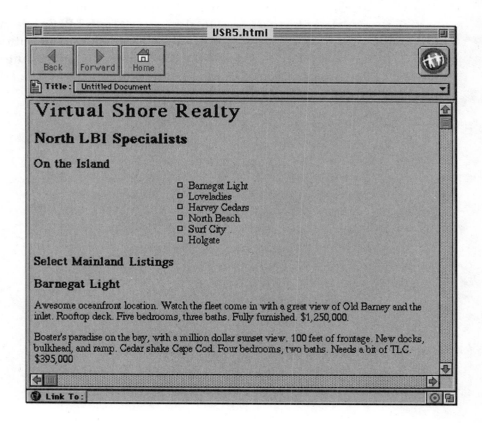

Figure 1-15: Indenting a bulleted list helps to visually center it on the page.

Text Alignment

HTML allows for three types of text alignment: left, right, and center. Text alignment works on a per paragraph basis. To change the alignment of a single paragraph, click within the paragraph and then click on the appropriate alignment button. To change the alignment of a number of consecutive paragraphs, highlight the paragraphs and click on an alignment button.

Select "Virtual Shore Realty" and "North LBI Specialists" by clicking and dragging. Click the Center Alignment button. Click on "On the Island" and click the Center Alignment button. Repeat the process for "Select Mainland Listings" (see Figure 1-16). When you're done, save the file.

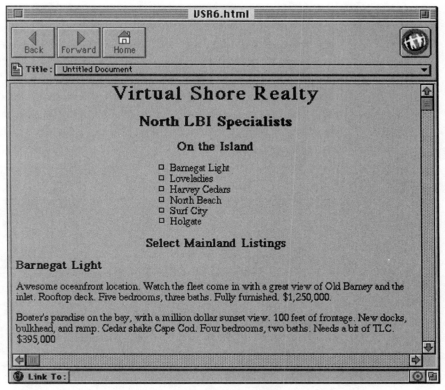

Figure 1-16: Centering the page heading provides a more formal appearance.

Adding Text

It looks like our copywriter left out a crucial tag line at the top of
the Virtual Shore Realty page. Click an insertion point directly
after the last *s* in "North LBI Specialists" and press Return. Type
LBI: One of the True Gems of the Jersey Shore, highlight the line
and assign the basic paragraph format (from either the button bar
or Format I Paragraph). Then, assign the Emphasis style (from the
Style menu). Press the Right cursor key once to deselect the text
and press Return. Save the file.

Adding Horizontal Rules

Now, let's set the heading off from the rest of the page by adding a pair of horizontal rules. The cursor should be in exactly the right place to add the first rule (on the blank line, between "LBI: One of the True Gems of the Jersey Shore" and "On the Island"). Click the Insert Horizontal Rule button on the button bar to set the first rule. Then, click after the last s in "Select Mainland Listings," press Return again, and click the Insert Horizontal Rule button again to set the second rule. The results should appear as in Figure 1-17.

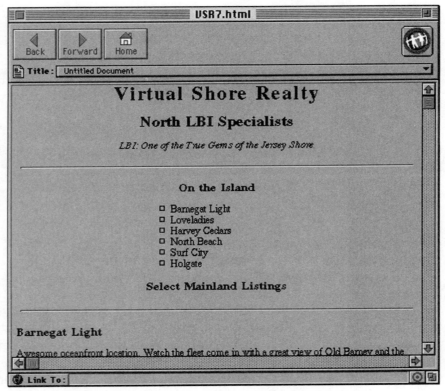

Figure 1-17: Horizontal rules help to differentiate areas of a Web page.

Through the Attributes Inspector, horizontal rules can be set to a specific width and size (or weight). The width can be defined as a percentage of the browser window or by an exact pixel width. You can also choose between a shaded (embossed) or no shade (solid) style.

Changing Text Size

The body text is looking a tad too small. Let's bump up the base font size by one level. At the Attributes Inspector's Page tab, change the base font to 4 (the default should be 3). Notice that the change will affect the body text only (not the headings). Experiment with different base font sizes to see how they affect the look of the page. When you have it looking just right, be sure to save the file.

Assigning Physical Character Styles

Now, it's time to take a run through the page to assign some physical character styles. Highlight the opening phrase of each house listing and apply a bold italic style by clicking on the Bold and Italic buttons. Highlight each of the prices and apply an italic style. When you're done, the text should appear as in Figure 1-18.

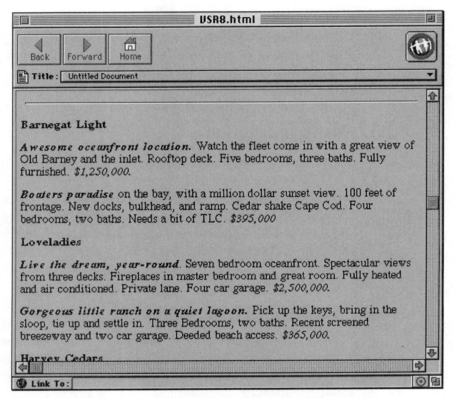

Figure 1-18: Larger text and selected styles help make Web page text more readable.

Copying Text Between Pages

Quite often, you'll want to copy a repetitive passage of text (or graphic) from page to page. If you only have to copy a piece of text once, it's an easy affair. If you have to copy the same piece of text a number of times, however, you'll probably want to use the Pasteboard. In this next section, you'll open an existing Web page and copy text from it into the main Virtual Shore Realty page:

1. Click File | Open.

2. Navigate to the CHAP-1 directory on this book's CD-ROM. Open the file named about.html.

Take a look at the bottom of the About page. We're going to copy the rule and text onto the main Virtual Shore page. To do so, scroll down to the bottom of the main page.

3. Click an insertion point at the very end of the main page.

4. Select the About.html window.

5. Highlight the rule and the last line of text ("Copyright, 1996...").

6. Drag and drop the selected rule and text onto the bottom of the main Virtual Shore Realty page.

7. Save the file.

Linking

At last the time has come to add those crucial links! In the following section, you will be creating internal links, external links, and anchored links. Let's begin with an internal link between the About page and the main page of the Virtual Shore Realty site.

Dragging & Dropping an Internal Link

With the rule and text having been copied, link the words "Virtual Shore (un)Realty" on the main page to the About page:

1. On the main page, select the words "Virtual Shore (un)Realty."

2. Click and drag the document page icon (from the about.html window "about" page) onto the selected text.

    The bottom of the main page should appear as in Figure 1-19.

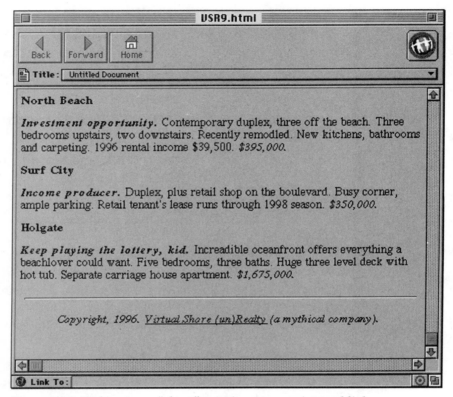

Figure 1-19: Linking to an "about" page is a common internal link.

Typing In an External Link

External links exploit the power of the Web by connecting sites around the globe with a single click. Let's link the acronym "LBI" in the line "LBI: One of the True Gems of the Jersey Shore" with the www.longbeachisland.com Web site:

1. Select the letters "LBI."

2. At the Link To line at the bottom of the PageMill window, type **http://www.longbeachisland.com**. Press Enter, and the link is complete.

3. Save the file.

Alternately, you can use PageMill's assisted URL entry feature, as described earlier in this chapter.

Creating Anchored Links

Now, let's create a little internal jumplist that links all the town names. You'll click an insertion point in front of each of the town listings, drop an anchor, and name each accordingly. Once the anchors are placed, you'll link them to the jumplist at the top of the page with a drag-and-drop technique:

1. Click in front of the Barnegat Light listing (not the jumplist).

2. Click Edit | Insert Invisible | Anchor. The anchor is placed (see Figure 1-20).

3. Select the new anchor.

4. At the Attributes Inspector, type **Barnegat** under Name and press Enter. The anchor is now properly named.

Repeat the four previous actions for each of the town listings. When you're done, it's time to create the jumplist. Dragging and dropping the anchored links is a straightforward procedure when both the anchor and the link are visible on the screen. Things get a little trickier when you have to scroll and drag the anchors:

1. Select the words "Barnegat Light" in the jumplist by triple-clicking.

2. Click and drag the anchor from the Barnegat Light listing onto the selected text. The listing is now linked.

Repeat the two previous actions for each of the town listings. To make the window scroll, place the cursor just below the window boundary. When you're done, the page should appear as in Figure 1-20. Don't forget to save the file.

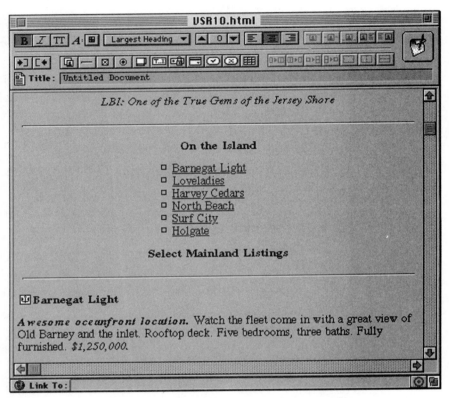

Figure 1-20: Jumplists are a great way to aid navigation on a long page.

Changing Colors

The Virtual Shore Realty Web page has come a long way in a very short time. Even though it doesn't contain any graphics, we've made it a functional page and we're on our way to giving it a distinctive look as well. In this next section, you'll assign colors on a global page basis, in addition to colorizing selected text.

Changing Colors on a Page Basis

To globally change the colors of the Virtual Shore Realty Web page, click on the Page tab in the Attributes Inspector. Try dragging some colors from the color palette onto the Body Text, Background, Normal Links, Active Links, and Visited Links buttons. When you're done fiddling, click and drag down on the Body Text button (drag down to Custom). This will summon the color picker. Use your system's color picker to assign some suitably beachy colors

chapter 2

Working With Graphics

A Web page without graphics is a pretty boring sight, and can lead, quite possibly, to a boring Web site. While the text content might carry the bulk of the informational value, the reader may never absorb the information if it is poorly presented. A text-only page does little to entice the reader. Pages that are visually pleasing, on the other hand, are sure to attract more attention, and hopefully, allow the reader to achieve a higher level of comprehension. As a Web page designer, you should always strive to provide a balance between the steak and the sizzle.

When planning a page, there are a number of graphic-related decisions to make. This chapter will help you get familiar with the different types of graphics and will explain how to implement each form. At the end of the chapter you can put your new skills to use in a special graphics exercise. Chapter 5 goes more into depth on the "Whys" of Web page design. In practice, you may use up to seven general types of graphics when designing your Web pages:

- Backgrounds
- Navigational aids

- Icons
- Dingbats
- Divider bars
- Illustrations
- Photographs

While Adobe PageMill is not a graphics creation tool, per se, it allows you to work with graphics from a wide variety of sources. Chapter 11 provides a rundown of some of the most popular applications used to produce Web page graphics.

WWW Graphic Formats

GIF and JPEG are the most common graphics file formats on the World Wide Web. GIF format should be used for solid color graphics, line art, and logos, while JPEG format is best used for photographs and continuous tone artwork.

Backgrounds Set the Stage

Custom backgrounds set the mood of a Web page. They provide the designer with the means to banish the boring default gray of the browser window and replace it with a distinctive look (as shown in Figure 2-1). In the exercise at the end of Chapter 1, you assigned various colors to the body text, links, and background. Image backgrounds take that one step further by allowing you to use a patterned graphic instead of a solid color background. The right background treatment will set your pages apart from the pack. The wrong background treatment, however, will compromise legibility, reduce effectiveness, and irritate the reader (as illustrated by Figure 2-2).

Figure 2-1: A tasteful background sets the proper mood.

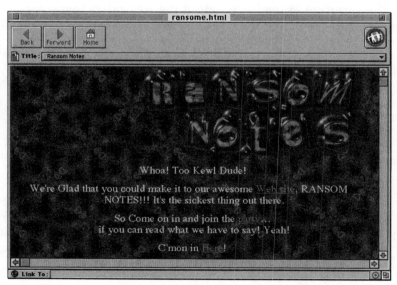

Figure 2-2: Say what? The wrong background treatment will muddy a page.

Color is one of the first decisions to make when designing a Web page. You should always try to choose a background color or image that works well with your text colors. Text legibility should be valued above all. Choosing a background color that is too close in hue to a text color will make the text difficult to read. On the other end of the color scale, you want to avoid using combinations that have too much contrast. Wild color pairings such as screaming yellow type on a plum purple background can contrast and vibrate so hard that they rattle the brain.

Setting (& Removing) Background Images

Setting background images in PageMill is a snap. Just drag the GIF or JPEG image file from the desktop and drop it into the Attributes Inspector's background image well. (The Attributes Inspector must be in Page mode.) Bingo...instant background image! To remove a background image, click on the Attributes Inspector's tiny trashcan button (at the lower right). You can also import background images via a dialog box by clicking on the button at the lower left of the Attributes Inspector.

What About PICT Files?

No problemo! PageMill allows you to drag and drop Macintosh PICT format images (such as screen shots) right from the desktop by performing the conversion to GIF on the fly.

Background images are often referred to as tiles, since the browser repeats the image to fill the open window. If the window is resized, the background image is retiled. Take a look at some patterned wallpaper, fabric, or carpeting, and you'll get the basic idea.

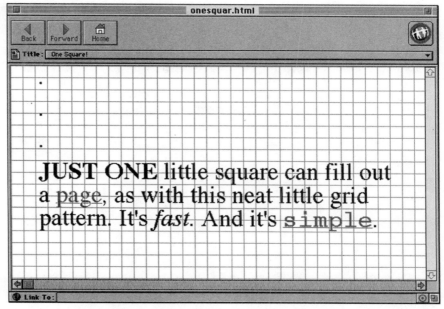

Figure 2-3: One little square tiles to fill out the window.

Backgrounds come in different aspect ratios and sizes, although square background images (see Figure 2-3) are among the most common. The browser will automatically tile background images, regardless of aspect ratio (the relationship of width to height). When using background tiles, you don't have to think in square terms. Take a look at the two margin lines running down the page in Figure 2-4. There would be no way to achieve this common "yellow-ruled paper" effect with a square texture. Instead, a short and wide rectangular tile (24 pixels high by 1024 pixels wide) was used.

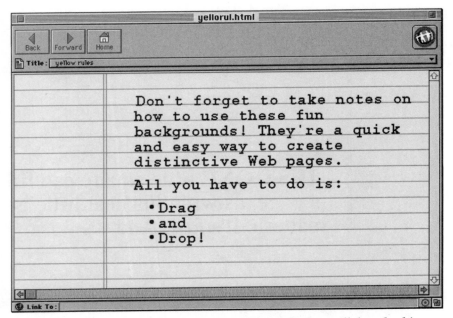

Figure 2-4: Wide patterns can be cool! And best of all, they will download in a flash.

Because the browser handles the tiling, it will repeat this pattern at the 1025th pixel (if the browser window is opened that far). The viewer won't notice that the pattern is repeating unless their browser window is open all the way to the repeating margin rules. There are many uses for these short-and-wide background tiles. Square tiles work fine when using symmetrical seamless textures. If the background design is asymmetrical, however, a tiling scheme similar to the yellow-ruled paper (as illustrated in Figure 2-4) is the best solution.

What Does Seamless Mean?

A seamless tile is one that tiles smoothly, with no visible edges. Creating seamless textures is not a trivial undertaking. It takes painstaking effort to achieve a result that does not look forced. Seamless texture tiles first came into vogue with three-dimensional rendering programs.

You are not limited to using just background tiles; you can use full-page images as backgrounds, as well. Using a full page image opens up your design possibilities. You might use a photograph of your town's skyline or perhaps an image of puffy clouds. A note of caution is in order, however. While it's nice not to be limited to tiled backgrounds, full-color, full-page background images can be huge. Use them sparingly and only when their impressive imagery makes waiting for the download well worth the viewer's time.

Where to Find Backgrounds

Background images are everywhere. You can pick them up on the Web for free, you can spend some time creating your own, or you can spring for a CD-ROM filled with commercial images. This book's CD-ROM features more than 2,000 very cool (and totally free, if you've already bought this book) textures along with hundreds of patterned backgrounds that you can use on your own Web pages.

Check Out These Background Sites!

Bumpy: The Land of Textures
  http://home.earthlink.net/~shaner/textures.html
Julianne's Background Textures
  http://www.sfsu.edu/~jtolson/textures/textures.htm
Pattern Land
  http://www.netcreations.com/patternland/index.html
Texture Land
  http://www.meat.com/textures/
The Virtual Background Museum
  http://www.teleport.com/~mtjans/VBM/

If you're thinking about building your own custom backgrounds, there are a handful of programs that are specifically designed to create seamless textures. Adobe TextureMaker and Specular TextureScape (included in Specular's 3D Web Workshop) are two of the most popular applications. You can also hack out your own textures with Photoshop and Kai's Power Tools's Seamless Welder. We'll get into more specifics in Chapter 11.

The commercial texture choices are burgeoning. It seems as if a new CD-ROM full of textures hits the streets every week. A good number of the commercial texture collections on the market are targeted at print designers who need high-resolution files to complete their projects. These high-resolution images contain three to four times more digital information than you need to complete your Web page. Print files are typically 225–300 dpi (dots per inch); Web files don't need to be higher than 72 dpi. Visual Software's Textures for Professionals includes scores of seamless textures including the ever popular woodgrains and marbles (as shown in Figure 2-5).

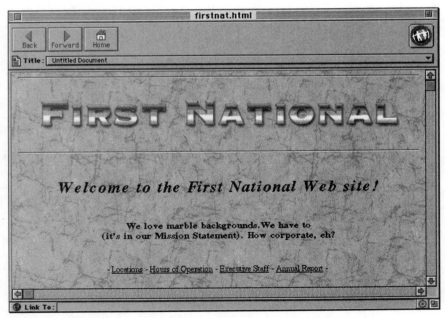

Figure 2-5: A marble background provides a corporate look.

Generate Custom Backgrounds via the Web!
The Background Generator
http://east.isx.com/~dprust/Bax/index.html

Don't overlook the print-oriented selections, however. While they may be more expensive, they're often of higher quality and usually contain low-resolution images in addition to the high-resolution images. You can always downsample high-resolution images in Adobe Photoshop or other paint editors.

Speeding Up Background Images

Since background images are just that (background images), you can use some tricks to speed up loading. The basic rules of graphic loading speeds apply. The smaller an image's file size, the faster it will load. Tiles with just a handful of colors load faster than full color tiles. The yellow-ruled paper tile (shown in Figure 2-4) loads quickly, regardless of its width, because it uses a very limited color palette.

What About Converting Windows Wallpaper?
While it's easy to convert Windows wallpaper (BMP) files to GIF format (with a file conversion utility, such as Paint Shop Pro), you should consider whether the wallpaper image makes for a suitable Web page background. Many Windows wallpaper files are far too dark to be used effectively.

With background images, it's usually a good idea to limit the color palette. The amount you limit it to depends on the image; some images will tolerate a tight color palette and some won't. Chapter 5 delves further into the subject of palettes and palette reduction, with a specific focus on what's come to be known as "The Netscape 216 Palette."

Placing Images

Once the stage has been set with a background image, you'll want to think about what types of images to use on top of the background. In the next section, you'll learn how images are manipulated once they've been brought into PageMill. Images can be placed on your Web pages either by dragging and dropping from the desktop or via a dialog box (which is summoned from the Place Object button on the button bar or from the File menu). You might want to try bringing in a few images now, just to get the hang of it.

To reposition an image within a page, you can either drag and drop or cut and paste to the new position. If you want to drag the image to a place on the page beyond what's visible in the browser window, drag the image to a point just inside the window border to scroll (it's a little tricky, but you'll soon get the hang of it).

It's important to consider where the actual image files reside, in addition to where you're going to place them on your Web pages. Otherwise, when you move your files up to the Web server, you'll end up breaking links and losing files. Chapter 5 goes into depth on creating a working directory structure.

Controlling Images via the Attributes Inspector

After an image has been placed on the page, your work is only half done. The Attributes Inspector's Object tab provides precise control over a number of image characteristics. In practice, you will use this tab for just about every image you place, although you won't alter all the settings for each image. The Object tab controls the following image characteristics (as shown in Figure 2-6):

- Width
- Height
- Alternate (text) Label
- Behavior
- Border

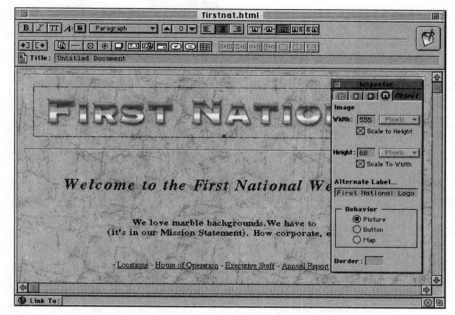

Figure 2-6: Take charge of your images with the Attributes Inspector's Object tab.

Width and *Height* can be set as an exact pixel size or as a percentage relative to the browser window. When an image is brought into PageMill, the width and height default to the actual size of the image. While it's easy to change the size of an image within PageMill, the safest method is to change the actual size of the image in an image editing application such as Adobe Photoshop before bringing it into PageMill. Otherwise, the image may become distorted in the browser. And even more importantly, scaling the image down in Photoshop will reduce file size and slash download time.

You should specify an *Alternate Label* for every image you place. The Alternate Label is the wording that is shown in the browser window if an image is not displayed (such as when the browser has images turned off or when a page download is stopped in midstream). While naming each image may seem like a tedious task, it's considered good Netiquette. With proper labeling, visitors can "see" what each image is, without actually downloading it. If they're enticed by the Alternate Label, they can reload the page at will. Figure 2-7 shows a partially loaded page that uses properly labeled images.

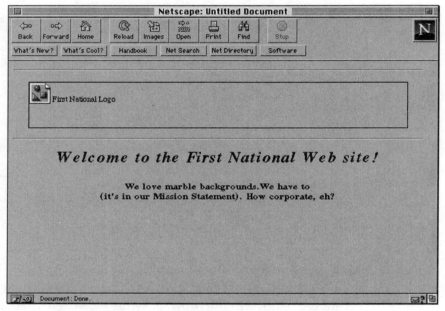

Figure 2-7: Don't leave your viewers guessing. Always specify an Alternate Label.

Specifying the *Behavior* of an object tells the browser what to expect—a picture, form button, or image map. Images come into PageMill as pictures by default. Forms are covered in Chapter 3, while image maps are dealt with later on in this chapter.

Images come into PageMill with a default *Border* of nil. While you can set the border as thick as you could possibly want, it's hard to imagine using a border thickness heavier than 1 or 2 pixels. The border color is determined by the object behavior. A picture will use the page's Body Text color, while a form button or an image map will use the page's Link colors (normal, active, and visited). While you wouldn't want to use a border on an irregularly shaped (transparent) graphic image, a border can look great around a rectangular photographic image. Figure 2-8 shows the same photograph with and without a border.

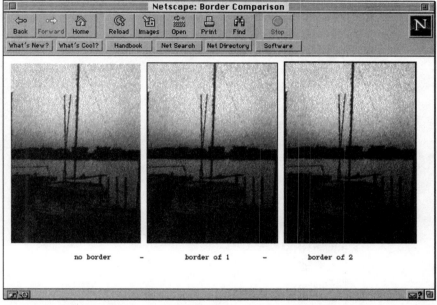

Figure 2-8: Borders help to "pop" a photograph.

Image Alignment

After you've set your image attributes (or perhaps before), you'll want to position the image on the page. Image alignment is set via one of the aptly illustrated buttons at the top right of the button bar. Just select the image and click away. PageMill provides five options to control how text reacts to an inline image:

- Top Align
- Middle Align
- Bottom Align
- Left Align
- Right Align

The first three choices—top, middle, and bottom—align one line of text with the image and are most appropriately used for short captions. You're likely to use either a left or right align (the last two buttons in the group) most frequently. These settings wrap text around the image. Figures 2-9 and 2-10 demonstrate the effect of the five alignment options. More complicated alignment schemes are possible through the use of tables (which will be covered in depth in the next chapter).

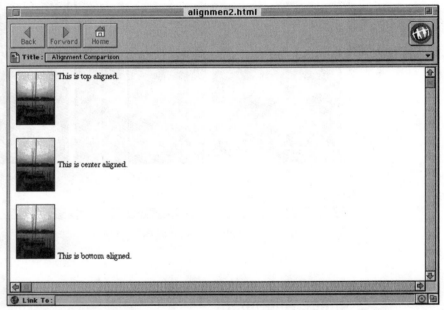

Figure 2-9: Choose top, middle, or bottom alignment when you have a short caption.

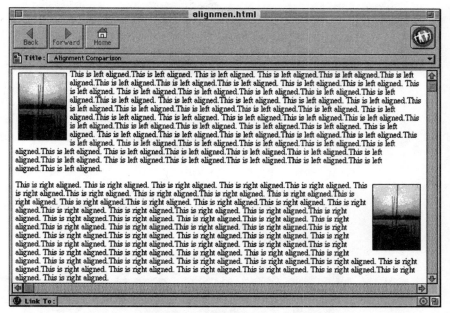

Figure 2-10: Left or right alignment allows text to wrap around an image.

What About White Space?

PageMill 2 is missing one crucial image alignment feature: control over the horizontal and vertical text offset. You can switch to HTML Source mode and add these settings to the image tag, by using the HSPACE="X" and VSPACE="X" modifiers within the <IMG SRC> tag.

Now that you've learned the basics of how to work with placed images, let's take a look at the various types of graphics you'll use to complete your Web page designs.

Navigational Graphics

Navigational graphics are the road signs of your Web site. They provide the means for your visitors to quickly find their way from place to place. In addition, they are an important part of the overall design scheme, providing much of the look and feel (as well as consistency) of a site. Navigational graphics are often referred to as button bars (as shown by Figures 2-11 and 2-12) and can come in both horizontal and vertical orientations. When implementing navigational graphics, you have a choice between assigning one URL or multiple URLs to each individual graphic (through the use of image maps). Once again, we'll get into some of the "Hows" here, while leaving the more philosophical "Whys" for Chapter 5.

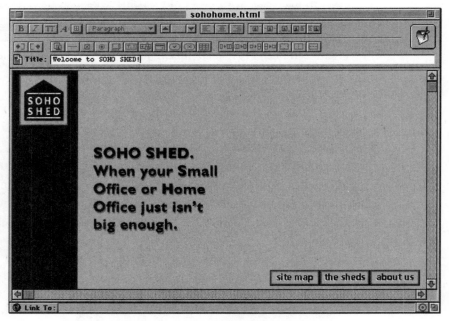

Figure 2-11: A simple three-button horizontal button bar.

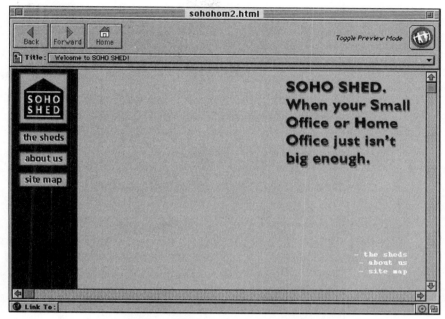

Figure 2-12: And a vertical variation, with a discrete text button bar.

Your navigational graphics may run either horizontally or vertically, depending on the overall design of your site. While early site designs tended to horizontal schemes (due to the constraints of early versions of HTML, most specifically, the lack of multiple columns), vertical navigation devices have come into vogue. Regardless of which orientation you choose, it's always a good idea to provide a text button bar, in addition to the navigation graphic. Text links may not look nearly as cool, but they're always faster and straight to the point.

Linking a Single URL to an Image

If you completed the exercise at the end of Chapter 1, you'll already know just about all you need to know about creating simple text hyperlinks. Creating graphic links is just as straightforward, since assigning a URL to an image is not unlike assigning a

URL to a piece of text. To link a graphic, begin by selecting it. You then have the choice of:

- Manually entering the link in the Link To bar,
- Dragging the page icon from that page onto the selected graphic, or
- Dragging the URL from Netscape Navigator.

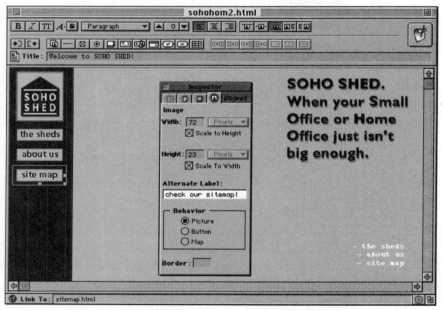

Figure 2-13: If the Border field is blank, PageMill will assign a border to linked images.

When you first link an image (as shown by Figure 2-13), PageMill will assign a border by default. To override the default border, go to the Attributes Inspector, type **0** in the Border field and press the Return key. And while you're there, don't forget to add an alternate text label!

Linking to Multiple URLs With Image Maps

Image maps are the coordinates that tell the server which page to deliver, depending on where the visitor clicks on a navigational graphic. The coordinates provide vertical and horizontal boundaries for each "hot spot" (areas that can be clicked to call up another page). Image maps come in two flavors, server-side and client-side. In general, the difference between the two has to do with where the coordinates reside, and how the browser reacts.

Server-side Image Maps

Server-side image maps are separate coordinate mapping files that must reside on the Web server. They require the use of a CGI script (which must also be on the server) to tell the browser which page to fetch. When a visitor clicks on a server-side image map, the browser sends the coordinates to the server, which then runs the CGI and consequently coughs up the appropriate page. Server-side maps are the original method, but these days, they're not the method of choice. They're slower for the visitor, they're more taxing on the server, and they can be a nuisance to maintain. Also, many ISPs require that your page be part of a commercial-level account if you want to use CGI scripting—a real expense if you're just looking to set up a personal page.

If you (for some unknown reason; perhaps you just like the abuse or have too much free time on your hands) want to create a server-side image map, you'll have to Command+double-click to summon PageMill's Out-of-Place image editor. Before you create a server-side map, however, you should consult with your webmaster as to where to store the map file (and be sure to ask if they'd really be happier with a client-side map).

Client-side Image Maps

Client-side image maps reside in the Web page itself. When a visitor clicks on a client-side image map, the browser sends a request for a specific page. Since no CGI script is required, this reduces the load on the server. And because the page URLs are hard-coded into the page, the browser is able to provide feedback as to where each link leads. For these reasons, client-side image maps are considered to be the more user-friendly of the two methods.

Creating a client-side image map is accomplished directly on the page. To access the client-side image map tools, double-click on the image you want to map; the image map tool buttons will replace the table tool buttons on PageMill's button bar (as shown by Figure 2-14). The image map tools provide the following functions:

- Selector Tool: allows you to choose an existing hot spot.

- Rectangle Hot Spot: assigns rectangular hot spots.

- Circle Hot Spot: assigns oval-shaped hot spots, great for bullets.

- Polygon Hot Spot: assigns irregularly shaped hot spots.

- Shuffle Hot Spot: changes the priority order.

- Hot Spot Color: these 14 colors show only in PageMill's Edit mode, not in the browser.

- Hot Spot Label: these toggle on and off, showing only in PageMill's Edit mode, not in Preview mode.

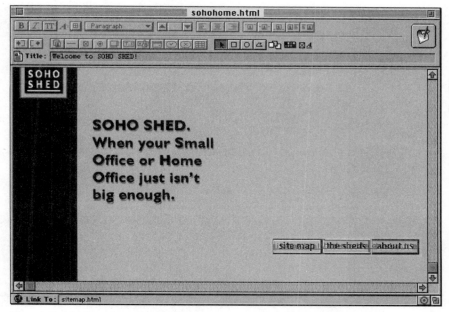

Figure 2-14: Creating client-side image maps with PageMill is a breeze.

To assign a hot spot, choose the appropriately shaped tool, then drag out a hot spot. You can resize a hot spot once it's on the page by pulling on its handles. Type the URL into the Link To bar, press the Return key, and you've got a link! Of course, you can also drag the appropriate page icon onto the hot spot itself. After you've finished assigning hot spots, you can toggle to PageMill's Preview mode to check the links. If you're feeling really brave, you can even take a look at the HTML created by the image map tool by selecting HTML Source on the Edit Menu; what you'll see will be similar to Figure 2-15. They're not all that hard to figure out. Each hot spot is defined by an area shape, starting and ending coordinates, and its URL.

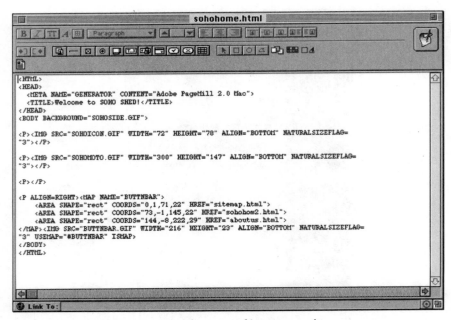

Figure 2-15: Yes! You too can make sense of image maps!

Button bars aren't the only type of navigational graphics that you're likely to use in your Web page designs. The possibilities are truly limitless. In the next section, we'll take a look at how you can use icons, illustrations, and photographs to spice up your pages.

Using Icons, Dingbats & Dividers

A well-designed Web site uses a carefully crafted aggregate of images to convey its message. So far, we've covered what one might consider the "printing stock" of a site: the background and navigational graphics. Those first two image categories form a container into which you'll pour the good stuff. It's time to look at the types of images you can use to allow each Web page to stand on its own by enticing and informing its readers.

Icons

Icons are pictographic objects that can convey more information than one might glean from a single-word text link (or graphic button). Unfortunately, great icons are not the norm. The responsibility of creating icons is too often left to chance (and a clip art book). The best icons are custom crafted specifically for the application at hand. It's essential to create meaningful images that tell the story properly, rather than haphazardly using prebuilt clip art that confuses and frustrates your visitors. The icons used on the mythical Onliner Diner page leave little to chance.

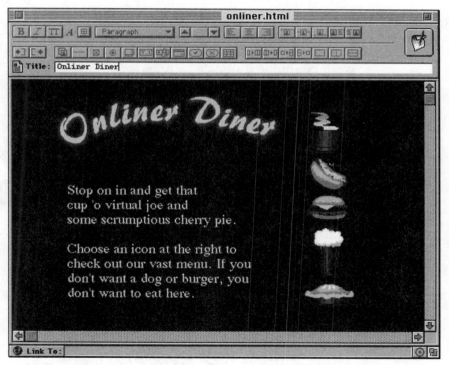

Figure 2-16: There's no confusion here: a dog's a dog and a burger's a burger. Cherry pie with that?

If you decide to use icons as links, you'll be wise to also include text links to the same URLs. These text links do not have to be placed physically next to the icons, just so long as they're not buried too deeply on the page. If you're in search of icons, be sure to check out Chapter 10. It focuses on online typographical re-sources and includes URLs for some wonderful sources for icon fonts, such as Emigre and Letraset.

Dingbats

If the only *dingbat* you know is Edith Bunker, you're showing your age. Any desktop publisher worth his or her weight in lead will tell you that dingbats are really just little typographical doodads, falling somewhere between bullets and icons. But the definition can get blurry in both directions. Figures 2-17 and 2-18 display a number of the dingbats included with Adobe's Zapf Dingbats and Microsoft's Wingdings fonts. In all likelihood, one or both of these fonts are already installed on your Macintosh or PC.

Figure 2-17: Adobe's Zapf Dingbats was, perhaps, the most popular dingbat font of all time, until...

Figure 2-18: ...Microsoft rolled out its Wingdings. Both fonts are stuffed full of nifty little doodads.

Dingbats are a wonderful replacement for the dull, boring bullets provided by HTML's list commands. In order to use a dingbat (from any font) in your PageMill designs, you'll first have to size and rasterize it with your favorite graphics application, such as Adobe Photoshop, Macromedia FreeHand, or CorelDRAW! You can choose to use a dingbat in basic black, or you can colorize it to your heart's content.

When using images as bullets, pay close attention to how the bullets align with the text. Depending on the bullet shape, you may want to try a top, middle, or bottom alignment. This book's CD-ROM contains basic round and square bullet-dingbats in a variety of sizes and 99 "Netscape-safe" colors. These little critters are designed to coordinate with the enclosed vertical striped backgrounds and horizontal divider bars.

Divider Bars

While HTML provides built-in horizontal rules (complete with
control over width and weight), you may find that they do little to
jazz up your Web page designs. Standard HTML rules can get a
little lost on the page. Graphic horizontal dividers, on the other
hand, add a nice touch by breaking pages into clearly defined
sections. And to top it off, you can even use animated GIFs as
bullets or dividers (should you choose to challenge the barriers of
good taste). Chapter 12 lists a number of Web sites where you can
find wacky animated bullets and rules. Figure 2-19 illustrates how
the integrated Web graphics found on this book's CD-ROM can be
used to build a refined little page.

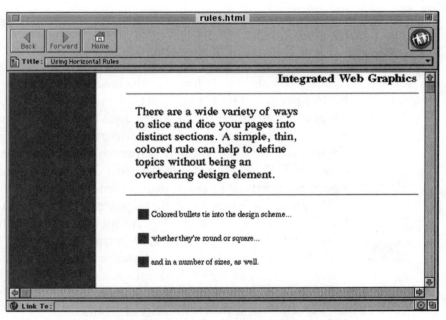

Figure 2-19: Thin, colored horizontal rules are an elegant solution.

Create Cool 3D Bullets & Bars Online!
Patrick J. Hennessey's insanely great Interactive Graphics Renderer (on vacation in Finland) http://www.great.fi/phpl.cgi?IGRNEW/ intro.html.

While the horizontal rules on the CD-ROM are available in three convenient widths (based upon the widths of the vertical striped background), they are all two pixels high. You can change the height (or weight) of the rule by typing a new height value in the Attributes Inspector (just remember to deselect the Scale to Height and Width options). Try adding a border to the rule for a different effect.

With the graphic appetizers out of the way, let's move on to the main course: tasty illustrations and photographs.

Using Illustrations & Photographs

An expressive illustration or an impeccable photograph can convey more in one glance than a Web page chock full of text. The old adage, "A picture is worth a thousand words," is only true, however, when it's the *right* picture. Take the time to find or create the right picture, and you will be rewarded. Use what you have at hand, just to fill space, and the Net will scoff.

Finding Illustrations & Illustrators

Illustrations can come in various forms. At the bottom of the list are the commercial clip art collections. Many of these aggregations aim to deliver a huge volume of material at a low price. While you get thousands upon thousands of images for pennies apiece, you may often find that you don't get *exactly* what you need. The illustration that's in your head is rarely found on a commercial disk. If you have the requisite graphics programs and skill you can try modifying or combining existing artwork, or you can try to create your own from scratch, like we did for the SOHO SHED page, as shown in Figure 2-20.

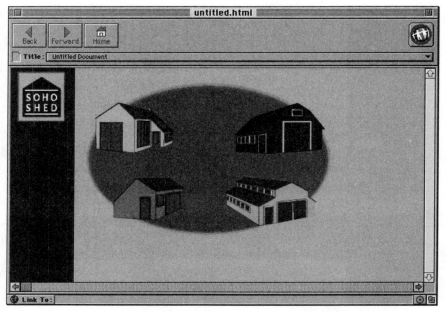

Figure 2-20: Don't look too closely at the perspectives, but these barn illustrations were all created specifically for this Web page.

The most appropriate and effective artwork is created specifically for the application at hand. That's why it's a prudent business decision to find the right artists and have them render something according to your needs. If you have a budget to spend on real illustration, get your hands on a bunch of artists' sourcebooks or some issues of *Communication Arts* (the *Illustration Annual* is a wonderful resource) to see who's who and who does what. These books will have telephone numbers (and maybe even e-mail addresses) of the artists or the agents that represent them.

Looking for an Illustrator?

Here are two places to start...

Publishers Depot
    http://www.publishersdepot.com/
Zaks Illustrator's Source
    http://www.zaks.com/illustrators/

A huge number of professional artists have made their way to the Internet. You can view samples and portfolios online, without ever having to leave your desk chair. For some good places to start, check out these pages on Yahoo:

- http://www.yahoo.com/Arts/Graphic_Arts/Illustration/Artists/

- http://www.yahoo.com/Business_and_Economy/Companies/Arts_and_Crafts/Illustration/Artists/

- http://www.yahoo.com/Business_and_Economy/Companies/Arts_and_Crafts/Illustration/Studios/

Photographs

Photographs are among the most compelling Web page graphics. More so than any other type of imagery, photographs quickly tell their story. By conveying a sense of reality, photographs put the viewer right into the picture and leave little to interpretation (unless, of course, it's an abstract photo). Photographs can be brought into the computer in one of four general ways:

- Scanners
- Digital cameras
- Video frame grabs
- PhotoCD

Looking for a Scanner or Digital Camera?
You'll find a great selection at:
PrePRESS **Main Street**
http://www.prepress.pps.com

Scanners convert either reflective or transparent art into digital form. While basic flatbed reflective scanners—used for digitizing photographic prints, sketches, and the like—start in the $300 range, transparency scanners (which are used for scanning 35mm slides, negatives, and 4"x5" transparencies) start at about a thousand dollars and run up to over a hundred grand for a full-blown commercial drum scanner. For Web page use, however, if you're scanning from 35mm slides, a thousand dollar transparency scanner will deliver all the image you need.

Digital cameras capture images directly into digital files. Although the most affordable digital cameras start at just a few hundred dollars, they are not capable of capturing the same quality of image as the combination of a traditional camera and scanner. The most attractive aspect of the less-expensive digital cameras is that they save time by avoiding the steps of photo processing and scanning. High-end digital cameras, however, deliver serious image quality and are a boon to the quality-oriented, time-constrained Web publisher. As with high-end scanners, though, top-notch digital cameras still cost many thousands of dollars, and are out of most peoples' reach.

Video frame grabs allow you to take still images from a video camcorder or VCR into your Web page designs. The most economical option is Play Inc.'s Snappy, which plugs into the PC's parallel (printer) port and delivers surprisingly good image quality. Kodak's *PhotoCD* is a great choice if you've shot conventional photographic film, but don't have access to a scanner. A Kodak photo lab can take your negatives and scan them onto PhotoCD media. If you use PhotoCD, you'll need a CD-ROM-equipped computer and software capable of converting from the PhotoCD format.

Regardless of source, photographs should almost always be saved as JPEG format files for Web page use. JPEG provides the highest levels of detail and compression, which means that your viewers will get the juiciest shots in the shortest possible time (as shown in Figure 2-21). You can also use digital stock photographs in your Web page designs, in addition to photos you've taken (or had taken) yourself. Just be sure to check those copyright agreements to verify that their use is well within the constraints of the fine print!

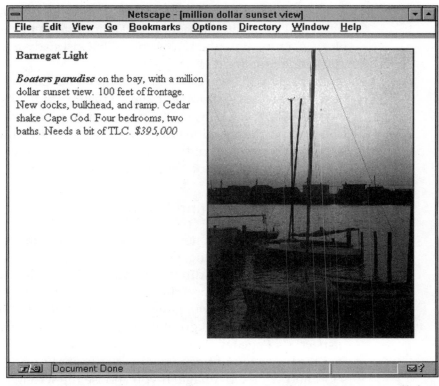

Figure 2-21: *Remember the waterfront property in Chapter 1? You can* **tell** *them about the million dollar sunset view, or you can* **show** *them.*

In the next section, you'll put PageMill to work as you create a simple pair of pages for SOHO SHED, a mythical purveyor of alternate working environments.

Project #2: SOHO SHED

SOHO SHED has decided that it's time to launch their own Web site. SOHO is a unique company. They manufacture sheds and small barns for the small office/home office marketplace. When you're working from home and run out of room, it's time to give SOHO a call. They can deliver a complete air-conditioned and heated shed in two weeks or less. These beauties are ready to move in, fully wired with Ethernet, an Internet router, phone jacks, and even satellite hookups. Their customers never have to pick up a tool, only the telephone. SOHO is ready to extend their marketing blitz to the World Wide Web.

Your task will be to create two sample Web pages: a Welcome page and an image-mapped page displaying SOHO's four basic models. Along the way, you'll learn how to place images, assign transparency to an inline GIF image, and create your own image map. You'll access all of the ready-made graphic files from this book's CD-ROM or Online Updates.

Setting a Background Image

Start out by opening a new page in PageMill. If the Attributes Inspector is not showing, summon it from the Window menu. Open up the CHAP-2 directory from the CD-ROM, drag (copy) it onto your hard drive and then drag the copied directory over to the side of your desktop. Drag the SOHOSIDE.GIF file from that directory onto the background image well in the Attributes Inspector's Page tab. Your page should look like Figure 2-22. Note that the background image well can only show a portion of this short and wide GIF image. If you choose the wrong file, click the little trashcan icon underneath the well and try again.

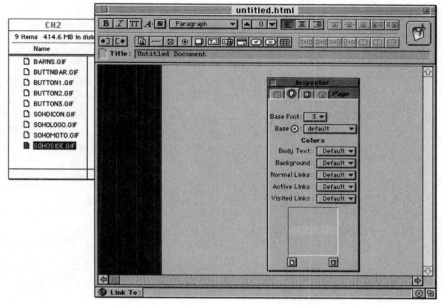

Figure 2-22: The background image in place.

Importing & Linking an Inline GIF Image

Now, let's bring in the SOHO logo icon file. Drag the
SOHOICON.GIF file from the desktop to the upper left corner of
the PageMill window. Did you notice that there are three handles
on the image? These can be used to stretch or scale the placed GIF,
if necessary. Since this logo file was designed to drop right into the
"barn siding," we shouldn't have to fiddle with it. Next, take a
look at the Attributes Inspector. It automatically displays the
height and width of the placed image. You can resize the image (to
the pixel) here as well. Take the time to assign an alternate text
label.

With the image still selected, type **aboutus.htm** in the Link To
field at the bottom of the PageMill window, and press Return.
When PageMill links the image, it automatically assigns a
hyperlink border to it, even though none shows in the Attributes
Inspector (as you can see in Figure 2-23). In the Border field, type **0**
and press Return to remove the border.

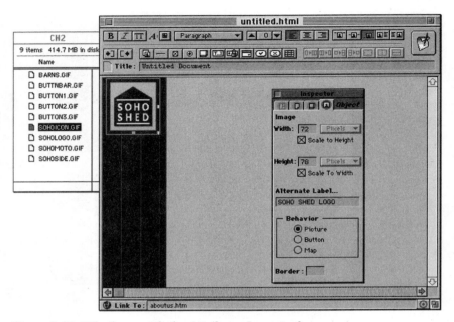

Figure 2-23: What's up with the Attributes Inspector?

Assigning Transparency

Click to the right of the SOHO SHED logo to deselect it. The text insertion point should begin flashing directly to the right of the logo. Press Return to move to the next line. It's time to bring in the company motto. Click and drag SOHOMOTO.GIF from the desktop into the PageMill window, just below the logo. When the image comes in, it will look like it's taking a chunk out of the barn siding (as shown by Figure 2-24). Take the time to label the image as "SOHO SHED. When your Small Office or Home Office just isn't big enough."

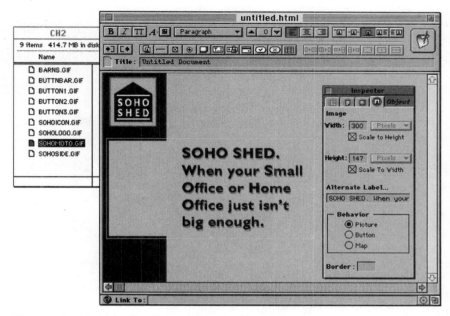

Figure 2-24: Ouch! What happened to the barn siding?

We really don't want to hack up the barn, so let's go ahead and assign transparency to the background color of the SOHOMOTO.GIF image. To assign transparency, you must first bring up PageMill's Out-of-Place image editor by Command+double-clicking on the image. The Out-of-Place image editor provides a transparency tool (the magic wand) and an interlacing tool (the toggling disk/venetian blind), in addition to the image-mapping tools that are available with PageMill's In-Place editor. Transparency is assigned by selecting the background color (which you want to make transparent) with the magic wand. Once you've assigned transparency (as shown in Figure 2-25), save the file by clicking on the button at the top left side of the Out-of-Place image editor window. When you save the file, it will overwrite the original file (which can get you into a loop if you've dragged the file directly from the CD-ROM, since it's impossible to overwrite a CD). Once you've saved the file, the page should appear as in Figure 2-26.

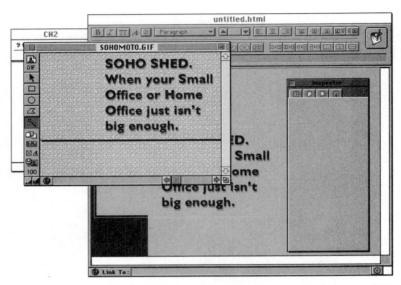

Figure 2-25: While the background looks a little funky in the Out-of-Place image editor, it really is transparent!

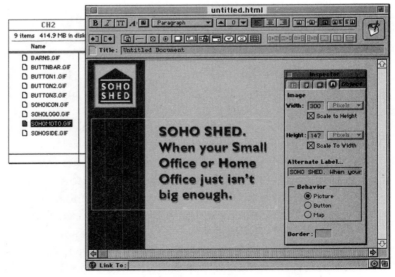

Figure 2-26: Now that's more like it. Once the transparent image is saved to disk, it looks perfect on the Web page.

Of course, you have the option of assigning transparency in your favorite image editor, but PageMill conveniently gives you that one last opportunity to set it as you build your page. In order for a GIF file to be properly transparent, it must have a consistent, non-dithered background. Otherwise, you may end up with a spotty or splotchy "not-quite-so" transparent area. We'll cover more on the subject of transparency and dithering in Chapter 5.

Creating Image Maps

While once deeply shrouded in mystery, the craft of creating image maps is now achievable by common folk. In just a few clicks and drags, you'll image map a simple button bar. Start by deselecting the SOHO motto and press Return. Click and drag BUTTNBAR.GIF from the desktop to just below the SOHO motto. The little button bar will drop onto the barn siding. Make it right align by clicking on the Right Align button at the top of the PageMill window.

To access the in-place image map tools, double-click on the image. Select the Rectangle Hot Spot tool, and drag out a rectangle around the Site Map button. Click in the Link To bar, type **sitemap.htm**, and press Return. It's that easy! Now, repeat the procedure for the last two buttons. Link them to thesheds.htm and aboutus.htm, respectively. The page should appear as it does in Figure 2-27.

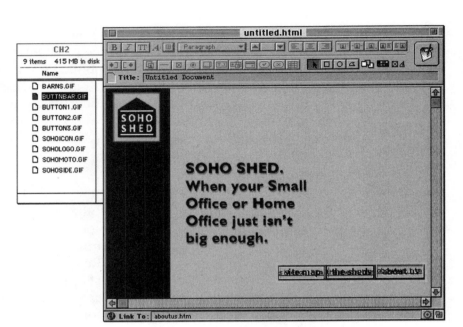

Figure 2-27: To resize a hot spot, just tug on its handles.

To finish off the page, type **Welcome to SOHO SHED!** in the title bar and save it as sohohome.htm. You're going to use the basic template of the page, with the background, button bar, and logo to complete the second page, aboutus.htm.

Delete the SOHO motto graphic from the page and save the file immediately as aboutus.htm. Replace it with BARNS.GIF and center the image. (You may want to try fiddling around with different image alignment settings to alter the spacing between the logo and the barns.) Command+double-click to access the Out-of-Place image editor, make the background transparent, and save the image. Double-click on the image to access the image map tools. Use the Polygon Hot Spot tool on each of the four barns. Just click, click, click around each barn to create the hot spot. From the top left and moving in a clockwise manner, assign the barns the URLs of solarshd.htm, gambrel.htm, horsey.htm, and saltbox.htm. The results should look roughly like Figure 2-28.

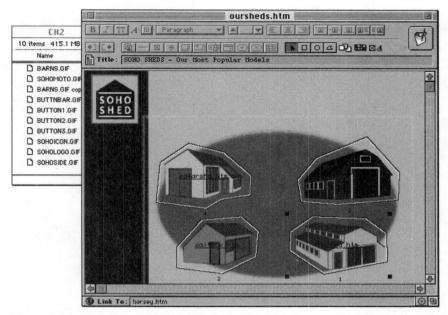

Figure 2-28: With four models to choose from in this image map, how are you going to keep them down on the farm, er, home office?

While the underbelly of the image map has a disconcerting appearance in Edit mode, all of the noise disappears when you toggle into Preview mode. Try it now to check it out.

Moving On

In this chapter, you learned how to work with graphics in Adobe PageMill. A successfully designed Web page includes a healthy mix of both text and graphics. You worked from the back (the background and navigational graphics) of a Web page through to the front (icons, illustrations, and photographs). It's good practice to attack the design of a page by taking into consideration how the different layers visually interact. A haphazard collection of graphics does not make an effective Web page.

In the next chapter, we'll cover some of the more advanced HTML text and layout features provided by the program, such as tables, frames, and forms.

chapter 3

Working With Tables, Frames & Forms

Typically, when a person starts out building their very first Web pages, they often "hit the wall" and become frustrated by the complexity involved in creating anything but the simplest page layout. Fortunately, PageMill 2 makes it easy to implement some of the most intricate features of HTML's command set, such as tables, frames, and forms. This chapter builds upon what you've learned in the previous two chapters and allows you to quickly master these advanced features.

Learning how to control tables, frames, and forms is key to the craft of advanced Web page design. With PageMill's visual controls, you can see exactly what you're doing, as you're doing it.

Why Should I Use Tables?

HTML tables impart a high level of structure in your Web page designs. When tables were first implemented (back in Netscape Navigator 1.1), Web designers quickly became enthralled with their control over text alignment, individual column width, overall table width, borders, and various spacing attributes. In the early days, it was a tough hack to write out all the HTML code necessary to build a nice-looking table. Thankfully, PageMill 2's Attributes Inspector and interactive design now make it easy to control each of these characteristics.

There are three basic reasons to use HTML tables. The first reason is implied by the name of the command, while the second and third, although they are every bit as important, may not be as obvious. You'll use tables:

- To create tables, such as spreadsheets, parts listings, statistical data, and financial reports (as shown by Figure 3-1).

- To constrain pages to a specific width.

- To create multicolumn page layouts.

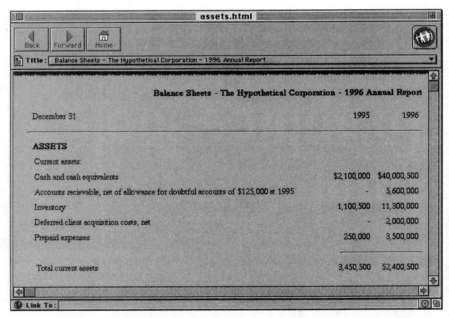

Figure 3-1: The Hypothetical Corporation uses their Web site to deliver their annual report to shareholders and the financial community.

Using Tables as Tables

When someone first mentions tables, one immediately thinks of the many types of information that are commonly presented in columnar form. The first thing that might come to mind is a spreadsheet, such as those from Microsoft Excel or Lotus 1-2-3. Perhaps you might think of the asset sheet from your company's annual report (as shown in Figure 3-1). If you're a sports fan, yesterday's box scores could be the ticket.

With PageMill 2, it's easy to create HTML tables that can be highly customized to suit your needs. The Attributes Inspector's table controls allow you to take charge over the entire table, as well as over individual cells. Table height, however, has to be set interactively. With the entire table selected, you'll be able to affect the following characteristics (as shown in Figure 3-2):

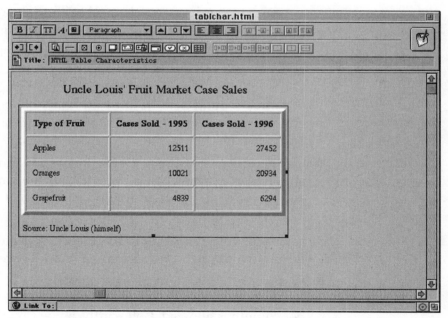

Figure 3-2: This simple table includes a border, cell spacing, cell padding, and a caption.

- Width—Can be set absolutely (as pixels) or relatively (as a percentage of browser width). You can click and drag on the table border to resize the relative width interactively, or you can change the width settings in the Attributes Inspector.

- Height—Optional. Can be set in absolute pixels (while in HTML Source mode— use the HEIGHT="XX" modifier within the TD command). Click and drag on the table border to resize the height interactively.

- Caption—Optional. Can be set to run either above the table (as a title) or below (as a footnote). Captioning is toggled on and off via the Attributes Inspector.

- Border—Runs around the outside of the table. Can be set anywhere from 0 (no border) to 50 (a huge, silly border). You'll rarely need to go wider than 5 (if that), although the wider the border, the more three dimensional the table will appear. The border is set via the Attributes Inspector.

- Cell spacing—The amount of space *between* cells. Appears as visible grid lines when the table border is set to anything larger than 0 and as white space when the border is set to 0. You might think of cell spacing as individual cell borders (keeping in mind that the attributes can only be set for an entire table, not specific cells). Cell spacing is set via the Attributes Inspector.

- Cell padding—No, it's not what we need in our offices after we've been working on our Web site for too long; it's the amount of white space added *inside* each cell. Cell padding is set via the Attributes Inspector.

You can apply cell controls to individual cells or groups of cells. Here's a rundown on cell controls (as shown in Figure 3-3):

- Width constraint—Can be set absolutely (as pixels) or relatively (as a percentage of table width). Only one width per column is allowed. Cell width can be set interactively by clicking and dragging on cell borders or by entering the width via the Attributes Inspector.

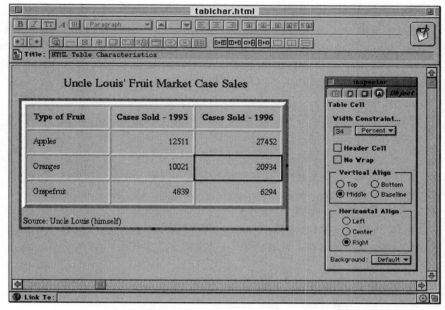

Figure 3-3: Individual cell controls are set via the Attributes Inspector.

■ Header cell—Automatically sets text in boldface. Set via the Attributes Inspector.

■ No wrap—Bases column width on longest line. Set via the Attributes Inspector.

■ Vertical alignment—Top, middle, bottom, or baseline (above the top!) of cell. Set via the Attributes Inspector.

■ Horizontal alignment—Left, right, or center. Set via the Attributes Inspector.

■ Background color—Can be set to any valid color. Background tiles are not supported. Set via the Attributes Inspector.

You can also plug the settings directly into the table commands while in HTML Source mode (as shown by Figure 3-4). HTML Source mode is a great asset when you're trying to fine-tune or troubleshoot a table. You can access HTML Source mode via the Edit menu or through the Command+H keyboard shortcut.

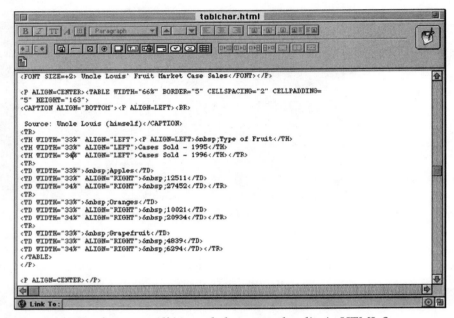

```
<FONT SIZE=+2> Uncle Louis' Fruit Market Case Sales</FONT></P>

<P ALIGN=CENTER><TABLE WIDTH="66%" BORDER="5" CELLSPACING="2" CELLPADDING=
"5" HEIGHT="163">
<CAPTION ALIGN="BOTTOM"><P ALIGN=LEFT><BR>

 Source: Uncle Louis (himself)</CAPTION>
<TR>
<TH WIDTH="33%" ALIGN="LEFT"><P ALIGN=LEFT> Type of Fruit</TH>
<TH WIDTH="33%" ALIGN="LEFT">Cases Sold - 1995</TH>
<TH WIDTH="34%" ALIGN="LEFT">Cases Sold - 1996</TH></TR>
<TR>
<TD WIDTH="33%"> Apples</TD>
<TD WIDTH="33%" ALIGN="RIGHT"> 12511</TD>
<TD WIDTH="34%" ALIGN="RIGHT"> 27452</TD></TR>
<TR>
<TD WIDTH="33%"> Oranges</TD>
<TD WIDTH="33%" ALIGN="RIGHT"> 10021</TD>
<TD WIDTH="34%" ALIGN="RIGHT"> 20934</TD></TR>
<TR>
<TD WIDTH="33%"> Grapefruit</TD>
<TD WIDTH="33%" ALIGN="RIGHT"> 4839</TD>
<TD WIDTH="34%" ALIGN="RIGHT"> 6294</TD></TR>
</TABLE>
</P>

<P ALIGN=CENTER></P>
```

Figure 3-4: Don't get scared! You only have to make edits in HTML Source mode if you want to.

Working With Tables

PageMill 2 lets you work with tables from a variety of sources. You can open up existing HTML tables (which have been created in other programs), you can use PageMill's conversion utilities to convert files, or you can create your own tables from scratch. If your word processing program supports HTML table export, you can save time by exporting a table and then opening up the HTML file in PageMill to make the last few tweaks. Chapter 9 reviews a number of ways to get outside data into PageMill.

One of the coolest (and fastest) ways to get table data into PageMill 2 is to cut and paste it from Microsoft's popular spreadsheet program, Excel (as shown in Figures 3-5 and 3-6). To move a table from Excel into PageMill, all you have to do is select the range of cells in Excel, copy them, switch to PageMill, and paste them in. Once the table is on the Web page, you can go in and tweak it to your heart's content.

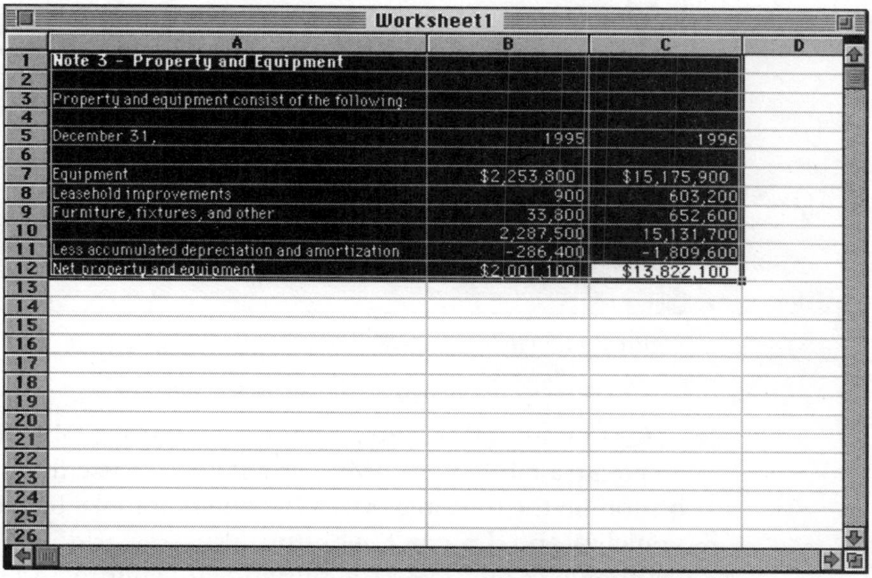

Figure 3-5: Here's the table in Excel. Just select and copy.

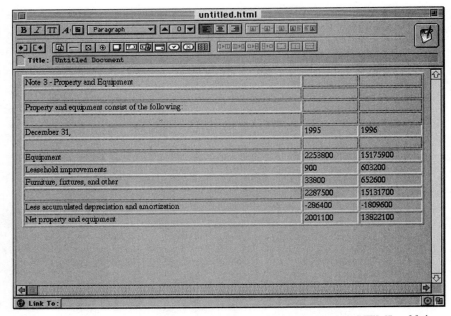

Figure 3-6: Switch to PageMill. Paste it in, and presto...instant HTML table!

Right now, let's see what it takes to create a table from scratch. To create a table in PageMill, you'll need to use the Insert Table button on the button bar (it's the one that looks like a little grid). If you click and drag on the button, a snappy grid will drop down (as shown in Figure 3-7), signifying table width and height in columns and rows, respectively. A maximum of 10 rows and 10 columns can be specified in this manner. When the mouse button is released, PageMill will draw the table with its default border, cell spacing, and cell padding (as shown in Figure 3-8).

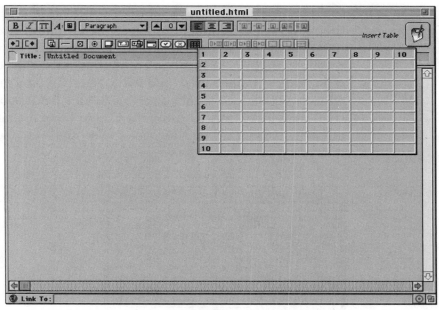

Figure 3-7: The drop-down grid looks like a flyswatter of sorts.

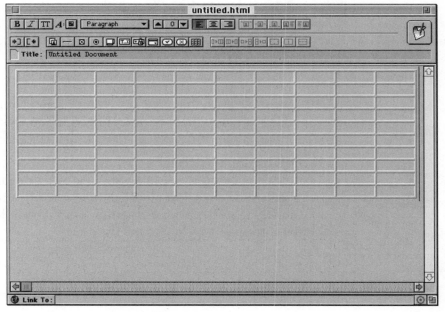

Figure 3-8: The 10 X 10 grid is drawn.

If you click on the Insert Table button (instead of clicking and dragging) you'll summon the Create Table dialog box. This convenient dialog box allows you to specify more than 10 rows or columns (up to 99 of each!) in addition to setting the cell spacing, cell padding, table border, and width (as shown by Figure 3-9). If you know how you want your table to look before you set it, you can save a bit of time by using the Create Table dialog box (instead of going to the Attributes Inspector to set these characteristics after the table is already on the page).

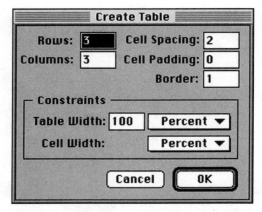

Figure 3-9: The Create Table dialog box lets you set table characteristics before you drop the table on the page.

Once the table is on the page, you can proceed to enter the data or edit what's already there (if you opened up an existing HTML file). There are a handful of tricks to editing a table's contents:

■ Edit the data in a cell by clicking an insertion point, by double-clicking to select a word, or by triple-clicking to select a line. To select all the data in a word-wrapped (multiline) cell, click an insertion point and Select All or use the Command+A keyboard shortcut.

- To change the characteristics—such as the width, alignment, or background color—of a cell (or cells), you must first select the cell (or range of cells) by clicking and dragging from one corner of the selection to the opposite corner. An outline will appear around the cell (or cells), letting you know exactly what is selected. Changes can then be entered in the Attributes Inspector.

- If working in a text editor more suits your style, you can always switch to the HTML Source mode (as shown back in Figure 3-4).

OK, That's Cool, but How Do I...?

Unfortunately, HTML doesn't provide all the niceties that you may have come to expect from your spreadsheet program. For instance, it's not possible to perform decimal alignment on columns of figures. You'll have to cook up a design compromise to handle situations such as this.

Adding & Deleting Columns & Rows

The first four buttons in PageMill's table-editing button bar (see Figure 3-10) make it easy to add or delete columns or rows. To add a column or row, begin by selecting a cell (or cells), then click on the appropriate button. The column or row will be added to the table immediately after the selected column or row. In other words, columns are added to the right of the selection, and rows are added below the selection. The process of deleting columns or rows is straightforward, as well. Just select a cell in the column or row you want to delete and click the appropriate button.

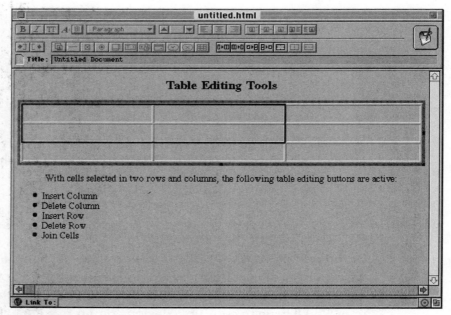

Figure 3-10: The table-editing button bar becomes active dependent upon the selected cells.

Joining & Splitting Cells

You're probably thinking, OK, now what do those last three buttons in the table-editing button bar actually do? Get ready to go back to high school biology class, because you're about to learn how to join and split cells! While this is not truly comparable to the mystery of life, it is the HTML magic behind the most complex table and page layouts. Coding this kind of stuff by hand is a laborious chore that often leads to premature hair loss and intense stomach distress. Thankfully, PageMill 2 makes this about as easy as it could possibly be (as shown in Figure 3-11).

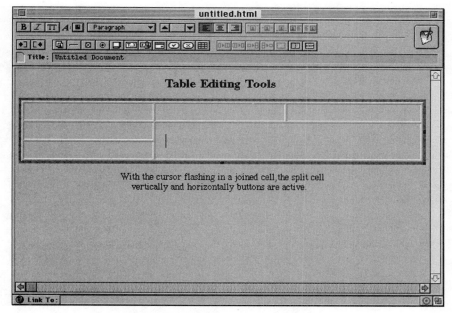

Figure 3-11: Joining and splitting table cells is a breeze.

To join two (or more) cells, all you need to do is select the cells and click the Join Cell button. If you take a look at the source code, you'll see that HTML uses ROWSPAN="X" and COLSPAN="X" modifiers to allow a joined cell to straddle rows or columns, where the *X* defines the number of cells to be straddled. These features are invaluable when you start building anything more than the most simple table and page layouts. Figure 3-12 demonstrates a common example of how you might use these features. The "Fruit Sold (by case)" heading straddles two rows, while the "Years" heading straddles three columns.

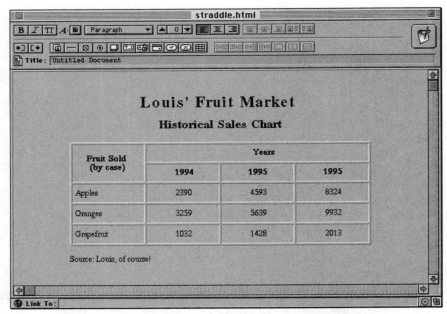

Figure 3-12: It would be impossible to create a table like this without joining cells.

To split a joined cell (either vertically or horizontally), click within the cell you wish to split and click the appropriate button. It's that easy! Now, let's take a look at why just about every Web page should use at least one simple table.

Exercise #3: Building a Table

Let's take what we've just learned and replicate the table shown in Figure 3-12. You'll want to start with a new page:

1. Click and drag on the Insert Table button to create a 4-column X 5-row grid. When you release the mouse button, PageMill creates a 4 X 5 table.

2. Click and drag to select the top two cells in the first column. Click the Join Cells button to vertically (row) span the cells.

3. Click and drag to select the top cell in the last three columns. Click the Join Cells button to horizontally (column) span the cells.

4. Following Figure 3-12, type the information into each cell. Click in the spanned cells to enter the data there. Use the Tab key to move forward through the other cells (Shift+Tab to move backward).

5. Once all the data has been entered, click and drag to select the 12 cells containing the years and sales data. Use the Attributes Inspector to set the Vertical Align to middle and the Horizontal Align to center.

6. Click and drag to select the two spanned cells and the three cells containing the years. Use the Attributes Inspector to designate these cells as Header Cells and set the Vertical Align to middle and the Horizontal Align to center.

7. Click on the page to deselect the table, then reselect it. Use the Attributes Inspector to set a bottom-aligned caption. Try fiddling around with different Borders, Cell Spacing, and Cell Padding options to see how they affect the table.

8. On the table, select the default word "caption" and type a new caption. To push the caption away from the table, place the cursor at the beginning of the caption and press Shift+Return to add a line. Use a Shift+Return to break "Fruit Sold (by case)" into two lines as well.

What's the Difference Between a Return & a Shift-Return?

When you press a normal Return, you'll get a standard line ending, which includes extra space between that line and the line that follows it. When you press a Shift-Return you'll get what's known in word processing terms as a *soft return*. Soft returns don't add any extra space, in addition to maintaining the current style. In HTML body text terms, this comes down to using either the <P> or <BR> commands, respectively.

9. To change the overall height of the table, click and drag downward on the left- or right-hand lower corners. You can also interactively change the overall width of the table in this manner. To set the width of the table precisely, enter the width in the Attributes Inspector (precisely with pixels or relatively as a percentage).

10. Try changing column width interactively by clicking and dragging on the intercolumn grid lines. Then, try changing column widths by selecting all the cells in a column and entering the width in the Attributes Inspector.

Once you've finished this little table, try experimenting on your own. Drag in some graphics, try changing cell background colors, and give nested tables a whirl as well!

Using Tables to Constrain Page Width

Have you ever seen a Web page that looked totally unbalanced—
one where the header graphic ended three quarters of the way
across the browser window, but the text flowed out to fill the
window (as demonstrated by Figure 3-13)? That's an example of
an unconstrained Web page and a prime reason why tables are
essential when building anything but the most elementary layouts. Tables allow you to design pages that "stick" to a defined
width. While an unconstrained Web page allows its text to flow
freely to fit the width of the browser window, you can set a specific pixel width for the text to flow (as in Figure 3-14), by adding
a simple table to the page.

Figure 3-13: An unconstrained Web page, with text spilling all over the place.

Figure 3-14: The same page, given a bit of manners with a simple table.

When creating a width-constraining table, you'll probably want to base the table width upon the width of the widest graphic on the page. It's a good strategy to have one overall page width that carries through every page on your Web site to provide a continuity of design. Otherwise, your pages will seem like they're jumping all over the place. Try building some page-width-constraining tables now, using the table-building skills that you've just learned.

Nested Tables

For intricate layouts, you'll often place tables within tables. Tables such as these are commonly referred to as *nested tables*. While that term might conjure up visions of those funny end tables at Aunt Edna's place, good old Edna never had the furniture flexibility that PageMill 2 provides when building complex Web pages. You won't end up with your proverbial drink and hors d'oeuvre in your lap.

Nested tables come into play when you place, say, a little spreadsheet into a page with a table-constrained layout. Tables can be dragged and dropped into other tables, or they can be cut and pasted. You have the option of dragging them from the Pasteboard, as well as from other pages. Figure 3-15 shows a simple pair of nested tables, as you might see used on a baseball Web page. To nest a table within another table, click in the cell you want to place the table into; then paste (or drag) the table into position. It's that easy!

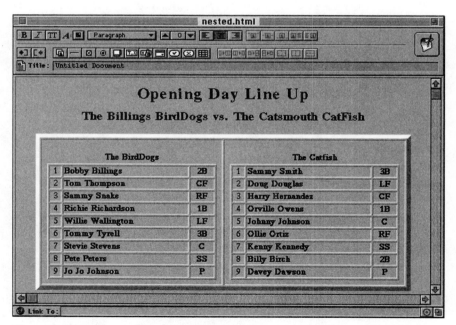

Figure 3-15: Batter up! Nested tables make it easy to compile complex Web pages from a number of sources.

Once the "inside" table is nested in the "outside" table, you can assign the inside table's horizontal and vertical alignment within its cell. You can also try some nifty design tricks by using different colored backgrounds for the inside and outside tables. Nested tables open up a whole new range of Web page layout possibilities. Try giving one a shot now. You'll be amazed at how easy they are to build.

Now that you've got the nitty-gritty on how to build tables, let's take a look at how you can use tables to build complex multi-column pages.

Using Tables for Multicolumn Pages

The slickest Web page designs use the HTML table commands to create multiple-column layouts. While we're all accustomed to multiple-column print publications, such as newspapers and magazines, multiple-column Web page layouts are a different beast altogether. Multicolumn Web pages most often consist of two- or three-column layouts. The dynamics of good Web page design frequently demand that the first column of a multicolumn page be used for a vertical navigational bar (as shown by the front page of the ESPN Auto Racing Web site, in Figure 3-16).

Figure 3-16: The front page of ESPN's Auto Racing Web site uses a vertical button bar in the first column.

ESPN uses a clean, uncluttered design on the front page of their Auto Racing Web site. The site is constantly being updated with breaking news stories, so the cleaner it is, the better. Buttons for NASCAR, Indy Car, Formula One, NHRA, and IRL standings and results line the skinny left-hand column, while the wider right-hand column contains headlines and teasers for feature stories. While most browsers aren't able to display the entire page without scrolling, those folks lucky enough to have a 21-inch monitor (running at a high resolution) can get it all in one glance.

The *San Jose Mercury News* Web site, Mercury Center, is a vanguard of great Web newspaper design. A lively layout, as shown by Figure 3-17, breaks the front page up into distinct sections. The info-laden page is lengthy, requiring the reader to scroll even on the largest monitor. Lead stories fill the left side, which is broken into a grid that allows the stories to span multiple columns as necessary. In contrast to the ESPN Auto Racing site, the Mercury Center site has its skinny navigational column on the right side, where it is used for short teaser lines and limited advertising spots. One can easily imagine how PageMill 2's cell joining and splitting tools could make intense layouts such as this possible for the average Web page designer.

Figure 3-17: Mercury Center defines great newspaper Web site design through the use of a nifty table-created layout.

While it's doubtful that the Web sites you create will be as high-powered (or well-funded) as the ESPN and *San Jose Mercury News* sites, you can learn a lot from the way that they've built their grids. Since both of these sites are constantly changing, they've been designed so that changes can be accomplished with a minimum of hassle. Careful annotation in your HTML file can help you to keep your sanity by adding comment fields (Edit | Insert Invisible | Comment).

With the basics of tables under your belt, let's take a look at how to create framed Web sites.

What's the Big Deal With Frames?

Frames afford the Web page designer the ability to create Web sites with a persistent structure. This enables a flexible site, where certain items such as headers, advertising banners, and navigational devices remain intact as your visitors scroll about through the content and jump from page to page. Figure 3-18 illustrates how Netscape uses a horizontal dual-frame design on their Destinations page (http://www.netscape.com/escapes/index.htm) to maintain a static advertising banner at the bottom of the browser window. Keeping the ad banner in view enhances the probability that the visitor will actually read it and (as the advertiser would hope) will click through.

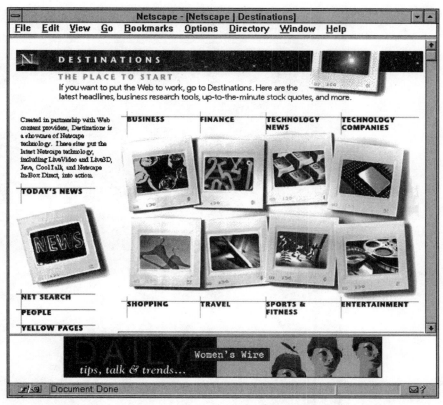

Figure 3-18: Ad banners placed in a static frame can't scroll away from view.

The Twentieth Century Fox Home Entertainment Web site also features a dual-framed design (as shown in Figure 3-19). The Fox site uses a skinny vertical frame to maintain its navigation bar. Interestingly enough, on the night we visited their Web site, the front page (http://www.tcfhe.com) featured a little tutorial on how to browse a framed site, in addition to providing visitors the choice of viewing Shocked or non-Shocked versions of the site. (You'll find more information on Macromedia's Shockwave in Chapter 12.) And to make things even more friendly, the navigation bar even includes a "browsing tips" section. Now that's downright neighborly!

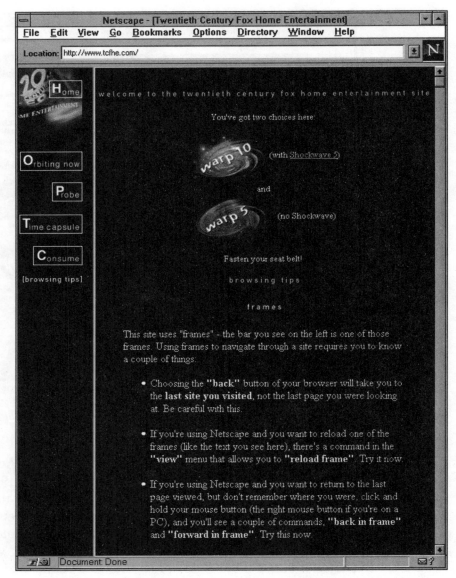

Figure 3-19: Just in case you were wondering how to navigate a framed site, Twentieth Century Fox Home Entertainment provides a few tips.

Microsoft's CarPoint Web site (http://carpoint.msn.com/) delivers its bounty of new car information via a triple-framed interface (as shown in Figure 3-20). The squat and wide top horizontal frame contains the site ID logo, along with Find, Home, Back, and Help hyperlinks. The tall, skinny frame at the left contains a menu of vehicle choices. When you click on a vehicle, the vehicle information is displayed in the main target window (as shown in Figure 3-21). We wanted to find out what ever happened to the 1996 Land Rover Defender 90. The mystery was solved after clicking the link; we found out that Land Rover chose not to bring over any 1996 models. We're saving our nickels and dimes for when the Defender reappears on our shores as a 1997 model.

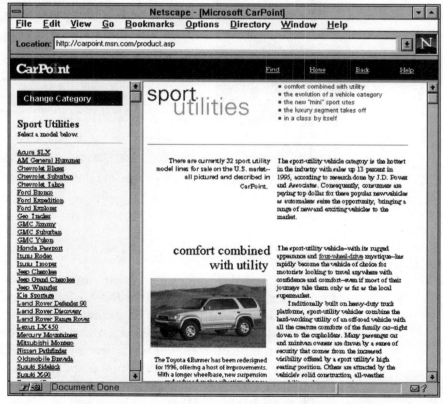

Figure 3-20: Three frames allow Microsoft's CarPoint Web site to pack a lot of information into a tight space.

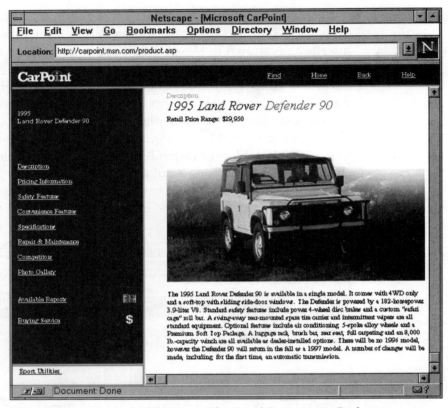

Figure 3-21: It's not a $30,000 Jeep. It's a Land Rover, mate. Back seats are optional.

How Do Frames Work?

In short, framed Web pages are nothing more than simple containers for other Web pages. It helps to think of a framed layout as a little curio cabinet. You're allowed to build as many "shelves" as you want (although common sense says to never exceed three; use four and you'll be on thin Net ice) in your cabinet, although each shelf (frame) is capable of holding just one item at a time. The curio cabinet is known as a *frameset,* with each shelf holding an individual Web page. When you click a link on a framed page, the new page is displayed within the *targeted* window. You specify the target window when you create your links.

A Framed Caveat

Using frames can throw up a big wall between your Web site and your audience. Before you consider adding framed pages, you should watch your server logs (if possible) to determine what percentage of your visitors are using a browser that is capable of displaying frames. If the figure is significantly high (say, over 85 percent), go for it. If not, wait a while...it won't be long before most everyone on the World Wide Web will be using a frames-capable browser.

The frameset is a rather terse little file, basically consisting of a page title, along with references to the initial frame source files, as well as sizing, naming, and scrolling information. When referring to the URL of a framed Web site, always refer to the URL of the frameset, not of the frames contained therein.

Creating a Framed Layout

PageMill greatly simplifies the creation of framed Web sites. Building the frames themselves is actually pretty easy—like most things PageMillian, all you have to do is drag 'em and drop 'em. It's getting the targeting right that might make your eyes cross, unless you have a solid understanding of the basic principles. It's best to sketch out a diagram of how you'd like your framed Web site to work *before* you go too far with page creation. While this is always a good idea, it's especially so when creating framed sites.

Drawing Frames

You have a number of options when drawing a new frame. To quickly split a window (or existing frame) in two, choose Edit | Split Horizontally or use the control-command-H keyboard shortcut; this will stack the new frame, as shown in Figure 3-22. If you want to create side-by-side frames, choose Edit | Split Vertically or use the control-command-V keyboard shortcut, demonstrated by Figure 3-23.

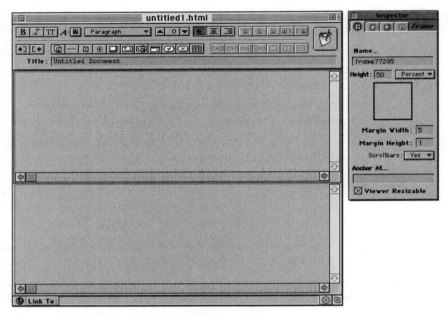

Figure 3-22: A new frame, split horizontally.

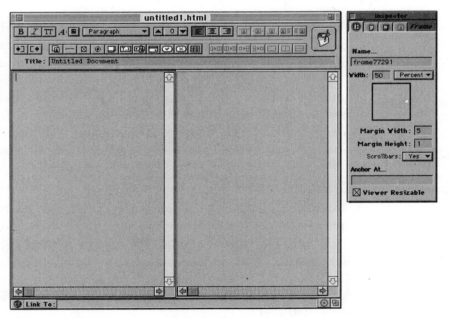

Figure 3-23: A new frame, split vertically.

You can also option-drag new frames out from the borders of the PageMill window. To do so, position the cursor over the horizontal (to create a horizontal frame) or vertical (to create a vertical frame) border, hold down the Option key, and drag to the approximate position where you want the border to appear. Once the frames are drawn (no matter which method you used to draw them), you can reposition the frame border by clicking and dragging it. Try creating some frames now, while experimenting with each method.

Take a close look at the Attributes Inspector as shown in Figures 3-22 and 3-23. With the Frame tab chosen, you're able to fine-tune each frame. The very first thing you should do is give each frame its own distinctive name. This step is especially important to do *before* you start building in your hyperlinks. If you change the name of the frame after it's linked, things could go awry. The name you specify in the Attributes Inspector will be the filename that PageMill uses when it saves the frame. Here's a rundown of the other options afforded by the Frame tab:

- Height—can be set for horizontal frames, in percentage, pixel, or relative terms.

- Width—can be set for vertical frames, in percentage, pixel, or relative terms.

- Margin Width—the amount of space between the left and right sides of a frame and its contents.

- Margin Height —the amount of space between the top and bottom sides of a frame and its contents.

- Scrollbars—can be set to yes, no, and auto. If the frame's content doesn't require scrollbars, be sure to uncheck this option.

- Anchor At—allows you to set up a framed page so that it opens at a specific point within a frame.

- Viewer Resizable—uncheck this box to prevent visitors from resizing specific windows (such as advertising banners).

Once you've drawn a frame, you can draw additional frames within that frame. Just click inside the framed area and create the new frame using the methods described above. Before you go wild (as shown by Figure 3-24) and start drawing too many frames, you should sit down and consider the alternatives. You may be able to accomplish a similar layout through the use of tables instead.

What's the Deal With the Squares?

Take a gander at the Attributes Inspector in Figure 3-24. Then, look back at Figures 3-22 and 3-23. Did you notice the twin squares in Figure 3-24? These nested squares are known as the Frames Widget. They indicate how deeply an individual frame is nested and allow you to set the width and height for each frame. Click on the inner and outer squares to toggle between the width and height settings.

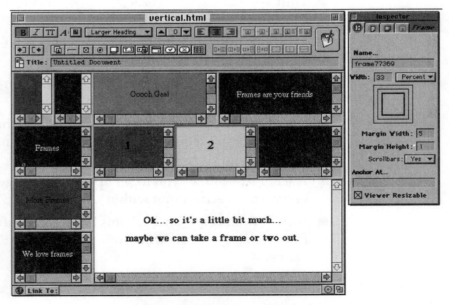

Figure 3-24: It's important to use frames in moderation!

With the frames laid out and properly named, you should immediately use File | Save Frameset or the shift-command-S keyboard shortcut to save your frameset. Once you start building inside the frames, you can also use File | Save Everything or the command-E keyboard shortcut to save the frameset along with the individual frames in one fell swoop. PageMill will not store the individual frames, however, until after they contain some content.

Targeting a Frame

It's one thing to create a nifty-looking framed interface, and it's quite another to make it work (right). PageMill affords you a number of options when targeting your framed links. Do you recall seeing a funny looking bull's-eye, both on the Page tab of the Attributes Inspector (in red and white) and at the bottom of the PageMill window (in tones of gray)? Surprise! That bull's-eye summons PageMill 2's targeting mechanism. The Attributes Inspector allows you to set the default target for each page, while the bull's-eye at the bottom of the window allows you to set the target for each individual link, should they need to override the default.

There are five basic ways to target a framed link:

- New window—opens the linked page up in a brand new browser window, which leaves the original framed browser window intact.

- Parent window—opens the linked page up in the current browser window, while wiping out the original frames.

- Same frame—opens the linked page up in the same frame in which the link resides.

- Same window—opens the linked page up in the same window. Similar to parent window option.

- Specific window—opens up the link in a specified window.

Now it's time to put that frame theory to work as you build a simple three-framed layout for the mythical Simple Links Web site.

Exercise #4: Building a Framed Web Page

Simple Links is a groovy little golf shop. They're just getting their online act together and have decided that a framed layout is the best solution for their Web site. True to the company's name, the three-framed layout they've chosen delivers their message with a minimum of fuss. You'll want to start this exercise by creating a new file: File | New or via the command-N keyboard shortcut.

1. Position the cursor over the left-side window border. Hold down the Option key—the cursor will turn into a right-facing arrow (as shown in Figure 3-25)—and drag toward the middle of the page to create a vertical frame. When you release the mouse button, the frames will be drawn (as shown in Figure 3-26).

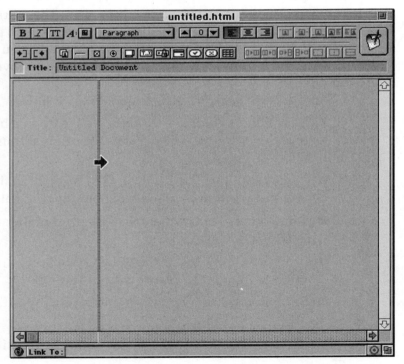

Figure 3-25: The frame-creation arrow points toward the center of the window (and away from the border you're dragging from).

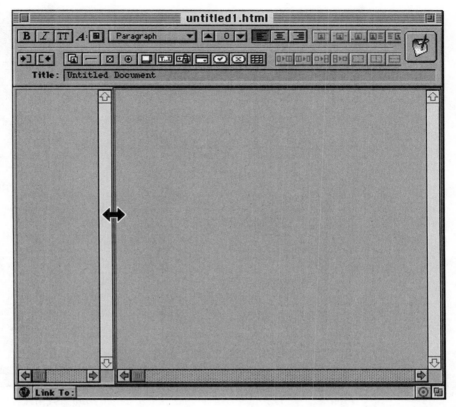

Figure 3-26: Instant frames! You can resize the frame by clicking and dragging on the border.

2. You need to set the width of the left frame before you go any further. Click within the left frame to ensure that it is selected. At the Attributes Inspector's Frame tab, choose Pixels, type **108**, and press Return. The width of the left frame is now set at 108 pixels.

3. Next, you'll create a smaller horizontal frame inside the left vertical frame. With the left vertical frame selected, choose Edit | Split Horizontally. Two horizontal frames will replace the one skinny, vertical frame (as shown in Figure 3-27). Adjust the frame borders to make the top frame fairly small.

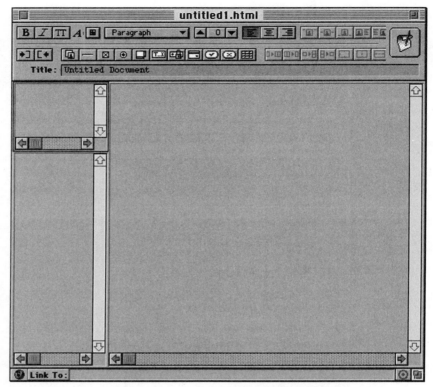

Figure 3-27: The highlight lets you know which frame is currently selected.

4. Now that all three frames have been drawn, it's time to name them. You're going to click in each frame to select it and then type a frame name—followed by a Return in the Name field on the Attributes Inspector's Frame tab. Name the little frame "logo," the big frame "big," and the last frame "menu."

5. Before you do anything else, let's save the frameset with a File | Save Everything or a command-E. You'll want to put everything in a brand new folder entitled "simple." At this point, PageMill will only save the frameset, unless you've entered something on one of the frames. If you have entered something on one of the frames, PageMill will automatically save that frame with the name you plugged into the Attributes Inspector. Save the frameset file as simplink.htm.

6. Now, it's time to drop in the logo and add a title. You'll need to get the simplink.gif from this book's CD-ROM. Copy it from the CHAP-3 folder on the CD into the simple folder on your computer's hard drive. Then, drag simplink.gif into the little frame at the top left. The logo looks pretty good, but the background of that frame should really be set to white. Bring up the color panel (Window | Show Color Panel), click the Page tab on the Attributes Inspector, and drag the white color chip onto the background button. In the Title field, type: **Welcome to Simple Links!** and press Return.

7. We've got to get rid of those hideous scrollbars and set the frame height. Click the Frame tab on the Attributes Inspector. Select No at the Scrollbars drop-down list. At Height, first select pixels and then type **84**. Set both Margin Width and Margin Height to 12. Make sure that Viewer Resizeable is unchecked. Fiddle with the frame border until the page appears as in Figure 3-28. Choose File | Save Frame As to save the frame as logo.htm.

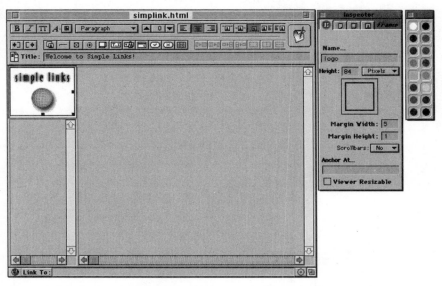

Figure 3-28: Center the Simple Links logo and adjust the frames to fit.

8. It's time to create our navigational text. In the skinny window on the bottom left, type the following words, each separated by a Return: **welcome**, **products**, **news**, **people**, **links**, **help**. Set them to bold and align them all flush right. Use the color panel and Attributes Inspector's Page tab to set the body text to yellow, the background color to dark blue, the normal link color to white, the active link to bright green, and the visited link color to light blue. Set the base font size to 4. Click the Frame tab. At Scrollbars, select No. Make sure that Viewer Resizeable is unchecked.

9. Now, select each one of the menu links and use the Link To field to link them to pages entitled welcome.htm, products.htm, news.htm, people.htm, links.htm, and help.htm, respectively. You can find these prebuilt pages in the CHAP-3 folder on this book's CD-ROM. Drag them into the simple folder.

10. Ready, steady, go...it's time to target those links. With the menu frame selected, we can do them all with one move at the Attributes Inspector's Page tab. At the Base Target, click and drag down to the "big" window, as shown in Figure 3-29, and release the mouse button. You've targeted the big frame! Take a moment to File I Save Everything.

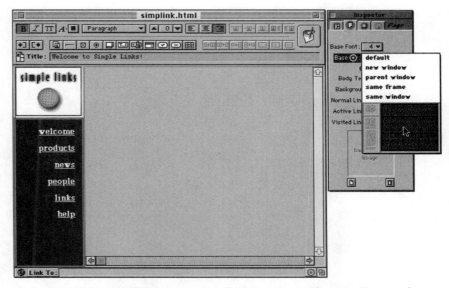

Figure 3-29: The Attributes Inspector allows you to set the overall target for an entire page of framed links. You can override it with the target at the lower right of the PageMill window.

Argh! I Can't See Everything!

Editing a small framed area (especially when you want to look at the HTML) can be nerve wracking, but it doesn't have to be! PageMill conveniently allows you to edit a frame in its own window by using File|Open Into Window.

11. Now for the fun stuff...switch to Preview mode and try out those links! When you're done clicking around, click the Welcome link, switch back to Edit mode, and File | Save Everything again. This will set things up so that the Welcome page is the first page your visitors will see when they hit the site, as shown in Figure 3-30.

Figure 3-30: Sure it's simple, but that's why it's Simple Links!

While you'll probably want to use this technique to point most of your internal links to your framed layout's "big frame," there are plenty of reasons to use the other types of targeting. If you have a page that was not designed to be viewed within a frame, you'll most likely want to target the full-window parent frame. If you're linking to another Web site, you might want to target the new site to open in an entirely new window; this way, your site's window will remain open, increasing the chances that your visitor will stay a while longer.

But I Don't Like Frames!

Always include a "No Frames" message for those unfortunate folks that might be visiting your site with a browser that is incapable of displaying frames. You can add a "No Frames" message by summoning the No Frames dialog box from the Edit menu or via the command-M keyboard shortcut. The "No Frames" message can even contain a complete, non-framed page (graphics and all!), which will automatically display in older browsers.

Here are some additional frame pointers:

- Name each frame with an identifiable label. Otherwise, PageMill will assign a nondescriptive name, such as "frame1137468."

- Pay careful attention to each targeted link. Don't run the risk of sending your visitors off to Web Sheboygan without a return ticket.

How Can I Edit a Frameset in HTML Source Mode?

Unfortunately, PageMill 2 does not allow you to edit a frameset in HTML Source mode. You'll have to open the file with an ASCII text editor such as BBEdit, Simple Text, or WordPad, instead.

- If a frame does not require the use of scroll bars, turn the option off via the Attributes Inspector.

- Disable the Viewer Resizable option on frames that you deem to be of utmost importance, such as those containing advertising banners or site ID.

- Consider providing site navigational tips for your visitors, a la the Twentieth Century Fox Home Entertainment Web site, as shown back in Figure 3-19.

■ Use the Attributes Inspector to assign sufficient margin width and height so that your text and images don't bump into the frames.

Removing a Frame

To remove a frame, drag the frame border to touch the opposite side of the frame (you'll see it change color slightly) and release the mouse button. A message will appear, asking if you really want to "Remove the adjoining frame from this document?" Click OK to kiss it good-bye.

Why Aren't There Many Framed Sites?

Frames made quite a splash when they were first introduced in Netscape Navigator 2.0, but the initial popularity among cutting-edge Web designers has worn off for a number of reasons. Here's a handful of hypotheses:

■ The inability of older browsers to display frames necessitated that Web site developers produce nonframed versions of their framed pages. This often meant more work, but questionable return on the developer's investment in time.

■ The navigational shortcomings of certain framed Web sites were exacerbated by neophyte Web surfers who were unaware that holding the mouse button down would allow them to go back in a frame.

■ Early on, a number of sites went overboard with frames. After a torrent of visitor frustration and outrage, most sites have backed off.

■ Serious techno-tweaks have a barnyard full of tricks to play with now that Java has taken the Web by storm. The initial "whoa, cool" phase has run its course.

That having been said, however, does not preclude the renaissance of framed sites. Until the advent of PageMill 2 there were few tools available to automatically create the structure needed to build with frames. As the Web flock completes the migration to newer versions of the browsers (that support frames), one can expect that framed sites will begin to flourish anew.

When Should I Create a Form?

There are many reasons to add HTML forms to your Web site. If your site contains a huge amount of information, you might use a search feature to query the database. You might be building a mailing list of potential customers, or perhaps you are interested in taking a survey of visitors to gauge their opinions. Whatever the situation, you'll probably need to use a form on any page where you'd like your visitors to enter variable information for the purpose of interaction with the site.

The Form is Only Half of the Equation

In order to use forms on your Web site, you'll need to have a program running on your Web server that knows what to do with the submitted information. These are often referred to as Common Gateway Interface (CGI) scripts.

Car Talk is an extraordinary Saturday afternoon radio show hosted by the Tappit brothers, Click and Clack. In the real world, *Car Talk* can be found on National Public Radio, while on the Web, they can be found at http://www.cartalk.com. Their site is every bit as fun and informative as their radio show. Take a look at the Car Talk Classifieds ad search form, shown in Figure 3-31. This nifty form allows visitors to the Car Talk site to search for the car of their dreams through a number of criteria, including minimum and maximum price, make, body style, mileage, age, and location. When you submit your query, the database returns any vehicles that meet your specifications. This is the place to go to search for that classic set of wheels!

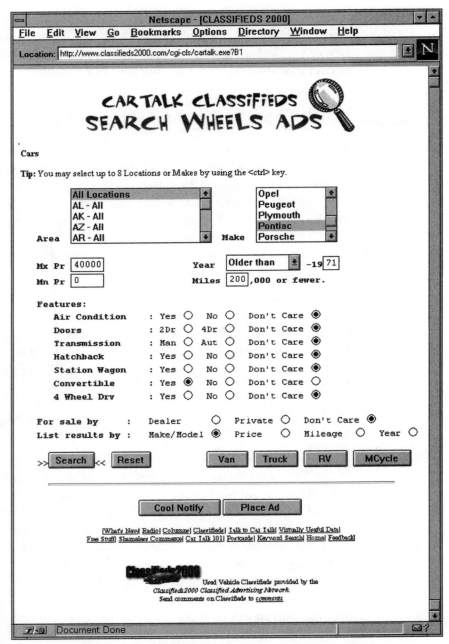

Figure 3-31: The Car Talk Wheels Search lets you look for that perfect old Pontiac convertible, just like the one you used to know and love.

Mo Hotta Mo Betta (http://www.mohotta.com/) is a mail order purveyor of hot and spicy foods, including hot sauces, salsas, chilies, peppers, snacks, and "mo hot stuff." The San Luis Obispo, California-based firm does the majority of their sales through their whimsical printed catalog. Although their Web site contains a nice selection of goods, the catalog features an amazing array of products to entice the widest range of customers. As such, compiling a mailing list for the catalog is an important part of their Web site. Figure 3-32 demonstrates how Mo Hotta Mo Betta includes a mailing list form at the bottom of their graphic home page (the site is broken into low- and high-bandwidth tracks).

If all you want to do is provide a means of visitor feedback, (rather than feeding your database), HTML's Mailto feature is the easiest type of feedback loop to implement. Although HTML forms are far more powerful, Mailto links are the fastest way to solicit e-mail from your visitors. When visitors click on a Mailto link, they are presented with a window that lets them send e-mail directly to a prespecified address. If you need more than just e-mail, however, you'll want to look into the options afforded by HTML forms and Common Gateway Interface (CGI) scripts.

How Do I Create a Mailto Link?

PageMill makes it simple! Just highlight the text that you want to link from, click in the Link To field, and press *m* (this will automatically fill in the "mailto:"). Then, type in the e-mail address and press Return. Bingo...you've created an instant e-mail link!

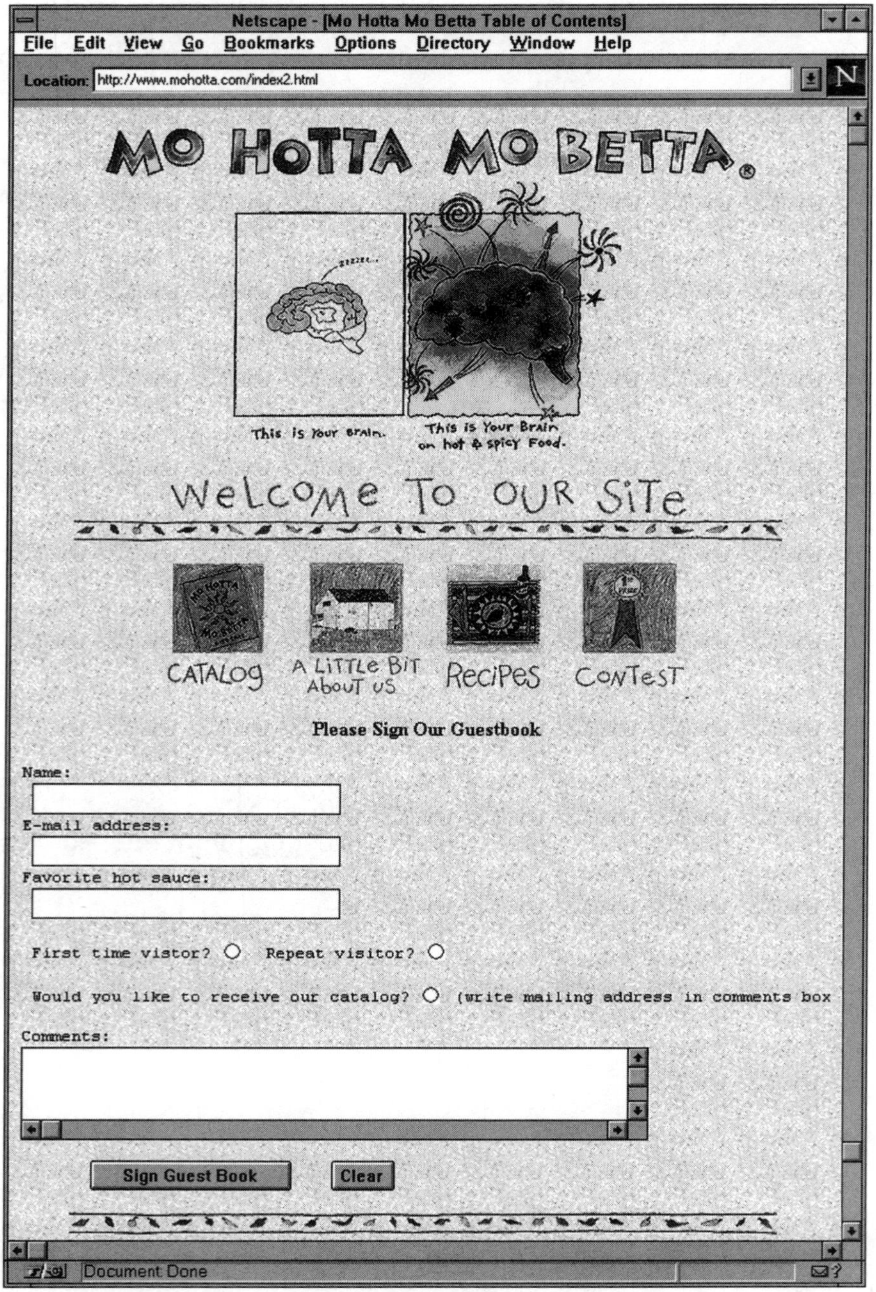

MO HOTTA MO BETTA.

This is your brain.

This is Your Brain on hot & spicy Food.

WELCOME TO OUR SITE

CATALOG   A LITTLE BIT ABOUT US   RECIPES   CONTEST

Please Sign Our Guestbook

Name:

E-mail address:

Favorite hot sauce:

First time vistor? ○   Repeat visitor? ○

Would you like to receive our catalog? ○   (write mailing address in comments box

Comments:

Sign Guest Book   Clear

Document Done

Figure 3-32: Hey, pepperheads...looking for some hot stuff? Go to http://www.mohotta.com/ and sign up now!

Form Creation Tools

HTML provides all the mechanisms you'll need to knock out a great-looking form. And PageMill makes those forms frighteningly easy to create. The program's form creation tools allow you to build complex forms without touching any serious HTML code. All you need to do is click a form object button on the button bar to bring it onto the page. Of course, you'll still have to assign names and values to the various fields, but that's a far cry from hacking this stuff out by hand!

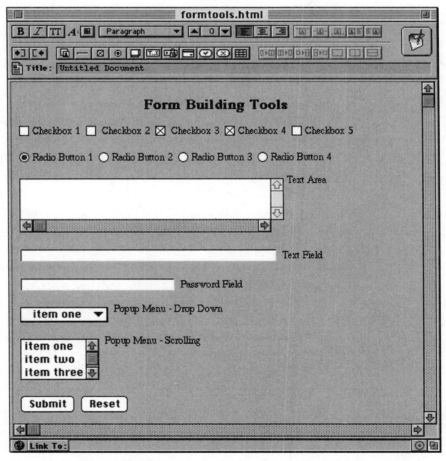

Figure 3-33: PageMill makes it easy to lay out forms. The real trick is making them work at the server!

Can I Have More Than One Form on a Page?
In a word, no. PageMill 2 only supports one form per page.

Once a form object is on the page, it's easy to alter or move it around with just a flick of the mouse. Figure 3-33 illustrates the following features:

- *Checkboxes*. These critters are often set as groups, which allow any, all, or none of the group to be selected. To set a number of checkboxes as a group, use the Attributes Inspector's Object tab to assign the exact same name to each of the items. You can also create and name the first checkbox, then option-drag to create additional members of the group.

- *Radio Buttons*. You'll want to use radio buttons when asking a "yes/no/maybe" type of question. While they're similar to checkboxes in that they can be set as groups, radio buttons allow only one button in a group (at a time) to be selected. To set a number of radio buttons as a group, use the Attributes Inspector's Object tab to assign the exact same name to each of the items. You can also create and name the first radio button, then option-drag to create additional members of the group.

- *Text Areas*. Use text areas for entering more than one line of text. While text areas can be quickly resized by pulling on their handles (or by entering specific values at the Attributes Inspector), by default, they do not provide text wrapping. You can thoughtfully allow the user's text to wrap within the field, by switching to HTML Source mode and entering WRAP="PHYSICAL" within the text area command.

- *Text Fields*. Use a text field when you only need your visitor to enter a single line of text. Text fields can be quickly resized by pulling on their handles (or by entering specific values at the Attributes Inspector).

- *Password Fields*. This is a special text field for entering a password. When a visitor types in a password field in their browser, only bullets or asterisks are displayed.

- *Popup Menus*. While this is a drop-down menu by default, it can be set as a scrolling list selection by dragging the bottom handle downward. A drop-down menu will only allow visitors to select one item, while the scrolling list selection field can allow visitors to select more than one item (by selecting Allow Multiple Selections on the Attributes Inspector's Object tab).

- *Submit Button*. This sends the visitor's variable information to the Web server and is required on every form. The text on the button can be altered by double-clicking the button and then double-clicking the text to select it. You can also switch to HTML Source mode, and enter the desired text in the VALUE="submit" field (replace the word *submit* with the text of your choice).

- *Reset Button*. This is a convenience feature that allows the visitor to automatically clear the form. The text on the button can be altered by double-clicking the button and then double-clicking the text to select it. You can also switch to HTML Source mode, and enter the desired text in the VALUE="reset" field (replace the word *reset* with the text of your choice).

- *Hidden Fields*. There are fields that visitors never see (unless they take a peek at the HTML source code). Edit | Insert Invisible | Hidden Field pops a cryptic little *H* in a box onto the page. This icon is visible only in PageMill's Edit mode. You'll need to add a name and value via the Attributes Inspector.

Check Them Off!
PageMill allows you to preset check boxes and radio buttons so that they are checked (through either the Attributes Inspector or by double-clicking on each while in Edit mode).

Each form object has a name and a value. You have complete control over how these variables are labeled. It is essential that you assign consistent names and values to each. Don't confuse the title that you see on the Web page with the name of the object. While the title is what your visitor will see, the object's name is what the CGI script will see. Although these may be named identically, it's possible that they may not. In any case, don't forget to give each object the proper name and value.

Where Does the Info Go?

Aye, here's the rub. A form merely provides the means of gathering information. You'll need to have a CGI script running on your Web server in order to do anything with the submitted data. The CGI must know what to do with this information, and it must be in synch with the form so that it understands what to do with the various names and values. In most cases, this necessitates that you huddle up with your webmaster to find out what kind of support they can provide with regard to scripting. It's important to note that CGI scripts are server specific. A script written for one platform may not run on another (i.e., UNIX Perl may be useless on a Windows NT server).

In the bad old days, the only way to create a CGI script was to write it with a programming language, such as AppleScript or Perl. Thankfully, things have changed. Nonprogrammers will be thrilled to learn that a number of applications are now available to build scripts without writing any code. And best of all, there are a slew of demos included on the PageMill 2 CD-ROM! Chapter 7 covers two programs (Maxum NetForms for Macintosh and O'Reilly's PolyForm for Windows 95/NT) that can be used to instantly create interactive forms without any programming, whatsoever.

How does the Web server know which CGI script to use? Take a quick look at the Attributes Inspector's Form tab. The Action field should be filled out with the name and location of the appropriate CGI, such as /cgi-bin/blahblahblah.gci, where /cgi-bin/ is the directory, and blahblahblah.cgi is the name of the script itself. You'll have to select either Get or Post, but it's essential that you contact your webmaster to determine which to use, as different servers have different requirements.

Exercise #5: Building a Form

In this little exercise, you'll build a Guestbook form for your Web site. This form will include text field, text area, radio button, and drop-down and scrolling list functions, as shown by Figure 3-34.

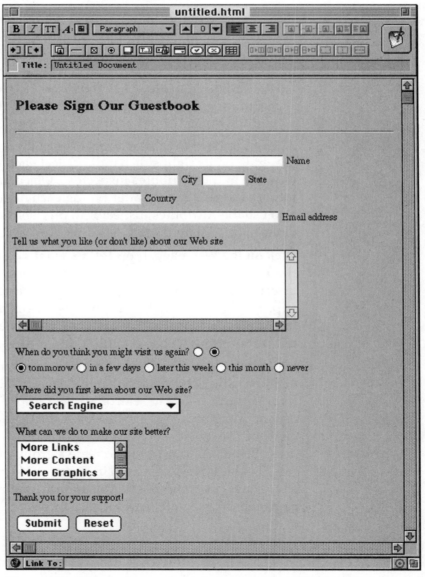

Figure 3-34: Guestbooks are among the most common Web page forms.

As you begin building the form, you'll quickly see how easy it is to create, adjust, and rearrange the different form elements. You'll want to start with a brand new page.

1. Let's begin by adding a simple heading. Type **Please Sign Our Guestbook**. Change the format to Larger Head. Press Return. Insert a Horizontal Rule. Press Return.

2. Now, you'll add five (one-line) text fields. Click the Insert Text Field button, type **Name**, and press Shift+Return. Click the Insert Text Field button, type **City**, press Shift+Return, click the Insert Text Field button, type **State**, and press Shift+Return. Click the Insert Text Field button, type **Country**, and press Shift+Return. Click the Insert Text Field button, type **Email address**, and press Return.

3. Adjust each text field so it appears as in Figure 3-34 by dragging on its right side handle. Select each field and type its name in the Attributes Inspector's Object tab. Don't forget to press a Return after typing each name. You can also use the Attributes Inspector to precisely set the size (length) of each field.

4. Back on the Web page, type **Tell us what you like (or don't like) about our Web site**. Press Shift+Return. Click the Insert Text Area button. Adjust the text area so that it is approximately 7 rows by 54 columns. Check the size with the Attributes Inspector's Object tab, and type **tellusaboutit** in the name field.

5. It's radio button time! Type **When do you think you might visit us again?** and press Shift+Return. Click the Radio Button button. Click to select the new radio button, and use the Attributes Inspector's Object tab to assign it the name of "nextvisit" and a value of "tomorrow". Option-drag the button four times to create a group of five buttons. Insert the text as shown in Figure 3-34 (**tomorrow, in a few days, later this week, this month**, and **never**) on the page and in the value field for each button.

6. Now, you'll add a drop-down menu. Type **Where did you first learn about our Web site?** and press a Shift+Return. Click the Insert Popup button. Double-click to select the new pop-up menu. Highlight the default text and type the following, each separated by a Return:

> **Search Engine**
> **Banner Advertisement**
> **Print Advertisement**
> **Television Advertisement**
> **Hot List**

Click the page to deselect the menu and then click once to select it again. At the Attributes Inspector's Object tab, give it a name of "wherefrom" and assign values to each of the five sources, as shown by Figure 3-35.

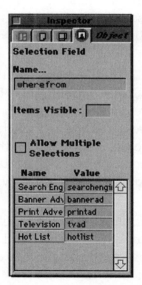

Figure 3-35: It's essential that every form object be assigned a name and value.

7. Let's add a scrolling list selection to the form. Type **What can we do to make our site better?** and press a Shift+Return. Click the Insert Popup button. Double-click to select the new pop-up menu. Highlight the default text and type the following, each separated by a Return:

   More Links
   More Content
   More Graphics
   Less Graphics
   More Shockwave
   More Software

   Click the page to deselect the menu and then click once to select it again. Drag the menu's bottom handle down so that the top three entries are showing. At the Attributes Inspector's Object tab, give it a name of "whatelse" and assign values to each of the six choices. Notice that Allow Multiple Selections is checked and that the Items Visible field is set to 3. Take the time to experiment with different sizes.

8. To finish up the form, you'll add a thank you line and those crucial Submit and Reset buttons. Type **Thank you for your support!** and press a Return. Click the Insert Submit Button button, press a space, and Click the Insert Reset Button button. Give the Submit button the name of "submit" at the Attributes Inspector's Object tab. (The Reset button doesn't need a name since it only works at the browser level.)

9. You're done, so save your file! If this were a real working form, you'd have to set an Action on the Attributes Inspector's Form tab. This lets the server know what CGI script to use with the incoming data.

Can I Use a GIF or JPEG Image as a Submit Button?
No problem! Just place the image on the page, select it, and specify it as a button on the Attributes Inspector's Object tab.

Try your new form out in PageMill's Preview mode. Then, try opening the form with a Web browser, such as Netscape Navigator or Microsoft Internet Explorer, to see how it performs. While some of the earlier browsers (AOL's in particular) had problems dealing with forms, just about all the browsers today support the HTML 2.0 form specification to which PageMill writes its forms.

Moving On

In this chapter, you learned how to implement tables, frames, and forms. These are among HTML's most powerful page layout commands. Advanced layouts are used in all but the simplest of Web sites. This chapter concludes your introduction to the program, as well as the medium. In the next section of *Web Publishing With Adobe PageMill 2*, you'll learn how to make your Web site fly. The next chapter deals with how to better define your Web site by identifying your audience and meeting their needs (as well as the requirements of the site's sponsor). Subsequent chapters will help you fine-tune your designs and troubleshoot your site.

part 2

Good Design

In this section of the book, you'll embark upon a journey to achieve the nirvana of clear, efficient, and effective Web site design. This is an honorable goal, indeed, and one that is only possible through thoughtful planning, diligent execution, and a touch of good luck. The three chapters contained herein are designed to help you identify your goals, implement your plans, and undertake any necessary corrections to your course.

What constitutes good design? Ask a thousand people this question and you will receive a thousand answers. Ask a thousand designers the same question and you will have to endure ten thousand answers. From workaday common folk to haughty big-city designers, everyone has their own idea of what constitutes good design. And each is certainly entitled to their beliefs and opinions. The higher one travels up the design food chain, however, the more excessive the explanation will be.

A certain amount of design critique will always be subjective in nature. Here's a common situation. If your client simply says, "But I don't like red," he or she is making a subjective remark. If, on the other hand, your client says, "I don't like the use of red on this page of financial information because of the common association of the color with 'red ink' (or a loss)," you've just heard an objective observation.

While subjectivity is often the subject, it's the designer's role to champion the cause of good design. And good design doesn't necessarily mean trendy, slick, or fancy. A good design is an effective design; one that gets its intended job done. It's merely a bonus if it makes the viewer say, "Whoa, cool!" Unless of course, the entire intent of the project is to make the viewer say, "Whoa, cool!"

chapter 4

Understanding Your Audience

You're going to build a Web site, but you're not so sure how to start. This chapter will help you get going in the right direction. We'll look into a number of issues that affect the design of your Web site, and we'll see how the design is truly dependent upon the subject matter you're planning to present.

Most importantly you will learn that an effective Web site designer understands the wants and needs of the targeted audience before ever building a single page with PageMill. We'll discuss how to plan your Web site carefully and promote it thoroughly, also critical to Web page success. Once you've captured the interest of your audience, you must deliver what they need (which isn't always, for your purposes, exactly what they *think* they want) in an engaging and orderly manner. And finally, you'll discover the importance of giving your audience good reason to come back to your site, again and again.

Content Is King

The first thing to consider when planning your Web site is that *content is king*. People will come to your site in search of the information it provides, not for its great design. They might come back to your site once, just to show a friend how cool it looks, but they will repeatedly come back to your site for more information. In the Web world, as throughout the entire Internet, the steak matters far more than the sizzle.

It is your first responsibility to determine what information your audience is looking for. You've got to think like them and look coldly at your site from their perspective. Then you must take stock of the resources you have at your disposal to provide the content your audience demands.

Your organization, be it a large corporation or a small hobbyist group, has a legacy of information. This information may be on paper, it may be on computer disks, it may be on videotape, or it may only be in the minds of you and your cohorts. What information goes up on your site is dictated both by supply and demand. If the information your audience demands exists in another form, repurpose it. If the needed information doesn't currently exist, create it. If you can't (for whatever reason) create it, set up a hyperlink (as you learned back in Chapter 1) to another Web site that has made available this information.

When you embark upon your site-building journey, avoid having a predetermined design in mind. Stay focused on what information your audience needs, not on how you think your site should look. This is not to say that design is irrelevant to the success of your site. On the contrary, it has everything to do with its success. The role of the designer is to allow the Web site visitor to access quickly and easily the information a good Web site provides. A clear, concise design enables visitors to get at the good stuff with just a few clicks of their mouse. A complex, dense design will boggle the user's mind and lead to frustration with your site.

The design of your Web site—and the pages contained therein—is secondary to and dependent upon the content. Like the best designs of any type, the form of your Web site should follow its function.

Design Your Site Around Its Content

Your responsibility as a designer is akin to that of an architect. You must design the overall layout of your Web site so that visitors can quickly find what they need. When a visitor lands at your front door, you want to greet him or her warmly and provide a floor plan of your site. Don't let the first doors your visitors encounter be those connected to a closet, basement, or boiler room.

If your most important content is in the kitchen, make sure that all visitors can get there immediately from your front door. You must not expect that your Web site guests will click happily away until they find what they're looking for. Since many cyberspace explorers aren't sure of what they're looking for, you need to provide a place where they can find *everything*.

Think about the grand old department stores. (If you've never had the pleasure of experiencing such, check out *Miracle on 34th Street*, or the Marx Brothers in *Big Store*.) At the entrance to the elevator, there was always a friendly operator who greeted shoppers and announced what they would find as they reached each floor. Your Web site should have a *central lobby*, with *escalators* to specific departments for the folks who *already know* where they're headed. And you should also design an *elevator* with a friendly attendant to help visitors quickly locate what they're seeking.

Provide a Site Map!
An effective *site map* provides the same level of assistance as a friendly elevator attendant. A site map should enable the viewer to find the information they are looking for with just a glance.

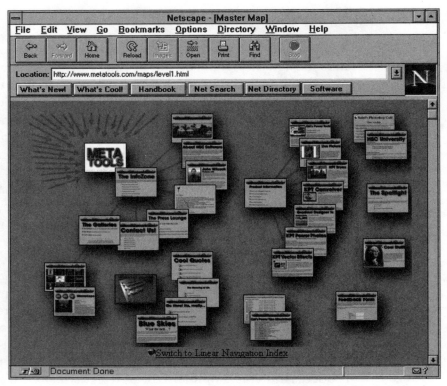

Figure 4-1: MetaTools' 133K graphical site map provides a high level of visual feedback. Notice the linear navigation switch option at the bottom of the screen.

Developing a site map is a good way to make your Web site function. There are a number of approaches to displaying a site map, but the key is to provide both graphics and text. Figures 4-1 and 4-2 show the route that MetaTools took to allow fast site access for both low- and high-bandwidth browsers. Those lucky folks who can quickly download the 133K image map through a corporate network will be pleased with the enhanced level of graphic information. And those of us with slow modem connections should be satisfied with MetaTools' slim and trim linear text directory. If this all sounds a little confusing for now, don't worry. We'll delve further into the concepts of browsers and bandwidth later in this chapter and of site maps in the next chapter.

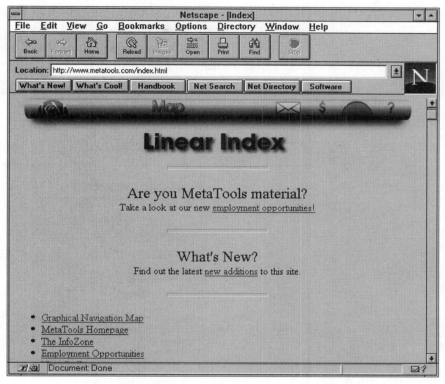

Figure 4-2: MetaTools' linear text directory allows users to quickly access the page they want.

As you design your Web site, you should aim to move folks through so that they see what you want them to see and do what you want them to do. There's a purpose behind your Web site, be it commercial or fun. You want to make sure that the value you receive is equal to the value your visitors receive from you. Here are some tips for making this happen:

■ If your goal is to build a mailing list and qualify sales leads, you'll need to offer a compelling reason for people to offer their names, addresses, and other pertinent demographic information.

■ If your goal is to sell products online, you'll need to make sure that you have all the mechanisms there to do so, and that your products are presented in the best possible manner, as illustrated by Figure 4-3.

■ If all you intend to do is build brand identity, you'll have it easier than most. In such cases, your primary purpose is not to have visitors give you anything, but to have them feel good about you and your product.

Once you have determined your content and layout, it's time to start thinking how you will bring in the crowds...

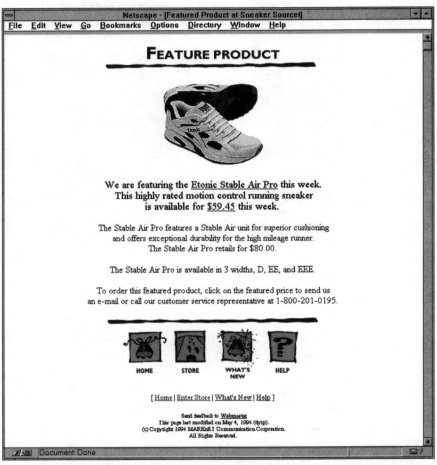

Figure 4-3: The Sneaker Source Web site delivers the goods. It is bright, clean, and attractive, encouraging the browser to buy.

Get the Word Out

You can put the most incredible Web site ever imagined on the Internet, and yet you can't be assured of true success unless its message reaches your intended audience. The secret is to get the word out, and then promote, promote, promote. The form that your promotion takes depends upon the type of Web site you're building. And like so many projects, your promotional efforts are almost always budget dependent.

It's not necessary to allocate a single cent of real money to promote your Web site, but should you decide to shell out the bucks, you'll want to send them in the right direction. In most cases—whether or not the project has a real budget—you'll begin your promotional efforts by focusing on the no-cost venues.

Register With the Search Engines

The first way your audience will find your Web site is through a *search engine*. Search engines are Web sites that have been designed to catalog the contents of the entire World Wide Web. They exist because they fulfill the needs of the Web community, providing an organized way of using this wonderful resource, which draws millions of information-hungry visitors every day. In many cases, advertising revenue is what keeps the search engines up and running. Those little advertising banners displayed at the top and sometimes in the middle of search engine pages are easy to endure when you realize the great service they afford. Certain search engines are not financed solely through advertising revenue, however. Some charge for their searches and offer subscription plans for enhanced levels of service.

Search engines use *automated robots* to crawl around the Web on a nightly basis; they check for new pages in cyberspace and gather updated information on pages that have already been cataloged. These software robots are often referred to as spiders, crawlers, or worms. One of the busiest spiders is Digital's Scooter, which scurries from site to site, gathering up information for Digital's high-powered Alta Vista database. The information is distilled and displayed, as shown in Figure 4-4, at no cost to the user.

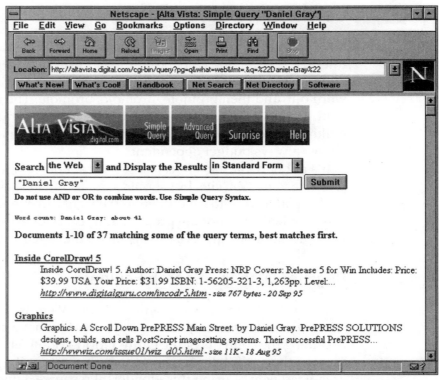

Figure 4-4: Digital's Alta Vista search engine (http://altavista.digital.com) is among the biggest and fastest of the bunch.

Some of the Most Popular Search Engine Sites

Here's a short list of the most popular Internet search engines, along with their URLs. Each has a different approach to organizing and delivering their information. If you can't find what you're looking for on one site, keep jumping until you do!

Alta Vista	http://altavista.digital.com
CERN	http://www.w3.org/pub/DataSources/ WWW/Servers.html
The Electric Library	http://www.elibrary.com
Excite	http://www.excite.com
Hot Bot	http://www.hotbot.com
Infoseek	http://www.infoseek.com
Inktomi	http://inktomi.berkeley.edu/
Lycos	http://www.lycos.com
Magellan	http://www.mckinley.com
NlightN	http://www.nlightn.com
Open Text Index	http://www.opentext.com
search.com	http://www.search.com
Web Crawler	http://www.webcrawler.com
Who Where?	http://www.whowhere.com
Yahoo!	http://www.yahoo.com
2ask	http://www.2ask.com/

The robots may find your site by chance, but you don't have to wait for them to come looking. You can (and should) ask the spiders to come crawling to your URL. This is an essential step in the launch of a new Web site, as well as when substantially re-vamping or moving a site. Submitting your URL is akin to sending out invitations for a party. People will only show up on your doorstep if they know there's a gig. Accordingly, if you move your site and leave no forwarding address, as in the case of a hostile parting of ways with an erstwhile ISP, visitors will think your Web site has fallen off the face of the earth. And if you open up a whole new section on your site, which is thinly linked to the existing site, you can't count on a visit from the spiders unless you give them a nudge and tell them where to look.

Each engine has its own online URL submission form to fill out, and each treats this task a little differently. It can take the better part of a day going from search engine to search engine, registering your Web site's specific information. While this may seem tedious, it's an essential step towards your site's ultimate success. Best of all, it's completely free! Figure 4-5 illustrates the Alta Vista registration form.

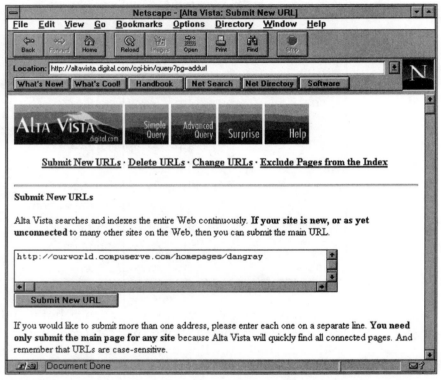

Figure 4-5: The Alta Vista registration form. Simply fill in the URL address, click on Submit New URL, and Alta Vista does the rest.

There are alternatives to registering with the search engines one-by-one. Services, such as Submit-It (http://www. submit-it.com/) and Postmaster (http://www.netcreations.com/ postmaster/) allow you to perform a wholesale submission. Submit-It feeds your information to Alta Vista, Apollo, BizWiz, Galaxy, Infoseek, LinkStar, Lycos, METROSCOPE, Nerd World Media, Open Text, Starting Point, WebCrawler, What's New Too!, and Yahoo!, among others (see Figure 4-6). The service lets you enter your site information just once, while their site submission robot does the chump work for you. Submit-It is also a free service, funded by advertising revenue.

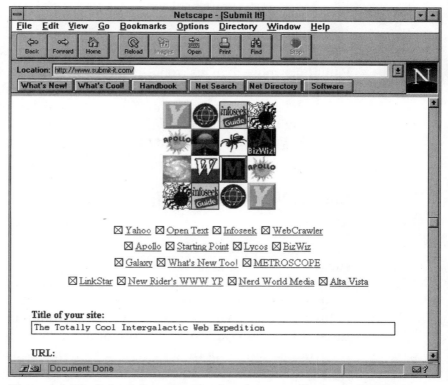

Figure 4-6: The Submit-It registration form lets you submit your URL to a number of search engines in one fell swoop.

Using Submit-It can save lots of time, which is great if you don't have time to lose. But there's something to be said for *knowing* that you entered exactly the information required for each specific search engine. You might, for example, want to write a description or announcement of your site differently for one search engine in deference to its particular audience. Each site also has its own indexing categories (and personality); it's very important to fill out the form as completely as possible. The more categories you can squeeze your Web site into, the better.

Find Yourself on the Search Engines!
Looking for a wacky way to waste time? Search for your own name on a number of search engines to see where you pop up!

Some search engines, such as Excite, Magellan's McKinley, and Point offer more than just robot-gathered lists. These sites provide reviews of Web sites, complete with satirical comments and numerical ratings. A number of the hybrid print/zines do the same. You'll need to register your site's URL with these services, and keep your fingers crossed that they like your stuff if they choose to review your site.

Spider Watch: Keeping Track of the Crawlers

Once you've registered your site, you may want to keep an eye on the robots to make sure they've done their job. The best-run Web sites are capable of generating server statistics that should include information about the audience you've attracted. At the very least, your webmaster should be able to provide you with a file listing of the server logs. Utilities can turn this raw dump into a structured listing. You can use this information in a variety of ways, but three of the most important items that you can learn are who's hitting your site, what pages they're hitting, and from where they're being referred. In this case, you should not be concerned with the raw level of hits. You should look only at the HTML page accesses, not at any graphic file accesses.

Hits: Raw vs. Real
Raw hits will report on every file access, including both HTML pages and graphic files. These numbers reflect a skewed approach to Web site statistics due to the wide variance in the number of graphic files per actual Web page. It's more important to look at real HTML page accesses, which provide a concise picture of true site traffic.

The robots should begin hitting your site within a few nights after you submit your URL. Depending on their backlog, some may not hit your site for weeks. After they've discovered your site for the first time, they will return time after time, each on their own mysterious (and often nocturnal) schedule. If you have access to your site statistics, you should watch to see if the robots are hitting, and also watch to see if they are referring people to your site.

Give a couple of weeks for the robots to do their initial work. Then, go to each search engine, and check to see that your site is indexed by doing a search on a number of key words. If your site doesn't show up in the search list, and if you're not seeing hits from that site, it's a good indication that the robot has not cataloged your site. Allow the robot a few more days to do its work, then check back again. If your site doesn't show up after a few weeks, you might want to try registering your URL again with the search engine.

Take note of how the various search engines list your pages. You should be cognizant of the title that you give each page in PageMill. This title will be picked up by the spiders and used to catalog your page. Neophyte Web designers commonly overlook the proper titling of their Web pages. It's a small touch, albeit an essential one.

With most search engines you'll only have to register your primary URL (or home page). Once the spider finds your front door, it will continue to crawl around your site, cataloging the linked public pages. The spiders are not smart enough to gain access to pages in non-public areas, however. If you maintain a number of password-protected pages, you can rest assured that the common robots will not be able to log in. Anything's possible though, and it's likely that a logging robot will eventually surface.

If, for some reason, you don't want the robots coming to your Web site, you can set up a special file to tell them to stay away. You'll find details on robot exclusion and a wealth of information about the various Web crawlers at WebCrawler's World Wide Web Robots, Wanderers, and Spiders page (http://info.webcrawler.com/ mak/projects/robots/robots.html).

Use Stats to Fine Tune Content

While we're on the subject of statistics, it's worth mentioning that all the data in the world is useless if you don't do something with it. This holds true for your server statistics, as well. You need to watch your audience. You need to see where they go and take note of where they don't go. If your audience is attracted by sugar, then you had better get ready to lay out plenty of the sweet stuff. If they want spice, you had better figure out what kind.

Web sites are opportunities in the making for social scientist wanna-bes, as people are infinitely more exciting to watch than lab rats. Having the ability to watch the hoards run through your site is essential in implementing an effective strategy. Thankfully, adding tracking and site management features does not have to be an expensive proposition. More depth on the ins and outs of tracking Web site visitors appears in Chapter 7.

Promote Your Web Site

Don't overlook any of the free promotional opportunities that are available to you on the Net. Remember to post announcements about the opening of your Web site only to those newsgroups and mail lists that are appropriate for the subject matter. Keep the posts brief and to the point. Don't sell...tell. Let folks know what your site is about and where they can find it.

Check the List of Mail Lists!

To see what mailing lists your news release may apply to, you'll want to check out the Publicly Accessible Mailing Lists Web site (http://www.neosoft.com/internet/paml/bysubj.html).

Once your site has been registered with the search engines, and you're satisfied the robots are doing their job, you'll need to look at promotional opportunities, from buying traditional print advertising to buying *webvertising*. Bringing attention to your site does not necessitate spending tons of additional money on advertising, however.

Take a look at every printed piece your organization publishes, from business cards to marketing collateral and traditional advertising. Consider adding your URL to each place your organization's phone number appears. If someone in your audience is looking for more information on your organization, they will see that you have a Web site and will have the correct address at hand.

Should you indiscriminately plaster your URL everywhere? In a word, no. Should your URL be the central design element of your T-shirts? Absolutely not. Should your URL be added to the majority of your printed pieces? Yes, but only if it can be done discreetly.

Cool Places to Put Your URL

Here are some of the best spots to sneak in your URL:

- T-shirts (discreetly—the hippest place is on the left sleeve, just above the hem).
- Hats (across the back is the coolest).
- Pens and other promotional trinkets.
- Stationery.
- Business cards.
- Press releases.
- Print advertisements (including the Yellow Pages).
- Television advertisements.
- E-mail signature.
- Any place you list your organization's phone number or address.

Want to Find Out Who's Linked to Your Site?
If your Web server can produce a list of referring URLs, you can identify where your visitors are finding your Web site. If you don't have the ability to check your site stats, however, you can always use the search engines. Just type in your Web site's name and submit the inquiry. The search engine will cough up a list of other Web sites that mention your site. Just follow these links to see what they have to say about you!

Uncool Places to Put Your URL

If you plaster your URL in the following places, get ready to get flamed:

- T-Shirts (when all you have is a big URL).
- Delivery vehicles (Figure 4-7).
- Bumper stickers.
- Inappropriate or unrelated newsgroups and mailing lists (not to mention cross-posting).
- Radio advertisements (having to listen to a disc jockey read a long URL is unbearable). The only really cool radio URL is http://www.cartalk.com.
- Everywhere.

Figure 4-7: Putting a big URL on your delivery van is not cool...even if you run it flopped on the grill, so folks can read it in their rearview mirrors.

Schemes to Draw a Crowd

After you've taken all this good advice to heart and tried to hold the line on your promotional costs, you may be tempted to spend some more money in the hopes of drawing a substantial crowd. Contests, giveaways, and other schemes are bound to crank up your hit rates and pull in the people, but they might not pull in the people you want to attract. There are always some folks who will come to your site just for something free, just because it's there. You'll get a marked increase in hits, but they won't be as profitable.

Promoting Your Page

For more great information on how to bring in the crowds, check out "How to Publicize Your Web Page" on Oregon State University's Web server at http://www.orst.edu/aw/stygui/propag.htm.

If you decide to run a promotion of this type, online or off, make sure that you hype it for everything it's worth. Get your news releases out early, and work the editors. Editors often appreciate a phone call or e-mail message to see if they've actually received a press release. When you make such a call, offer to answer any questions they might have. You may need to send out another release, since busy editors sometimes lose loose papers on their desks. Time your events so that you can get maximum coverage in both print and electronic realms.

What You See, Your Audience Might Not

The Web is unique among communications media in that there are no other channels where so many variables are left to the discretion of the reader/viewer. On the Web, your audience may be browsing your site with graphics turned on or off. They might be using the current version of Netscape Navigator—complete with all the coolest plug-ins (which support all the latest enhancements). Or they may be using *Lame-O no-brand* browser, version 0.9 alpha.

Perhaps the most apparent symptom of "browser individuality" is the way the Web treats text. Each browser can be set up with unique individual preferences for typeface and size. When you put your pages up there for the world to see, you have no idea of how those pages will ultimately be viewed.

If you pick up a morning newspaper to read on your train ride to work, you always read the news in the typeface and size that the production editor specified. If you sit down to watch the evening news, you could be watching the day's events on a little portable screen or you could be soaking it in on a huge home theater screen. Regardless of the size of the television screen, however, you always see the news graphics in the typeface and style that the graphic designer intended.

But if you jump to your favorite Web page, it's more than likely that you won't view that page with the same typefaces that its designer originally created it with. Each computer is just a little bit different. Although many folks never mess with the preference settings in their browser, it still seems as though every machine is configured differently.

Controlling Typeface Selection

Sad fact time. You have no control over how your pages will be viewed. Until a new specification is standardized, typefaces are going to be a willy-nilly subject. While there were at least three competing typeface specification schemes, Adobe's PostScript, Bitstream's TrueDoc, and Microsoft's TrueType, recent developments promise to dramatically alter the situation.

Adobe has teamed up with Microsoft to produce a new font format, OpenType, which combines the font technologies of Adobe's PostScript Type 1 and Microsoft's TrueType formats. The companies are creating extensions to the HTML standard based on OpenType and have proposed the extensions at the Fifth International World Wide Web Conference in May 1996. This is a problem just waiting to be licked. Since this is a book on creating Web pages with Adobe PageMill, you can probably guess where we're putting down our bets. The combined efforts of Adobe and Microsoft will most likely get the nod.

Serving Browser-dependent Pages

If you are running your own Web server, rather than using an Internet Service Provider to put your Web site online, it is possible to equip your Web server so that it delivers different pages to different browsers. Applications such as Maxum's NetCloak allow a Macintosh-based Web server to identify what brand of browser is requesting a page and can be configured to serve up a specific page for a specific browser.

Having this level of control lets you fine-tune your message to meet your audience. You can automatically deliver the right page to the right client, without them ever having known that you've been watching their vital statistics. We'll talk more about this in Chapter 7.

Serve Up a Lite!
If you don't have the ability to automatically detect browsers (and most Web sites don't), you should consider giving visitors the option of viewing an alternate "lite" version of your site with minimal graphics.

Design for the Bandwidth

Bandwidth is one of the Web buzzwords you often hear bandied about. "We don't have enough bandwidth to implement that solution" or "With a T3 line, we have all the bandwidth we need" are two hypothetical examples of how the word might be used by propellerheads. The term refers to the size of the "pipe" (capacity of the Internet hookup) being used on a Web site or browser. The more bandwidth you have, the happier you'll be, both on the server and client side. Of course, the bigger the pipe, the more money you'll spend.

A good Web designer must always remember that the bandwidth they have at their disposal is often not the same as their audience's. Your Web site may be sitting on the fastest line west of the Pecos, but it won't matter if your audience is dialing in on slow 14.4 and 28.8 modems. Bandwidth is always limited by the smallest diameter of inline pipe.

ISDN—What Does It Stand For?

Who cares what the acronym stands for? This very cool technology allows you to cram almost 10 times as much data down your copper phone line, albeit at 10 times the cost. It's no cakewalk to set up, however, and you'll need to trash your trusty modem in favor of a new ISDN box or board. This is a perfect case for knowing your audience. If you are relatively certain that your target market will be coming to your site via fast T1 lines or ISDN, you can create a far more robust environment. Your graphics can be larger, and you can use such goodies as gargantuan Shockwave animations and pipe-eating QuickTime movies without the fear of bogging down. Very few folks have fast lines running to their homes, but large corporate networks are typically hooked up via T1 lines or better. Table 4-1 indicates common transmission speeds from modems to the *superfast* T3.

Device	Speed
Modem	14.4 Kbps
	28.8 Kbps
ISDN single line	64 Kbps
ISDN double line	128 Kbps
DirecPC satellite dish	400 Kbps
T1	1.5 Mbps
T3	45 Mbps

Table 4-1: Common transmission speeds.

As you can see from Table 4-1, the pipe doesn't have to be a physical wire, be it copper or fiber. Hughes, the GM division responsible for the little DSS home satellite dish, has come up with a wonderful scheme to hook your computer up to the Internet via satellite. The DirecPC package (as shown in Figure 4-8) consists of a satellite dish and expansion card that combine to give you a whopping 400 Kbps of throughput. It's the perfect accessory for your slopeside ski chalet, just so long as you have a good clear shot to the southern sky (where the DirecPC satellites hang out).

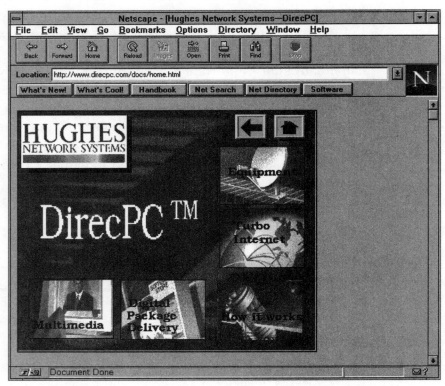

Figure 4-8: DirecPC provides 400Kbps Internet access in the boonies.

Eventually, we'll be living in a totally wired world, where we all have really fast lines coming into our homes and businesses, be they from the telephone company, from the cable company, or through satellite services. Once that high-tech day comes, we won't have to worry about the restrictions of limited bandwidth. Right now, the faster ISDN service is a residential reality in many parts of the country.

How Much to Lay the Pipe?
There is a wide range of costs associated with laying a bigger pipe. These costs can fluctuate geographically and should be inherently lower where forced by the dynamics of competition. Your best bet is to check the Web sites of the big (and smaller local) ISPs.

Enough of That Technical Nonsense. What Does It All Mean?

Easy. You must always strive to keep your pages as light as possible. If you know that your audience is coming to you at 14.4, be sure that you don't try to cram too much down the pipe. It's a common practice to offer two versions of a page, one for high-bandwidth browsers and one for our less fortunate low-bandwidth brethren (two versions of MetaTools's site are shown in Figures 4-1 and 4-2). Once we proceed onward into the hands-on design chapters following this one, you'll learn how to create pages that are fast and tight.

Access to Browsers & Plug-ins

If your site uses all the latest gizmos, you should warn your audience right away. If it's been designed to use Netscape-specific features, Chapter 5 will show you how to pop in a link on your front page to get "Netscape Now!" If a plug-in, such as Macromedia's Shockwave, is necessary for the full experience, you'll learn how to provide a link there, too. You don't want folks to have to go hunting for the software they need to enjoy your site to its fullest. Make things easy for them and they'll be more likely to have a good experience, add a bookmark, recommend your site to their pals, and pen your site into their personal home page hotlist. Make it tough and your Web site will turn into a ghost town, and even worse, you could get flamed to cinders.

CD-ROM

This book's CD-ROM puts a large variety of plug-ins at your fingertips. And you'll always be able to gain access to the latest versions of those plug-ins (and likely more) on this book's Online Updates.

A Site Done Right

Enough of the hypothetical examples. Let's take a trip to a real live site! We're going to take a look at Sneaker Source (www.sneaker.com), a snappy little Web site that was initially created with Adobe PageMill 1.0 and BBEdit. Web page design wasn't always as easy as it is now with PageMill 2. The first version of PageMill could not handle such essential design elements as wraparound text and tables. BBEdit quickly became the text editing tool of choice for hard-core HTML hacks. We'll delve into BBEdit in Chapter 9.

The following site achieves a high level of performance by using a couple of image file tricks. Its graphic icon files are small, limited palette images. This keeps download time to a minimum. In addition to limiting image palettes, the site design reuses its icons and navigational elements. This can deliver a dramatic decrease in site response time. Once an image has been downloaded and stored in the Web browser's cache, it does not have to be resent.

Don't Run Short on Cache!
Browser cache has nothing to do with making an online purchase! It's the area of your computer's hard drive that your browser uses to store frequently accessed pages and images. Your browser will allow you to adjust your cache according to your personal preferences and available disk space.

Sneaker Source

Sneaker Source is an online purveyor of athletic footwear. Their Web site, created by MARKnET Communications, illustrates many of the points that have been made in this chapter and presents an enjoyable experience for its visitors. The Sneaker Source welcome page, as shown in Figure 4-9, is a crisp introduction to the Web site. The page provides just enough information to spark visitor interest without going overboard on the details. As the site was designed to be viewed with Netscape Navigator 3.0, a "Get Netscape Now" button is kindly provided to whisk non-Netscape-equipped visitors to Netscape's server so that they may download a copy of the world's most popular Web browser.

Figure 4-9: The Sneaker Source Welcome page is concise and to the point.

The Sneaker Source Welcome page includes a number of polite features. The page is warm and friendly with limited palette graphics that load very quickly. A menu bar across the top of the page and a row of whimsical icons at the bottom of the page allow visitors to quickly navigate to their section of interest. A convenient Mail To link allows visitors to send feedback to the webmaster. Clicking on the "About Us" icon brings visitors to a page explaining the philosophy behind the site (as shown in Figure 4-10). Take a look at how the About Us icon is "grayed out" (or faded) on that page, and notice how (for the most part) the icons are reused from page to page.

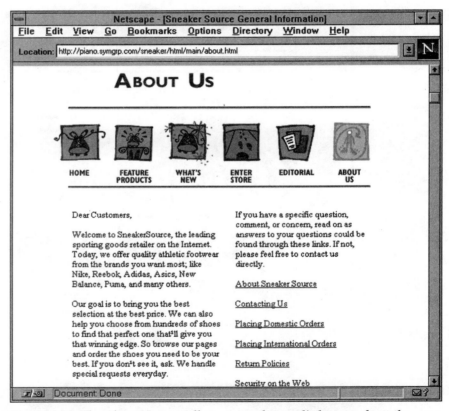

Figure 4-10: The About Us page allows you to learn a little more about the company and what they're all about.

Clicking the "Enter Store" brings you to the actual front page of the online Sneaker Source store, as shown in Figure 4-11. The front page of the store is a basic site map that allows visitors to search the site with a handy form, or choose from among a dozen different sports categories. At the bottom of the page, the Incentive Program, Order Status, Feedback, and Help Icons whisk visitors to those special departments. As you can see, the illustrated icons are carried throughout the site, which provides a consistent motif, in addition to speeding up the visitor experience, overall.

Avoid "Under Construction" Faux Pas
It's best not to leave any cliché "Under Construction" signs lingering on your Web site. Yellow and black striped bars are tres passé.

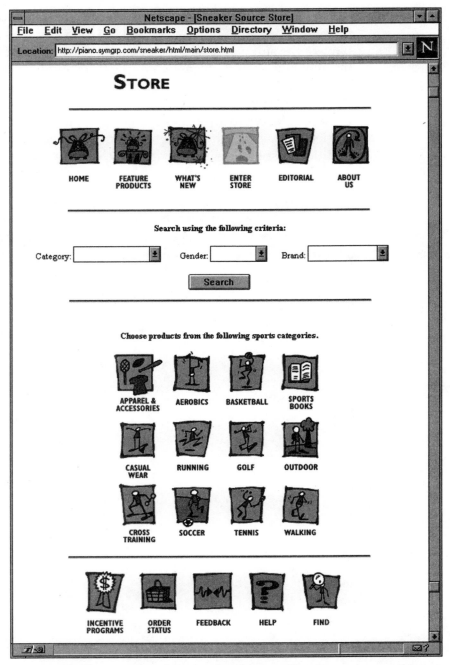

Figure 4-11: The entryway of the Sneaker Source online store puts everything at the visitor's fingertips.

Buying sneakers online opens up a whole new kind of shopping experience. There's no waiting for a grumpy, underpaid clerk, and no fighting the crowds. We clicked on the Running category, to bring up the front page of the Running section of the online store (as shown in Figure 4-12). Let's go Web shopping!

Figure 4-12: Did you ever think there were this many categories of running shoes?

Let's Go Shopping!

The front page of the Running section provides a huge list of running shoes in table format. The entries are sorted by manufacturer and include pricing information. Visitors can scroll through the listing to review the many running shoes. Each listing is hyperlinked to bring visitors to pages with photographs and rather extensive specifications.

As you navigate through the Sneaker Source Web site, the pages load almost instantaneously, as the majority of the graphic images are already in Netscape's cache. Once you've hit a few pages, you'll only have to wait for the tiny HTML file to be transferred (as well as a tiny grayed out icon and possibly a sneaker photo). We browsed the Sneaker Source for quite some time, and found the Saucony Jazz Trail model, as shown in Figure 4-13, to be an intriguing choice.

The presentation of the Saucony Jazz Trail sneakers is just as crisp, clean, and enticing as the rest of the Sneaker Source Web site. A photograph of the sneakers leaves little question as to what they look like from a variety of angles. Pop-up selection fields conveniently allow potential customers to check on available colors and sizes. Clicking the Shopping Cart icon adds the sneakers to your cart, which shows you a list of items you've selected. Choosing the Check Out icon brings you to the virtual cash register, where you can actually make the transaction online in a secure environment. All without leaving your desk chair! With all this shopping convenience, we'll have plenty of leisure time to put those new sneaks to good use.

In all, the Sneaker Source Web site provides a pleasant online shopping experience. The site is fast, well designed, and worthy of the attention of any true sneaker-wearing cybernaut.

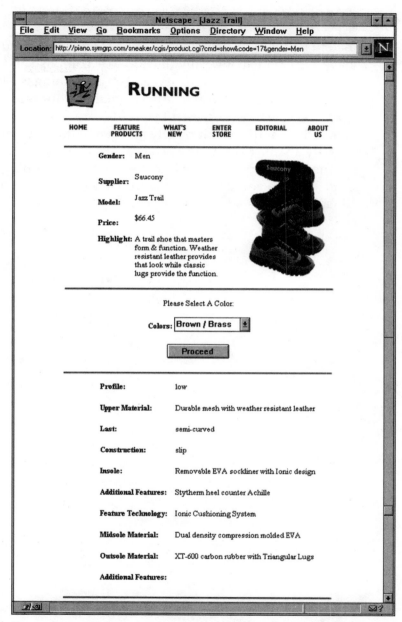

Figure 4-13: The Saucony Jazz Trail model had us reaching for our credit cards!

Moving On

Before you design a single Web page for your site, you should have a good idea of what you want to accomplish and of the audience you've chosen to serve. Web publishing is a dynamic medium that allows you to quickly change your direction while en route. The most successful Web sites are designed by folks who know their audience intimately and can build a dynamic site that rapidly adapts to changing needs.

The next chapters move into the magic of designing your Web pages, where you'll blend art with science. The real fun's just ahead, when we take the theory and put it to work.

chapter 5

Web Design 101

Welcome to Web Design 101, where we will delve into some of the "Whys" of Web page design. In the last chapter, you learned how to identify the goals of your Web site and how it might best serve your audience. Now, we're going to put that knowledge to work as we discuss some of the important steps taken in the design and construction of a Web site. We'll spend a bit of time discussing basic design concepts and the ins and outs of working with images. You'll also learn a number of tricks you can use to help create the optimum working environment.

The "Whys" of Web Page Design

Once you've identified exactly why your Web site exists, you can begin designing the site to meet those needs. As you begin laying the plans for your Web site, you must always keep in mind that the site design should reflect the purpose. Don't spend too much time on designing attention-getting features and pages that are ancillary to the site's needs. While we all want to generate lots of traffic, big hit numbers don't always reflect a successful site. Focus instead on what's going to pay the rent.

■ If your site exists to sell a product, it is only successful if the product gets sold. Make sure that visitors can get all the information they need to make a decision; then, provide the means for them to make the purchase, whether online or not.

■ If your site exists to generate a database, it's only successful if a sufficient number of visitors submit those forms. Get them to the form as quickly as possible. Make the form easy (and perhaps even fun!) to fill out. Thank them and send them on their merry way.

■ If your site exists to provide technical support, it is only successful if the visitors can quickly remedy their problems and come away from the site feeling good about the experience. Remember, they've come to your site in search of help, not a cold online shoulder.

■ Of course, if your site exists to sell advertising space, big hit numbers are crucial. The higher the hit rate, the more your site can charge for those ad banners. Go for broke.

Many Web sites have mixed purposes. Take Netscape, for example. While their site exists primarily to sell and support their server and browser software, they also sell Mozilla memorabilia (see Figure 5-1), books, and most importantly, advertising (as shown by Figure 5-2). In fact, a significant amount of Netscape's revenues come from selling banner advertising space. We're talking millions upon millions of dollars. Every time you click on one of those What's Cool? or What's New? buttons, you just helped to ring up another nanocent for Netscape. More power to them. At least it's not another penny in Bill's pocket.

Thinking of Advertising on Netscape's Web site?

Running an advertising banner on Netscape's Web site will yield a huge amount of exposure, but it costs accordingly. Get out your checkbook and take a gander at http://home.netscape.com/ads/ad_rate_card.html.

Figure 5-1: Move over Barney, Mozilla's in town!

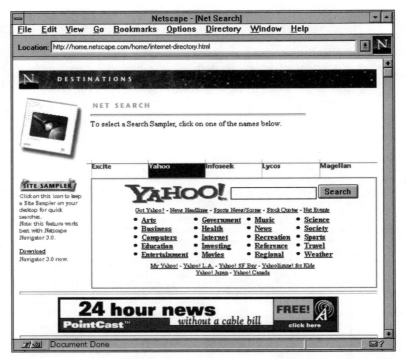

Figure 5-2: Netscape's ad banner revenues provide a constant flow of income for the company.

In order to keep track of what is and isn't being hit, you'll have to analyze the Web server logs. You can read more about the subject of Web site tracking in Chapter 7.

Keep It Simple & to the Point

If you're going to err in your Web site design process, you'll always want to err in favor of simplicity. A complex design—besides being harder for the visitor to deal with—is usually harder to create and maintain. A simple, elegant design lets the content shine without getting lost in a hackneyed presentation. Speed and readability should always be paramount.

- Use consistent, limited-palette color schemes for backgrounds, graphics, icons, and buttons.

- In general, use solid color backgrounds or skinny background tiles. Save those wild seamless tiles for special pages.

- Don't use more than one or two animated images per page. Avoid the carnival midway look.

Cnet (as shown in Figure 5-3) is a great example of a Web site design that works. A clean background, limited palette, consistent navigation, and graphic restraint help visitors quickly find what they're looking for. You'd do well to mimic certain aspects of the cnet site (http://www.cnet.com). The 99 sets of integrated backgrounds, bullets, and horizontal rules contained on this book's CD-ROM are a great place to start. They provide a simple vertical stripe along the left side of the page (along the lines of cnet's), along with matching bullets and rules (in various sizes), much of what you'll need to knock out a crisp site.

Figure 5-3: Cnet is one of the most heavily trafficked Web sites in the world, and its design is one of the most effective.

Streamlining Navigation

When the Beach Boys' Brian Wilson wrote "I Get Around," back in the early '60s, never in his wildest dreams could he have imagined that the song would become a Web surfing mantra. The whole idea of the Web is to quickly get from one place to the next without "getting bugged driving up and down the same old strip." If you fail to provide a smooth navigational interface, your visitors are likely to go off in search of a whole new Web site where the pages are hip.

Tiny Text Navigation Bars

If you set your text navigation bars with the Smallest Heading format, you'll get a nice, unobtrusive look that's easy to implement across your Web site.

When you design your navigational features, you want to keep them consistent throughout the Web site to the greatest extent possible. As was mentioned in Chapters 2 and 4, there are scads of ways to design your navigational bar—both horizontally, as well as vertically. Take a gander at "the electronic feedbag" example. While it uses big, gawky buttons, Figures 5-4 and 5-5 demonstrate two different ways to implement a horizontally oriented navigational scheme. Figure 5-4 was built from five separate GIF buttons, with one button swapping out each time the visitor hits a new page (to convey a "dimmed" appearance for that page's button). Figure 5-5, on the other hand, uses only two GIF images for the entire Web site. The pointer bounces around as the visitor moves from page to page.

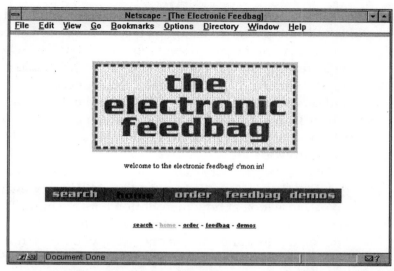

Figure 5-4: This approach uses five GIF images on each page, for a total of 10K. In addition, a new button has to download with each page.

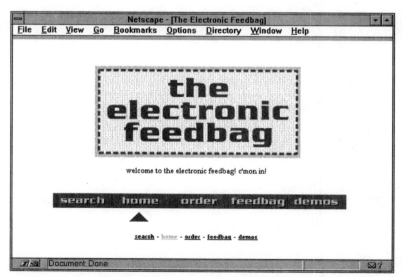

Figure 5-5: The button bar approach uses just two files (the button bar and the pointer), for a total of 8K.

While these two examples may look very similar, there's a definite advantage to using the second method. The composite button bar and pointer download only once. This scheme should be incrementally faster for the visitor when downloading the first and subsequent pages. The fewer the connections that the browser and server have to negotiate, the faster the download. The pointer moves from position to position through the use of fixed-width tables. Reusing navigational graphics is a great (and free!) way to speed up your site.

The Adobe Web site uses a neat trick to reuse navigational graphics. Figure 5-6 displays the PageMill Overview page. Let's take a close look at how their button bars are built. There are five separate GIF files used to create the header. While it's easy to isolate the top two and the last one, what you might not have noticed is that the "world" graphic is separate from the "overview" graphic. Since four of the five images are persistent as you navigate through the PageMill subsite, you'll only need to download the big "what's new," "details," "at work," "getting help," and "adding on" images as you jump between pages (within the subsite).

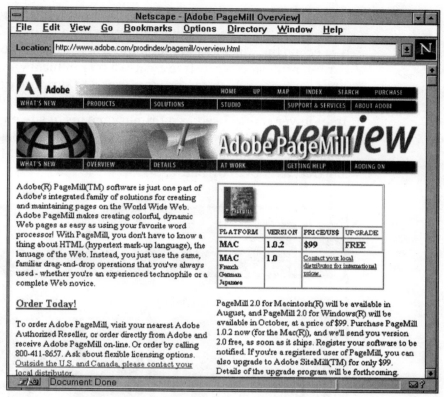

Figure 5-6: Adobe's Web site reuses its navigational graphics to great effect. Can you see where one graphic ends and the next begins?

The Adobe navigational scheme works fairly quickly once a visitor has downloaded the persistent images, although it can take a while to load all of the images when first hitting the site. The images eat up a significant amount of onscreen real estate, as well. If you're visiting the Adobe site on a machine that's equipped with a 21-inch monitor, it's not a problem. Unfortunately, if you're visiting the site with a 14-inch screen running at 640 X 480, you won't get to see much of the page without scrolling. This is not necessarily a problem. Since much of Adobe's intended audience works with big monitors running at high resolution, they can get away with the overly large navigational graphics.

Kobixx Systems (http://www.kobixx.com) has introduced SiteTree, a slick Java-driven tool to provide a visual Web site map that echos the Macintosh Finder and Microsoft Windows 95 Explorer interfaces. SiteTree creates a hierarchical view of a Web site's contents, which can be rearranged to simplify navigation. Once the tree has been fine-tuned and implemented, the TreeViewer can be used as a primary means of site navigation (it is not essential to have Java-support at the browser). Besco Graphic Systems was among the first Web sites to implement Kobixx SiteTree, as shown by Figure 5-7.

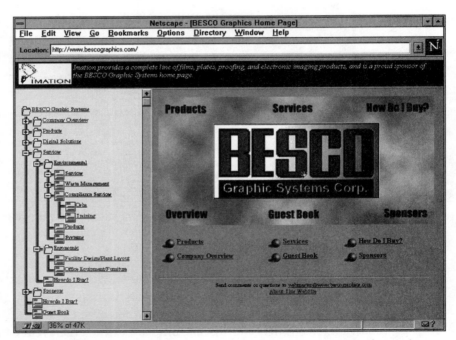

Figure 5-7: SiteTree's TreeViewer (from Kobixx Systems) provides fast and graphical site navigation, regardless of whether the browser features Java support.

The Caveats of the Cutting Edge

If you design your Web site with special features that are best viewed with a certain browser or plug-in, you owe it to your audience to provide a quick link to that browser or plug-in. For instance, if you've designed around the features in Netscape Navigator 3.0, you'll want to be able to send your visitors to the right place to download the browser. Check out http://home.netscape.com/comprod/mirror/usage.html for information on the "Netscape Now!" program. As shown in Figure 5-8, the page provides full details on how you can display the Netscape Now! button on the front page of your Web site.

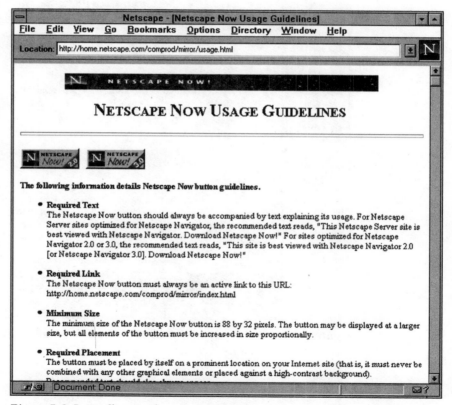

Figure 5-8: Just adhere to the rules and you too can sport a "Netscape Now!" button on your front page!

The HotWired Web site has long been on the bleeding edge of online design. The site uses a cool JavaScript to pop up a totally separate navigational window (as shown by Figure 5-9). This little window is persistent as you navigate throughout the site. It's so persistent, in fact, it even sticks around after you've left HotWired. Perhaps it's just their way of saying "Y'all come back now, ya hear?" Of course, if HotWired's visitors are not using a browser capable of supporting Java, they won't have the benefit of the navigational window. This should not be a problem, as by nature, visitors to the HotWired site are likely to be trendy folks, running the latest browser revisions.

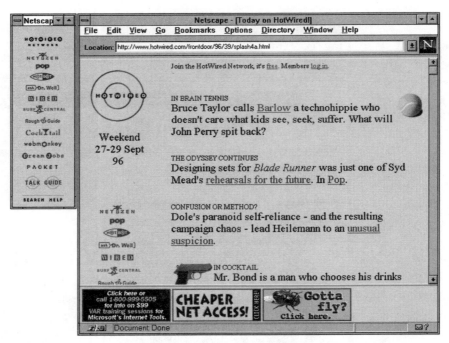

Figure 5-9: HotWired's separate navigational window stubbornly sticks around, even after you've left its Web site.

Unfortunately, the more trickery we load into our pages, the more we run the risk of crashing our visitors' browsers. As you begin to add high-end features to your site, it becomes more and more important that you test your pages thoroughly, on multiple platforms and browsers.

Fine-tuning GIF Images

"Taste's Great! Less Filling!"goes the advertising jingle. While we're not selling beer here, the same statement can be made about great Web graphics. The best electronic artwork should not only look good, it should also perform, by displaying properly and downloading quickly. This section will hit on some of the most important matters relating to image preparation. There's a wealth of other graphics information elsewhere within this book. Chapter 2 provides a rundown on how to work with images in the Page-Mill environment, while Chapter 11 delivers the goods on a number of programs that you can use to create great Web graphics.

Tweaking GIF Palettes

Palette tweaking is a topic that's a bit dry, a tad technical, and arguably boring. But it's an important subject, nonetheless. Rather than burden you with a bunch of technobabble, we'll cut right to the chase. The primary reason to tweak the palette of a GIF image is to reduce its file size and, consequently, reduce the time it takes to download. GIF palettes can contain no more than 256 colors (although as you'll soon learn, the browsers only support 216 colors). A browser can only use one palette per Web page. It's your responsibility to shoehorn as much image as possible into that very limited palette.

To illustrate the positive effects of palette tweaking, an experiment was conducted to see how small a marble tile image could be made. Starting with a 247K, 24-bit tagged image file format (TIFF) marble tile from Visual Software's Simply 3D CD-ROM, we successively cut back on the number of colors in the palette using Adobe Photoshop.

Original	GIF Images (87a non-interlaced)			
24-bit TIFF	Number of Colors in Palette			
Image	64	32	16	8
247K	83K	45K	33K	18K

The original RGB file was a 72 dpi image, 320 X 256 in size. To cut down the color palette, we began by using Photoshop's Posterize (Image | Map | Posterize) function on the original file. A preview option allows quick experimentation with different levels of posterization. If you push the image too far, you can see the results before you apply the effect. (You don't have to use the posterize function, but it's a good way to get a feel for the reduced color palette before you actually index the image.) After posterizing the marble, we converted the Image Mode to Indexed Color. The number of colors (or bit resolution) was limited specifically to the number of colors we used when we posterized the image. The image was converted with an Adaptive Palette and a Diffusion Dither. The Diffusion Dither was used to reproduce the image in a more faithful manner. Diffusion is usually preferable to Pattern Dithering, which can add unwanted artifacts and patterns (as its name implies). Figure 5-10 illustrates the difference in how the images look, albeit in grayscale. While we used Photoshop in the previous example, any competent image editor should provide similar functions. Compare the 256-color version at the far left with the 8-color version at the far right. The 256-color texture is smooth and realistic, while the 8-bit version is rather chunky. To see the real difference in full color, be sure to visit this book's Online Updates.

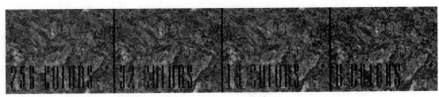

Figure 5-10: Which looks best to you?

Indexing an image without dithering often yields an over-posterized look, although it will help to reduce file size even further. In our 16-color image test, a non-dithered image resulted in a 31K file, as opposed to a 33K file for the dithered image. Is 2K worth the loss in image quality?

So What's the Netscape Palette?

While the GIF format supports 256 colors, one shouldn't get the wild idea that it's possible to use all 256 colors! This is due (in part) to the fact that the Windows operating system eats up 20 colors, just to display its graphical user interface. Since this is not a universally Microsoft world—and we're not all stuck eating a steady diet of white bread—Netscape had to make some concessions.

The *Netscape Palette* (as it's referred to in some circles) is a non-dithering combination of 216 colors that are designed to appear consistently across platforms (Macintosh, Windows, UNIX, and so on) in Netscape Navigator (as well as Microsoft's Internet Explorer on Windows systems). When specifying colors with the Netscape Palette, you can be assured that the colors will look similar whether viewed on a Power Mac, Pentium, Silicon Graphics, or Sun work station. There's a file (216color.gif) on this book's CD-ROM, which is indexed to the Netscape palette. You can use this file to perform custom palette conversions on your GIF images.

PANTONE's ColorWeb

http://www.pantone.com

PANTONE's ColorWeb is a groovy resource for Web designers. ColorWeb is a package that includes a system color picker and coordinated swatchbook that allows you to quickly specify the 216 "Internet-safe" colors. It was available initially only for Macintosh, although a Windows version is likely.

When you design your Web graphics, try to stick to the colors in the Netscape Palette. However, if you are converting photographs for use on your pages, don't bother with the Netscape Palette or with the GIF format. The best way to display color-rich images (such as photographs) is to use the JPEG format (which is unencumbered by browser color limitations).

Avoiding Palette Clash

Browsers load palette colors on a per-page basis. The colors that come in first are the colors that are used to display all the GIF images on a page. That is, if a Web page includes a number of images whose color palettes use a total combination of colors higher than 256, the images that come in late (after all the slots are filled) may suffer from a distorted display as the browser converts the orphaned colors to their closest match.

In short, you need to proceed with caution when indexing colors. While we all want the smallest possible image file sizes, the safest method for preparing GIF images may be to first index them to the Netscape Palette, then save them with the smallest number of possible colors.

Cropping & Scaling Images

It's always noble to avoid using images that contain an overabundance of wasted space or are excessively large. While this may seem obvious to some, it's a point worth making. This is not to say that you should crop every portrait to the ears and chin, nor every house to its porch and chimney. Any image editing application of merit will include the ability to quickly crop and scale a picture. If you keep your images generously large enough to discern, but small enough to quickly download, you'll keep the attention of your audience.

If you want to provide a nice big image, you should consider "hiding" it behind a smaller thumbnail. If your visitors are truly interested in the subject, they'll click on the thumbnail to see the big picture. If they're not interested, they won't click on the thumbnail, the result being that you save the noninterested visitor the time and trouble of downloading the big picture.

Please note that scaling an image within PageMill is not the same thing as scaling within an image editor. When you scale an image in PageMill (whether by pulling on the image handles or by changing the pixel width and height in the Attributes Inspector), you are not changing the actual size of the image file. Hence, if you scale an image down in PageMill, your visitors will be downloading a file that is unnecessarily large. While scaling is a convenient feature to have within the page-authoring environment, you'll achieve better results by handling most of the scaling chores within your image editing application. If you're planning on using thumbnail images, you should always create those images from the original files.

Transparency—Getting It Right

In your travels about the Web, there's little doubt that you've seen plenty of transparent GIF images, both good and bad. A good transparent GIF will float on the page with nary a hint of an outline. A bad transparent GIF will look fuzzy or chunky around the edges with a perceptible edge. Although PageMill makes it easy to assign transparency to inline GIF images, the program doesn't care whether they're good or bad transparent images (as shown by Figures 5-11 and 5-12). That particular responsibility is yours and it can only be accomplished in an image editing application.

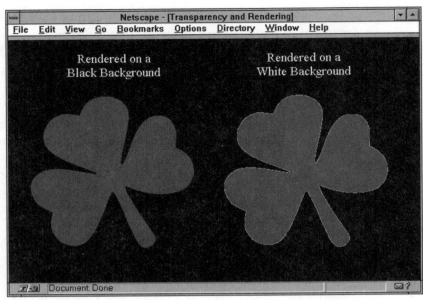

Figure 5-11: Check out the jaggy white outline around the second clover. That won't fly.

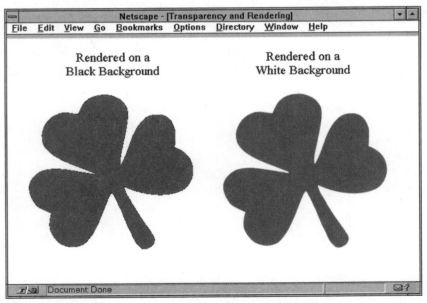

Figure 5-12: The black jaggy background around the first clover isn't acceptable, either.

There's a simple method you can use to ensure that your transparent GIF images are truly transparent. Always render your transparent images on the same color background they will be displayed upon. Figures 5-11 and 5-12 show the same image rendered on both a light and a dark background, then displayed on both a light and a dark background (in Netscape Navigator). The images that were rendered on the same background they are displayed on look great. The images that were conversely rendered and displayed aren't up to snuff.

Bad transparency rendering becomes extremely noticeable when soft drop shadows are used. Figure 5-13 demonstrates what happens when a drop-shadowed image is rendered upon too light a background. This image was rendered on a white background in Photoshop, but placed on a gray Web page background. Figure 5-14, on the other hand, was rendered on the same white background as it is displayed upon. Obviously, Figure 5-14 represents how the image should look. You can even use this technique for transparent graphics that you plan on using over textured backgrounds, as shown in Figure 5-15. If you want to try this method, choose a background color that matches the predominant color in the texture image. While this technique isn't perfect, it can be faster than the alternative (which is rendering over the background itself while using a transparency mask).

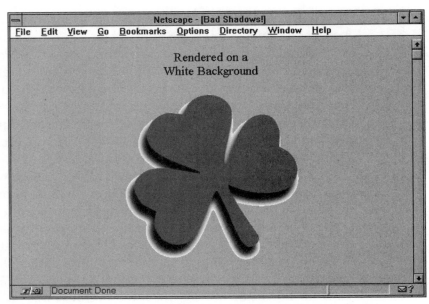

Figure 5-13: Ouch! Using this image would be grounds for dismissal.

Figure 5-14: That's more like it! It's tough to tell where the GIF image ends and where the background begins.

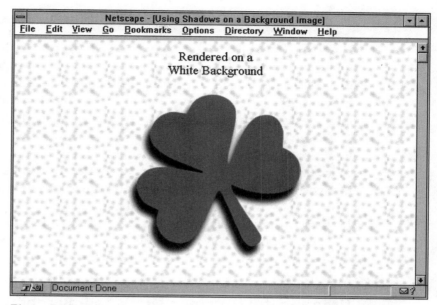

Figure 5-15: Using a transparent image over a textured background is a powerful effect...if you can successfully pull it off!

PageMill's built-in Transparency Editor is great for assigning the attribute at the last minute, but it falls short of what's possible within an advanced image editing application, such as Adobe Photoshop or Macromedia xRes. If possible, try to assign transparency well before you bring your GIF images into PageMill, so as to avoid any headaches at deadline time. Always fine-tune the images at their source to achieve the best results.

Use Transparent Space!
You can use transparent space around an image as a sneaky way to perform various alignment functions (in lieu of setting up a table). Just leave a little extra space on the side of the image that you want to space out from the adjacent text.

The Low-Resolution/High-Resolution Swap

Have you ever hit a Web page where a fuzzy grayscale (or one-bit) image downloaded and displayed immediately, only to be replaced by a crisp, full-color image? Have you ever wondered how they did it? There's nothing special about this little trick of "Web page design as performance art." It's accomplished with one of Netscape's cute modifications to the <IMG SRC> tag. Although you'll have to hack a bit in PageMill's text editor to make this work (since there's no option for this in the Attributes Inspector), it's worth the effort if the full-color image is fairly large. Just follow this syntax: <IMG SRC="fullcolor.jpg" LOWSRC="grayscale.jpg">. You can use either GIF or JPEG images, as long as you make sure that the images are exactly the same pixel width and height.

Creating the Optimum Working Environment

Everyone has their own idea of what the ultimate design studio should be like. Whether your dream studio is packed with Macintosh or Windows computers—and whether it's at the beach, on the mountain, or in the city—there are a variety of steps you can take to optimize your working environment to inspire and enable you to create great Web page designs. While you might not be able to achieve design studio utopia, you can use the following suggestions to help boost morale and increase productivity.

Go for a Fast Internet Connection

Waiting for pages to download (and upload!) is a bore. If you're hamstrung by a slow Internet connection, you owe it to yourself to investigate the alternatives. Plain old telephone service (POTS) just doesn't cut it once your workload reaches a certain point. While the promise of new, faster modem chips from Rockwell and others is encouraging, it may be a while until they're commonly available. And then the question will be whether or not your Internet Service Provider (ISP) will have the same type of modem as you.

The best bet might be ISDN (Integrated Services Digital Network) service, and depending on where you're located, it may be available right now. An ISDN line will cost you significantly more than POTS, although it shouldn't break the bank. The real trick may be finding an ISP that supports ISDN within your local calling area. There's a happy downside to having a fast connection to the Net. Cruising on a fast line is inherently pleasurable. Once you get a fast connection, you may find yourself (and your cohorts) spending more time cruising around the Web than you can afford!

Get a Big Desktop

As someone who has designed Web pages on everything from laptop computers through beefy design workstations, I've found that a big desktop is, perhaps, the quintessential Web page design productivity booster. To get a big desktop, you'll need two things: a large monitor and a high-resolution video card. While it's always nice to have plenty of desktop, the need for a big monitor is accentuated by PageMill's drag-and-drop methodology. A big monitor allows you to have lots of windows open at one time— which is quite handy when you're linking pages by dragging and dropping their respective page icons. You'll be far more productive, since you won't be constantly shuffling windows around.

How big is big enough? For serious PageMill design work, a 17-inch monitor should be considered the bare minimum. A 21-incher is the optimum environment. Big monitors are available from a wide range of sources. Radius (http://www.radius.com), for one, has a long reputation in the design community as a purveyor of quality monitors. Of course, there is a host of other sources. Once you've chosen your monitor, you'll need to choose a serious video card with enough memory to support 24-bit color at the high resolution required with that large monitor.

Number Nine's (http://www.nine.com) Imagine 128 video card is a superb choice for Windows-based design work (see Figure 5-16). The 4MB Imagine 128 PCI card sets the standard for speed and performance. The card delivers all the color and resolution you'll need for most resolutions (although if you're running at ultra-high res in 24-bit color, you should check into the 8MB version). If you're working on a Macintosh, you may be interested to hear that RasterOps is now marketing its own version of the Number Nine 128 card, as well.

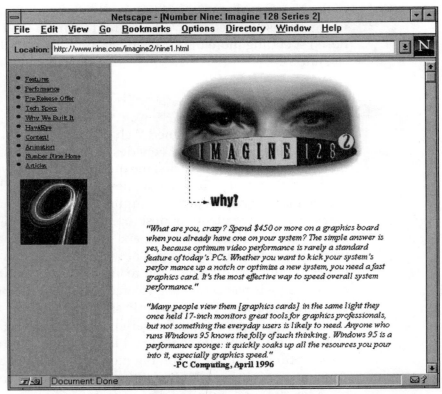

Figure 5-16: A fast, high-resolution video card, like the Number Nine Imagine 128, will make you more productive.

Serious video cards need sufficient video RAM to deliver 24-bit color at high resolutions. One and 2MB cards just don't have enough memory. If you're shopping for video cards, check the magazine reviews, visit the companies' Web sites, and above all, avoid the no-name brands. A bargain video card can quickly become a nightmare when the drivers don't work right or the next time a major system software revision comes out (and the bargain brand has mysteriously disappeared).

Stopping Monitor Glare

The best graphic designs are grown from a magic combination of inspiration and perspiration. (We're talking abstractly, of course; don't shut off your air conditioner!) Most professional designers will tell you that it's tough to be inspired in a typical corporate setting, while wallowing in the inferno of a thousand fluorescent overhead lights. While it's not worth getting into the ramifications of corporate politics, the first thing you need to do is put out those lights. The enemy is glare. If you can't convince your boss that you need to nix the overhead lights, try moving your monitor. You should also be cognizant of how your monitor is positioned with regard to any windows or skylights.

The Radius PressView SR monitors (as shown in Figure 5-17) are designed for prepress professionals who require the highest level of color fidelity and performance. While these are awesome monitors, they are a tad pricey (approximately $2,500 for the 17-inch model and $3,500 for the 21-inch model). However, the PressView SR series offers a great hint for designers on a budget. Check out the nifty "hood" that surrounds the monitor; it's there to reduce glare. With a little ingenuity, along with some cardboard and a simple utility knife, you can create your own custom hood for any monitor.

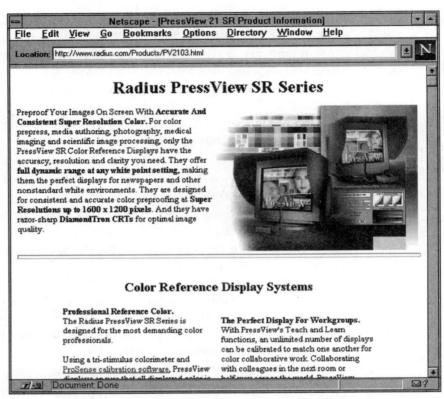

Figure 5-17: If you can't work under the proper lighting, a monitor hood will help to obfuscate glare.

Take a Break!

If your eyes are bugging out, your neck is hurting, and you're starting to show symptoms of carpal tunnel syndrome, get up from your computer and go for a walk.

Testing Your Site's Performance

No matter what type of system—be it Mac or PC—you've built your Web pages on or what resolutions and color depth you're running, you should always test your Web page designs on multiple systems. There is a vast difference between computers (even on the same platform) when flipping between resolutions and color depths. If you're designing pages on a Macintosh design station with a 21-inch monitor, running at 1152 X 870 (or higher) and 24-bit color, you should check out how those pages look on the lowest common denominator for Web browsing: a Windows machine running at 640 X 480 and 256 colors. Don't worry about designing graphical pages for anything less.

Are your pages taking too long to download? PageMill's Download Statistics Window (shown in Figure 5-18) provides a handy way to estimate how long it will take visitors to access each page. The window allows you to quickly get a feel for how long a page, object, frame, or frameset will take to download at various Internet connection speeds (9.6, 14.4, 28.8, 33.6, 68.0, and 128.0 Kbps). Download Statistics can be found on the Edit menu, and may also be accessed via the Command-U keyboard shortcut.

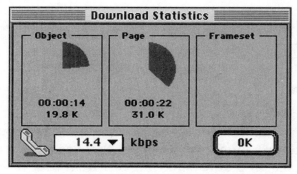

Figure 5-18: If you think a page may be getting too fat, check the Download Statistics.

Mirroring Your Server's Directory Structure

Are you constantly breaking links when you upload your Web pages to the Web server? This is one of the most common operational snags and is inherently avoidable. The best solution is to mirror your Web server's directory structure on your local hard drive. Of course, you don't have to mirror the whole thing—just the directories that are pertinent to your Web site! Create a "root" directory for your site and replicate any subdirectory that you might have within the root. Name the subdirectories *exactly* as they are named on the server. (Pay particular attention to capitalization!) PageMill 2 also has a Server Preferences feature that allows you to set up local aliases for various server directories (as shown by Figure 5-19).

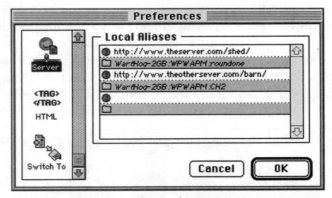

Figure 5-19: Server Preferences can be set for multiple sites.

For more information on transferring files, check out Chapter 7 for details on a number of programs that you may be able to use to simplify the procedure of moving files from your workstation to your Web server. And Chapter 8 delivers a rundown on how you can use Adobe SiteMill to keep those stray links mended.

Don't Write Off the Text Editors!

While we all know why we bought PageMill—to avoid ever having to tangle with HTML coding—one of the most productive aspects you can add to your shop is a bit of HTML expertise. Having the ability to hack it out by hand (and understand what you're doing) is a true virtue. This is not to say that you have to learn how to do it yourself, however! Instead, you should foist this responsibility on someone with the right disposition (should you not be the one predisposed). Just as importantly, you should arm yourself with the right tools for the job. Chapter 9 provides a rundown on a variety of applications that you can use to quicken the flow of existing documents into Web pages.

Moving On

This chapter covered an array of design hints you'll put to good use as you begin creating Web pages with PageMill. The more knowledge you have, the more effective you'll be. The next chapter, "Design Problems and How to Conquer Them," delves into the solutions for some of the most common maladies that may beset a Web site.

chapter 6

Design Problems & How to Conquer Them

Unlike traditional print publishing, nothing is permanent on the Web. If a mistake, such as a typographical error, is made on a Web page, it can be corrected immediately without the cost or time involved in sending a printed piece back to the press. If a Web site design flaw rears its ugly head, it too can be dealt with in a timely manner. Implementing a design change to a Web site does not have to be a monumental undertaking as long as you've designed your site to accommodate such changes. In the previous chapter, you learned how to build your pages to enable easy page adjustments.

This chapter will warn you about some of the most common pitfalls a Web designer encounters and will (hopefully) help you to avoid them. Out on the Web, every mistake has been made a thousand times. And that's a good thing, because we can all learn from the haphazard online efforts of others. By working through this chapter, you should gain an understanding of what to avoid, and what to do if you've already crossed the line of questionable Web site design.

Common Design Problems: A Baker's Dozen

Here are 13 of the most common Web site design problems, in no particular order:

1. The Web site is too darn slow.
2. It's hard to read.
3. It's just plain ugly.
4. The navigational system is confusing.
5. It was designed for a specific browser.
6. It doesn't feel like one site.
7. It's tough to find.
8. It's password protected.
9. It goes 404: Page Not Found.
10. It doesn't do what you wanted it to do.
11. It's a pain in the neck to maintain.
12. It's stale.
13. It flashes.

By no means should you consider this a complete list. There are plenty of Web site design faux pas to avoid, but these are among the most common. You may recall that some of these points are mentioned in previous chapters; they are well worth repeating, and the rest of this chapter is dedicated to solving these common design problems.

As you read along in this chapter, you'll quickly notice that many of the solutions are similar in nature. Solving one design problem often helps to solve another. Take heed of this advice, and it will take care of you.

It's Too Darn Slow

This first common problem shouldn't be a surprise to anyone with more than 15 minutes exposure to the Web. It's one of the unfortunate realities of the Internet at present. Nevertheless, you must always strive to make your pages as fast and light as is possible.

Here are several ways to make your Web site move along nice and fast.

- *Keep your GIFs and JPEGs as small as possible.* You can easily keep graphics files small by using the lowest practical number of indexed colors in your images. The fewer the number of colors, the smaller the file will be. Experiment with your image editor to get the right balance between file size and appearance.

Figure 6-1 displays the difference in appearance when a button is saved with a variety of color palettes. File sizes range from 883 bytes at 3 bits per pixel, to 3331 bytes at 8 bits per pixel. It's up to the Web page designer to determine where the trade-offs should be made. In this case, at 1629 bytes, Photoshop's 5 bits per pixel setting provides the best compromise of file size to image quality.

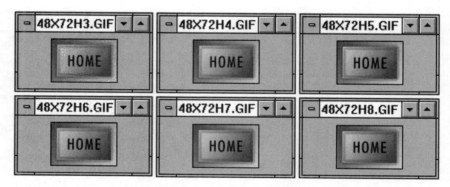

Figure 6-1: The smaller the color palette, the smaller the GIF file, but the trade-off is in image quality.

Color Palette Size vs. File Size	
8 bits per pixel	3331 bytes
7 bits per pixel	2755 bytes
6 bits per pixel	2143 bytes
5 bits per pixel	1629 bytes
4 bits per pixel	1213 bytes
3 bits per pixel	883 bytes

■ *When possible, consider using a composite button bar, rather than individual buttons.* The more separate images you have on the Web page, the longer it will take to download them all. This has to do with the overhead that each graphic file has to carry. The three small individual (5 bit per pixel) buttons shown in Figure 6-2 weigh in at 1597, 1629, and 1564 bytes respectively, while the composite button bar saves some space at 4004 bytes. While this doesn't sound like a dramatic savings, it adds up. When you start working with beefier files, it can make a substantial difference.

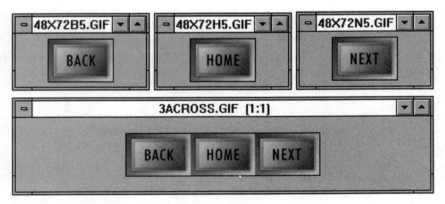

Figure 6-2: A composite button bar can save download time.

■ *Use a repetitive button bar (or individual buttons) that is identical from page to page.* Once the browser downloads the button bar or individual button, it caches it (stores it in memory) and doesn't have to download it on subsequent pages. If the button bar calls a different file on each page, it will result in slower performance. The mythical Pete's Aquatic Pets page, shown in Figure 6-3, uses a repetitive button bar that is downloaded only once. As visitors jump from page to page, the pointer is moved from icon to icon through the use of a nifty little table.

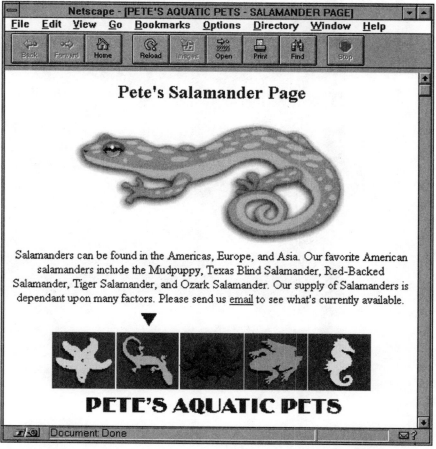

Figure 6-3: As you jump from page to page on the Pete's Aquatic Pets Web site, only the pointer moves.

■ *Use thumbnail images and warn users about the file size of large graphics*. In other words, give those folks a chance to at least think twice before they've committed themselves to downloading a great big graphic file. Figure 6-4 shows a common example of when and how you might want to use a thumbnail.

Figure 6-4: Don't make visitors wait for those big images, unless they've asked for them!

■ *Consider providing alternate text-only versions of your pages.* As creative as they are, graphics still are the time killers. The folks who come to your site for a quick answer to their queries will be grateful, while others who have more time on their hands will enjoy the graphics version. Let visitors make their text/graphics choices on your front page, as well as on each page.

■ *Don't create huge text pages.* Break large pages up into smaller chunks. Text pages that take a week and a half to load are just as bad as pages that are loaded with graphics. Try to keep your text files under 40K or so.

■ *Make sure you have a big enough pipe run to your server.* Look into upgrading your line if you're seeing a high enough hit rate to justify the expenditure. The added costs are akin to making a larger press run on a printed piece. Your systems administrator should be able to provide you with your options and the associated costs.

■ *Check to see if your server is getting bogged down with requests.* If it is, find out why. If there are other busy sites running on the same server, your site's performance may suffer. Once again, talk these issues over with your systems administrator to see if there are ways to improve your site's performance without dropping a huge chunk of change to switch servers.

Does Your ISP Cut the Mustard or the Cheese?

If you're in the market for a new Internet Service Provider, check out The List at <http://www.thelist.com/> for a huge list.

■ *Consider adding a graphics server.* If your site is heavy on graphics and is running on Macintosh, investigate the possibility of adding a Maxum RushHour graphics server. RushHour uses RAM caching to greatly accelerate site performance.

It's Hard to Read

Gee, you mean you can't read mauve type over a seafoam plaid flannel textured background? So much of good site design is so obvious, it's amazing how some folks never give it a second thought. The bottom line is that if your audience can't read what you've got to say, you've failed in your role as a designer. Strive to make things visually interesting, not illegible. Figure 6-5 illustrates the Magnificently Obscure Page, which may not be all that magnificent, but is certainly obscure. You'll have a tough time reading the text on this page without reverting to the source code.

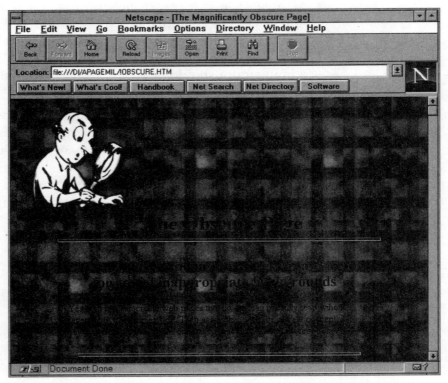

Figure 6-5: You mean to say that you can't read this? Good Web design means site visitors can read what you have to say.

Here are some strategies to ensure that your Web site visitors can actually see what you've designed.

- *Lighten up your backgrounds and choose your text colors carefully.*

- *Stay away from heavy-handed textures and steer toward more monochromatic motifs.* Make sure that there is enough contrast between the background pattern or color and the text color. When in doubt, always go with a lighter background. This book's CD-ROM contains a number of conservative predefined color schemes that have been tweaked for maximum readability. In addition, a good number of the 2,000 textured backgrounds have also been designed with readability in mind. But fear not, zany texture aficionados...there are plenty of wacky textures on the CD-ROM as well!

Want to Learn More About Color?

Check out Gary Priester's *Looking Good in Color*, Ventana, 1995. It's a great reference guide. While the book is subtitled as *The Desktop Publisher's Design Guide*, most of the principles apply to online design, as well.

- *Use a larger text size with the <FONT SIZE="X"> command.*

You don't have to resign yourself to having tiny body text! While PageMill 1.0 did not have a provision for cranking up text size, PageMill 2 does this with ease. You can ratchet your type size up quickly by using the Increase Relative Font Size button. Just select and click. Figure 6-6 shows how different font sizes display within Netscape Navigator.

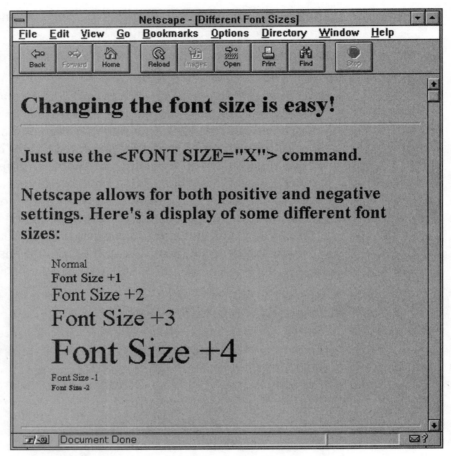

Figure 6-6: Use a larger font size when appropriate.

■ *Use typefaces that hold up under low resolution.* When creating text graphics, such as buttons and click bars, stay away from very fine serifs and frilly faces. Stick with fonts that were designed to be used for onscreen viewing. Chapter 11 will give you an online tour of some of today's best font foundries. Figure 6-7 shows the differences between City Medium, a slab serif face, and Snell Bold, a fine script face at different point sizes. Snell actually holds up pretty well for a script!

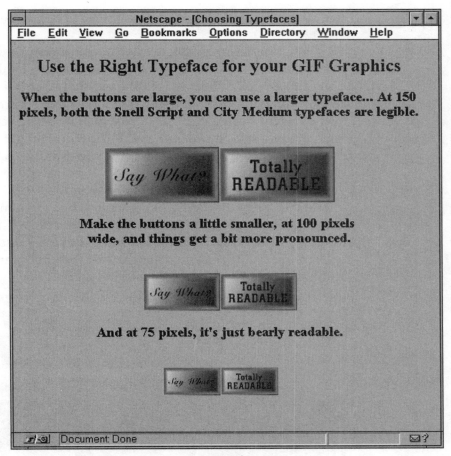

Figure 6-7: In smaller sizes, slab serif typeface, such as City, will hold up better than a fine script, like Snell.

Preview Your Site on the Most Popular Browsers

Take a trip to your site with Netscape Navigator, Mosaic, and Microsoft's Internet Explorer to see how it looks on each of these browsers. If you can, check with the most current versions of the browsers, along with a previous release. Watch closely for weird things that may happen with text wraps and graphics.

It's Just Plain Ugly

This Web site design problem often goes hand in hand with hard-to-read text, although it's possible to have a very legible but very ugly site, as well. If beauty is in the eye of the browser, consider consulting your office's version of Snow White's mirror, by asking, "Who has the fairest Web site?" To which it should reply: "You have the fairest Web site of them all." If you can't get your mirror to tell you truthfully (or at least lie to you as it did to the Evil Queen), you're just going to have to roll up your sleeves, clean up your Web site and make it truly gorgeous.

The Web page displayed in Figure 6-8 displays a number of design problems turning it into a rather displeasing site, even though you *can* read its bilious green text over its purple plaid background. Note the bad drop shadow (botched transparency) and unsuitable border on the headline graphic.

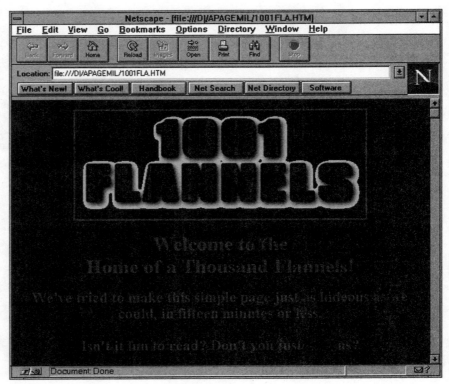

Figure 6-8: Well, it could have been even uglier!

Sure, PageMill makes it easy to crank out your own Web pages, but it doesn't turn you into an award-winning designer. If you are seriously design challenged, give some thought to hiring an experienced designer. Or take the advice of one. Once the design of your Web site is set, you can take over the maintenance. Meanwhile, here are some helpful tips.

- *Start with an integrated template.* You'll want to use a template that provides matching (or complementary) bullets, bars, and accents. Using an integrated template can make it easy to knock out a polished site without spending a ton of time or cash. You'll find a nice selection of these on this book's CD-ROM, along with a demo of Specular International's 3D Web Workshop, which includes a good number of modifiable buttons and doodads.

- *Remember that less is more.* Hideous backgrounds are to blame for the most offensive pages. Think twice about using that tartan plaid or busy floral print!

- *Use proven color schemes for backgrounds, graphics, and text.* If you're having trouble putting together a color scheme, there are a number of ways to jump-start the process. PANTONE, the company behind the PANTONE Matching System, has a nifty little program called ColorUp that suggests color schemes for you. Another sneaky idea is to take a trip to your local paint and home decorating store. Peruse their selection of paint chips. Often, they have chip sheets that illustrate a variety of color schemes. Take a few chip sheets back to your studio and try matching some of the combinations to see what you get. Just the thing for that Victorian, Southwest, or Colonial look!

Check the CD-ROM!

This book's CD-ROM contains a selection of proven color schemes.

The Navigational System Is Confusing

Watch Out! Your Web site visitors can't figure out where things are. They can't get to where they want to go, and they're leaving your site faster than you can say "Please don't leave! You just got here!" It's time to look at how you can make your navigational system more navigable! Nothing, after all, beats a good set of directions (Figure 6-9).

Figure 6-9: You can get there from here. The Issaquah Online Web site makes it easy with a solid set of directions available to the visitor.

The Issaquah Online Web site makes it a snap to find your way. The site, which was developed by Blue World Communications with PageMill (and other tools), is friendly and easy to get around. When visitors land at the Issaquah Online front door, they are immediately presented with a whimsical and graphical site image map, along with access to the site index and a handy search feature.

Here are some tried-and-true ways to help ensure that your Web site visitors find their way around your cyberplace with ease.

- *Use a consistent navigational interface.* Don't throw your visitors any spitballs. After they've plowed through a number of your pages, you've established a pattern in their minds. You don't want to undo it! It's important to establish a consistent navigational interface and maintain continuity. Avoid changing your icons midstream and don't mix your graphical metaphors. The Issaquah Online Web site (as shown in Figure 6-10) uses a vertical row of icons to great effect.

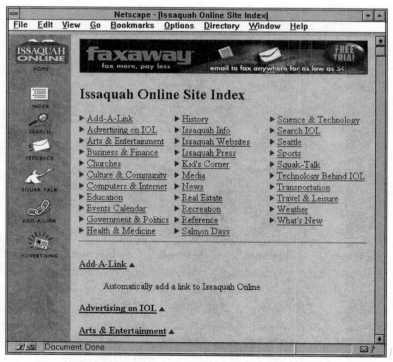

Figure 6-10: The Issaquah Online Web site index provides total access, while maintaining a consistent interface.

■ *Always use a text navigation bar.* Use this navigation bar in addition to a graphic navigational interface. Some folks like to cruise the Web at high speed, with the graphics turned off. If you only have image map navigation, you'll invoke their wrath.

■ *Stay simple, straightforward, and obvious.* Don't be seduced by way cool, overly complicated schemes. Navigation has to be instantly comprehensible. Your visitors shouldn't have to figure out how to cruise your site.

It Was Designed for a Specific Browser

There are other browsers in cyberspace besides Netscape's Navigator. While you don't want (or need) to build a version for each browser, it's polite to have both a high- and a low-bandwidth track.

Let Them Know!
If you're using Java or Shockwave animations within your Web site, be sure to let visitors know right away. Be a courteous Web designer, and post a notice on the front door.

Here are some tips for accommodating your (browser-impaired) Web site visitors who don't happen to be using Netscape.

■ *Preview your site on a number of browsers.* While there are scores of browsers on the market, you should concern yourself with only the most popular. Start with Netscape Navigator, Mosaic, and Microsoft's Internet Explorer. If you have the opportunity, try accessing your site from both Windows and Macintosh platforms. You'll be amazed at the difference between machines, even when running the same software on similar platforms. There are many video-related variables that will affect how your site looks.

- *Create a text-only version of your site.* This important task might not take all that much time, and it's one of the most considerate things you can do as a Web designer. Remember to use the Attributes Inspector palette to label your images with an alternate text field.

- *Put a button on your front page to "Get Netscape Now!"* If you've designed your site to be viewed exclusively with Netscape Navigator, you need to make it as easy as possible for the browser-impaired visitor to get a copy. Adding the "Get Netscape Now!" button is a convenience for our less fortunate Web-browsing brethren.

It Doesn't Feel Like One Site

You don't want to boggle the minds of your Web site visitors. The Web is a confusing enough place as it is. As your visitors jump from one page to another, you want them to feel as if they're in the same warm fuzzy place.

Here are some easy strategies for bringing consistency to your Web site.

- *Keep the navigational interface consistent.* A consistent navigational interface will help to unify the look and feel of your site. You don't want your visitors to have to figure out a different set of controls on each page, or even in each section, of your site.

- *Use your logo.* One of the easiest ways to enhance continuity is to carry a theme or motif throughout your entire Web site. If you have a nice looking company logo, for instance, use it once on every page, if it can be done discreetly. Take a look back at the Issaquah Online pages illustrated in Figures 6-9 and 6-10 for a great example.

- *Reuse common design elements.* You'll add to the site's continuity by reusing elements such as buttons and click bars. This will help to speed up your site, as the browser will only have to download the graphic once. The Issaquah Online Web site effectively implements this strategy with its vertical button bar.

- *Try not to vary backgrounds too widely*. Use the same background pattern or make slight variations. Change backgrounds only when you have a really good reason to do so, such as wanting to differentiate between sections of your site. An added benefit of using the exact same background pattern file is that you'll speed up your pages, as you do with reusing buttons and click bars.

- *Use the Title Bar to your best advantage*. If someone bookmarks your page, you want your site and page name there. This one is often overlooked and is totally unobtrusive. Page titles are picked up and used by the search engines (see Chapter 4) and are an essential way to differentiate your pages.

It's Tough to Find

Hey, it's great that you've built an awesome site, but just building it doesn't mean that you'll instantly attract an audience. The Web isn't a field of dreams (except for those IPO millionaires, like the Mozillanaughts and Yahooligans we all know, love, and are envious of)...if you build it, they won't come unless they know you're out there. There are a number of ways to get your site on the map, without resorting to hucksterism (Figure 6-11).

Figure 6-11: Let everyone know where you can be found.

You'll find that your site will gain attention as you begin adding your Web site address (URL) to everything your organization puts out. This includes letterhead, envelopes, business cards, print advertisements (including magazine, newspaper, and yellow page ads), marketing collateral, promotional trinkets, T-shirts, and other goodies. But don't make the address the central focus. It's just part of your contact information, as are your telephone and fax numbers.

Name Your Domain

A named domain, like *mycompanynamehere.com*, helps to set your Web site apart. Expect to spend 50 bucks to register, and 50 more on an annual basis to maintain the name. You can register the name with InterNIC (the regulatory agency) yourself, or your Internet service provider should be able to register your name with InterNIC for you. Expect to drop another 50 for the convenience of having your ISP do the legwork. Check out <http://rs.internic.net/domain-info/faq.html> for the InterNIC FAQ.

It helps to get a Web site address that makes sense, since most people don't enjoy typing in a URL that's as long as a football field. If you have the opportunity to register a suitable domain name, do so immediately. The domains won't last forever, and there could be a slew of organizations that need or want to use the same name as you.

It's Password Protected

Using password protection gives you the opportunity to monitor your visitors more closely. Unfortunately, password protection will lower your hit rate and aggravate a certain percentage of users. On the other hand, it will qualify your visitors (Figure 6-12) to a certain extent. If they're willing to register, they're more likely to be legitimately interested in what you have to offer.

Figure 6-12: What's the password? Using password protection can both help and hurt a Web site.

You've got to determine what the specific benefits of password protection are as they relate to your site. There may be a way to achieve your end goal without putting up a big electric fence. Since password protection is done at the Web server, it's important to talk this over with your site administrator to see if there are alternatives. You may be able to use products such as Maxum's NetCloak to accomplish your needs. Chapter 7 covers NetCloak and other packages that have staked their claim by providing additional Web site utility.

It Goes 404: Page Not Found

Clicking on a link to a Web site only to find that the linked page has disappeared is a big turnoff. Bad links happen for a number of reasons. The linked page may have moved or the server may be unreachable. Or you may have made a typo and missed entering a character when adding the link in PageMill's Attributes Inspector. Chapter 8 covers the basics of Web site housekeeping, but here are several key points.

- *Make sure all links work.* Before you put a page out in the open, take the time to click through each page. It may take a little extra time, but it's worth the effort.

- *Don't key the text in by hand.* If you're using repetitive button bars—both graphical and text—make sure that you always copy the information from the same place. Use PageMill's pasteboard.

- *Use software "helpers."* If you don't have the time to do things manually, you can enlist the help of any one of a number of programs such as Adobe SiteMill and InContext WebAnalyzer.

- *Keep checking for problems.* When you have downtime, make use of it by checking through your pages to see if anything's gone 404. You may have control over the pages on your site, but if you're linking to outside sources, who knows what may be happening on the other side of the WWW.

It Doesn't Do What You Wanted It to Do

You may think you know what you want out of your Web site when you start your quest, yet along the way, things will change. Every site is different, and the needs of the sponsoring organization (even if it's just little ol' you) must be fulfilled to make a Web project a worthwhile endeavor.

Sometimes, It's Obvious...
If the goal of your Web site is to sell product, for example, and you're site isn't selling, then a correction is in order. You've got to find out why items are not selling, and make changes.

To get on course, take stock of your Web site on a regular schedule. Ask yourself, "Is it doing what I wanted it to do?" If your site isn't doing what you want it to do, make a change in course. If it is, do more of the same. Use your site statistics to fine-tune your content. The statistics will tell you which pages people are hitting. This can help you to determine where to lay more bait to get them to the pages where you want them to go. Chapter 7 delves further into the subject of site statistics.

It also helps to go back to your audience, through some sort of survey mechanism, to find out what they want. Then plan your efforts so that you can give them what they need. Remember that what they want and what you are prepared to offer are not always the same thing.

Your agenda may be obvious, or it may be hidden. While your visitors may be on your Web site to glom up your freebies, you might be building a mailing list of people interested in such. They want the freebie. You want their name. Nothing in life is free.

It's a Pain in the Neck to Maintain

A Web site is not a "do it once and it's done" project. By nature, a Web site requires regular maintenance. It's imperative that you design your site so that you can tend to it on a regular basis without breaking half your links with just a few keystrokes. Simply maintaining the links on your Web site can be a huge time killer.

If you start by building a simple site, the maintenance aspect will remain easy. In other words, the more straightforward your site design and layout are, the happier you or your webmaster will be. That doesn't mean that you're going to make everything a straight linear path; just that the only place you want to see spaghetti is on your dinner plate.

Of course, it helps to maintain a site map on paper. Sketch out the relationships between your pages. If you can't draw it, you're bound to run into problems. Documenting your steps is especially important if you're not working alone. Your associates will need to know where to go to make alterations in your absence.

Consider using a database to publish your pages, rather than creating all of your pages manually one-by-one. PageMill does a great job of creating design-driven pages, but in certain cases, such as extensive online catalogs or informational corporate intranets, you'll need to resort to serious muscle. You can use PageMill to create the templates, however, and use a database to do the repetitive tasks. Chapter 7 includes coverage on the subject of database-driven Web site design.

Finally, use programs such as Adobe SiteMill and InContext WebAnalyzer to manage your Web site. When you move a page, SiteMill will adjust the links for you. This eliminates the chump work of manually cutting and pasting the links, and saves an incredible amount of time. Check out Chapter 8 for the skinny on SiteMill.

It's Stale

How many Web sites have you visited that seem like they've never been changed since the day they were first put up? And how many times have you been back to those sites to see if they have anything new to offer? Your local bakery wouldn't survive if they didn't bake fresh goods every day. You wouldn't pick up your local newspaper if you knew that it didn't contain any current news. It's imperative to always have something in the proverbial oven. While your site might not require a daily change of sights and sounds, you do need to make sure that a lack of new material isn't keeping your most valuable visitors from "stopping back again soon!"

To keep your Web site fresh, start by setting a schedule for updating your site and then stick to it. If you're working with others, you'll probably need to delegate responsibility among a number of individuals so that each person has a set task.

Build Browser Muscle Memory
If you want your visitors back, day after day, think about setting up a page that *does* change on a daily basis. This can help to lodge your bookmark into your visitor's daily routine.

Another way to keep your site fresh is to provide content that changes on a regular basis. Think about what you can accomplish each day or each week. You want to establish the concept of "there's always something new" for your audience so they become repeat visitors.

Finally, don't let old pages linger. If you have pages that are date-driven, such as organizational calendars, make sure that you delete the old information immediately after the dates expire.

It Flashes

Flashing text was never cool. It still isn't, and it's darn close to cliché to mention Flash as a no-no. There may be certain instances where you feel that you absolutely must include a Flash command, but none easily come to mind. If you're going to use flashing text, just make sure that you do so sparingly.

DANGER!
If you have "warning label" of some type on your site, the flash command *may* be appropriate. Or maybe *not*.

Moving On

There you have it. Just follow these simple directions and you'll be a star Web site designer. Ah, if only life were that easy. Successful Web site design takes time and planning. While in conventional publishing, forethought is more valuable than afterthought, this is not the case with Web publishing. If you make a mess out of your Web site design, you can always fix it (unless it was so incredibly bad that it cost you the account). By the way, you should always spend the time to preflight and beta test your Web site behind your firewall before turning it loose on your audience.

The next section of the book focuses on extending the functionality of PageMill. By itself, the program is cool. When you team it up with the right applications, however, it's insanely great. You'll learn about the programs you can use to create incredible pages that captivate your audience and effectively tell your story.

part 3
Pumping Up PageMill

chapter 7

Doing What PageMill Doesn't Do

Back in the spring of 1996, when this book was first in the planning stages, there were a lot of things that PageMill didn't do. While PageMill 1.0 was a very innovative program, it fell short in a number of places. The shortcomings were felt in the area of rapidly evolving Web standards. Specifically, the program didn't handle HTML tables or frames. Although some may argue that the latter hardly matters, the former is undeniably important for Web designers with any hope of taking complete control over their page layouts. If you've read through Chapter 3, you've discovered how PageMill 2 now handles those tough page designs with aplomb. With most of the page design issues laid to rest, we'll turn to some of the administrative issues at hand.

PageMill allows you to put a pretty face on your Web pages, but it doesn't handle much of the nitty-gritty of running an entire Web site. Rest assured, this isn't a chapter on how to become a webmaster. We won't get into the fine points of running a Web server and we won't start talking a bunch of overly techno mumbo jumbo. That's a topic for an entirely different shelf of computer books. Instead, it's our aim to acquaint you with a number of techniques and technologies that will help you to become more effective at implementing your Web designs.

And although PageMill doesn't perform any site management chores, you'll learn in the next chapter, which is about site management, how you can quickly get your house in order with Adobe SiteMill. For the price of a software upgrade, your site can be whipped into shape with drag-and-drop ease.

We'll take an overview of the many applications that can make your life easier and your Web site more effective. Demo versions for many of the programs discussed herein are available online. This chapter will focus on those areas in which most PageMillers can use a helping hand:

- Moving Files
- Creating scripts without hacking code
- Tracking your visitors
- Database Web publishing

Moving Files Via FTP

If you're lucky enough to be working on a corporate intranet, where you can move all of the pages associated with your Web site from your "creation station" to your "live site" with a simple drag and drop, this section isn't for you. Folks sitting on Mac or PC networks such as these have it easy. For the less fortunate, those who have to use a File Transfer Protocol (FTP) program to move their files, read up. If you've been using a command-line interface program to transfer files, you can shelve it in favor of something out of the 1990s. While the method that you use to transfer files may depend upon your Internet Service Provider (ISP), we'll begin by taking a look at how CompuServe handles file transfers for its personal Web spaces. Then, we'll have a look at Ipswitch's WS_FTP and Dartmouth College's Fetch (not to be confused with Adobe's old Fetch image-cataloging software, which was recently sold to Luminous).

Transferring Files With CompuServe's Publishing Wizard

http://www.compuserve.com

When CompuServe (CIS) designed its Home Page Wizard system, the company knew that they had to keep things as straightforward as possible to avoid massive confusion among its user base. With millions of subscribers, CIS instantly became one of the largest entities in the Web site hosting business when it began offering free personal Web site space. While the Home Page Wizard is aimed at the low-end—to enable total Net newbies to quickly hack out a page—it includes all the functionality you need to move your PageMilled site up to CompuServe's massive Web server.

There are two modules in the CompuServe Web package. The Home Page Wizard module is used to create basic Web pages. Since you're using PageMill, you'll probably never use it. The Publishing Wizard is the keeper because it's a simplified FTP program. Once you enter your personal information, the Publishing Wizard asks you to select the files you want to upload to your Web site (as shown in Figure 7-1). After you've compiled the list of files, click next and select the page that you want to be the home page for your personal site (see Figure 7-2). The Publishing Wizard will set that page up to be the default home page, without requiring any special naming conventions.

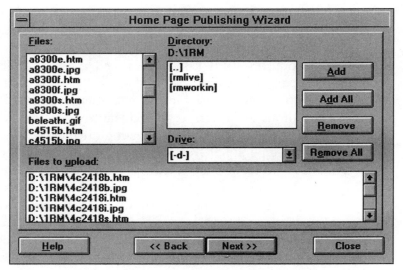

Figure 7-1: With CompuServe's Publishing Wizard, all you have to do is click, click, click to move your pages to their Web server.

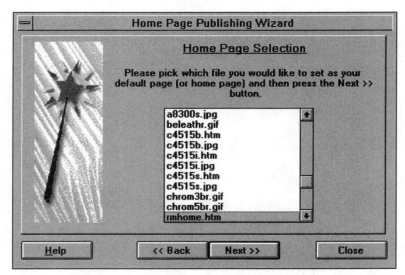

Figure 7-2: The Publishing Wizard lets you set up any page as the default home page.

CompuServe has made things easy for its subscribers by building a hard-coded system for transferring files. Most Web site hosting services, however, do not have the luxury of a custom-crafted file transfer program and rely instead upon the generally available shareware applications.

Transferring Files With Ipswitch's WS_FTP

http://www.ipswitch.com

Ipswitch's cryptically named WS_FTP is probably the most popular Windows FTP tool today. The software—which makes FTP chores a breeze—is widely available from a vast array of sites (try www.shareware.com). Both 16- and 32-bit versions are available for use with Windows 3.x, Windows 95, Windows NT, and OS/2. WS_FTP is freeware for educational (students, faculty, or staff), government (federal, state, or local), or for home (noncommercial) use. Otherwise, commercial users get a 15-day evaluation period before they choose to purchase the commercial version of the program.

Transferring files with WS_FTP is strictly point-and-shoot. While it's a tad more complicated than CompuServe's Publishing Wizard, that's to be expected of a true FTP utility that is intended to be used with the widest array of servers. The program can automatically detect the type of server you are logging on to and will configure itself appropriately. Version 4.04 is designed to hook up to the following host types, among others:

- BULL CP6 and GCOS
- CDC Cyber
- Chameleon
- FTP PC/TCP and PC/TCP 3.0
- HellSoft
- HP/3000
- IBM AS/400, MVS, MVS/KNET, PC TCP/IP, R1000, Spartacus KNET, and VM
- Ipswitch

- MAC NCSA, Peter Server, and VersaTerm
- Microsoft NT
- NCSA/CUTCP
- NetWare v4
- OS/9
- PDP11 RSX 11M
- Sun Solaris
- Tandem
- Unisys 5000 (EXOS)
- VMS MultiNet and UCX
- WFTPD

Moving files to your Web server is a straightforward procedure. With your computer online, click WS_FTP's Connect button. This brings up the Session Profile window. Pop in your Host name (the address of your Web server), along with your User ID and Password (if required). Press the OK button and WS_FTP will find your server and negotiate the connection. Once you're connected, select the files you want to transfer from (in the left-side window) and maneuver to the directory you want to transfer to (in the right-side window) as shown by Figure 7-3. The Auto-sensing option allows you to select and send all your files at once (although it may be prudent to manually send the HTML files as ASCII and the GIFs, JPEGs, and other non-ASCII files as binary). After the files are selected, just press the right arrow button (between the two windows) and WS_FTP will send your files to the Web server (as shown by Figure 7-4).

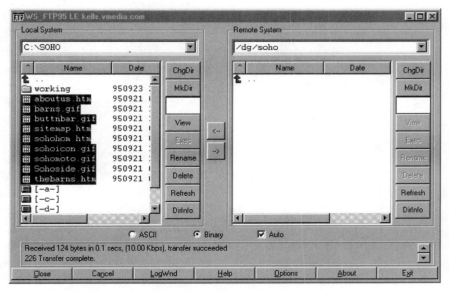

Figure 7-3: Pick and choose the files from your hard drive.

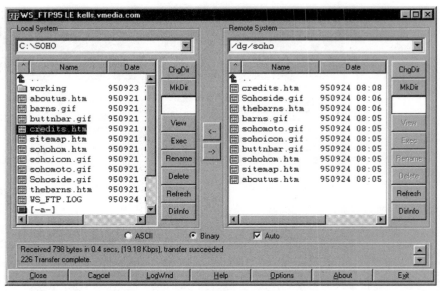

Figure 7-4: The files you selected and sent are now sitting on the Web server.

In addition to simply moving files, WS_FTP allows you to perform a number of important functions, such as renaming and deleting files, viewing and creating directories, and viewing files in ASCII format, while the Log Window keeps track of your FTP sessions. In all, WS_FTP is an essential utility for Windows-based Web publishers who need to maintain sites across the Internet.

Dartmouth's Trusty Fetch

http://www.dartmouth.edu/pages/softdev/fetch.html
Macintosh-based Web publishers rave about Dartmouth College's widely popular Fetch program for FTP work (see Figure 7-5). It's so good that it even won MacUser's 1996 Shareware award for best Internet software! Like WS_FTP, Fetch is free for educational uses (as well as for charitable organizations). The program supports drag-and-drop file and directory transfers and is scriptable via AppleScript or Frontier for automated FTPing.

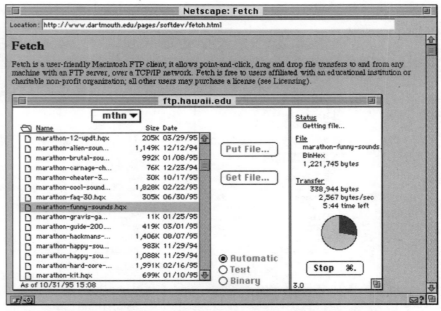

Figure 7-5: If you're building Web sites with PageMill on a Macintosh, go Fetch!

Creating CGIs Without Hacking Any Code

Although PageMill does a bang-up job of creating Web page forms, it doesn't provide anything to handle the data on the other (server) end. In the early days, we were all hostage to the (largely UNIX) scripting gurus who we relied upon to create custom Common Gateway Interface (CGI) scripts. Thankfully, applications have quickly come to market to automate the script creation process, allowing mere mortals to complete their own interactive form designs. CGI scripts are server-specific beasts. A script created for a UNIX server will not necessarily run on a Windows NT server, a Macintosh script won't run on a UNIX server, and so on. We'll take a look at a number of packages, such as Maxum's NetForms, that can have your site performing as if it were tended by the high priests of UNIX themselves.

Revving Up Mac Servers With Maxum

http://www.maxum.com
Maxum Development is the premiere developer of Macintosh-based Web server add-ons. Their popular NetCloak and NetForms products are among the most widely deployed server products in the industry, and have helped the Macintosh to establish a respectable foothold as a viable Web server platform. The company's focus is on extending the Web site functionality "by making them dynamic, interactive, secure, accessible, and fast." NetCloak and NetForms cover the first two bases, by providing a means to create dynamic documents on the fly and by delivering an easy-to-implement solution for interactive forms, respectively. The Maxum Web site, shown in Figure 7-6, contains downloadable demo versions of their applications along with online manuals, FAQs, and a host of other goodies.

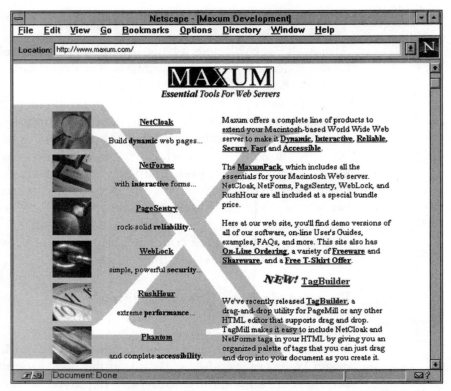

Figure 7-6: Maxum's Web site allows you to try each of their server add-ons before considering a purchase.

NetCloak

Remember the dreaded Romulan Cloaking Device from the original *Star Trek* TV series? It allowed the Romulans (or whoever had captured the device) to invisibly sneak about space with nary a hint of their presence. NetCloak runs in a similar manner— "below the radar"—allowing Macintosh Web servers to deliver customized content based upon a set array of parameters. When a visitor hits a NetCloaked server, they get custom pages, built on the fly just for them. How does this happen? Each time a client (browser) sends a request to a server, the request carries a certain amount of information with it. This information (which normally just gets dumped into the server log file) includes:

- Client domain: IP address from which the browser is accessing the site.
- Referring document: the exact page from which the browser was referred.
- Client type: browser version and platform.

NetCloak works by implementing its own little set of HTML commands. These commands access the NetCloak CGI running on the Web server. By using this client data, the server can run a script to deliver a customized page based upon locale of the user, the source of the incoming link, or the type of browser. This allows you to pull some pretty cool tricks. If you're running an international site and want to serve up pages in multiple languages, you can set up NetCloak to deliver pages based upon the domain. A domain ending with .es (Spain) would get a Spanish page, and so on. If you want to issue a special greeting to folks who have jumped from a specific site, you can make use of the referral information (this is a great one to handle clicks in from ad banners at multiple locations). If you want to serve up different versions of your site for different browsers, you use the client information to deliver terse text pages for Linux browsers and full-blown, Java-stuffed, framed nightmares to Netscape 3.x users.

What's Perl?

Perl is a powerful UNIX (although there are versions for other operating systems) script programming language that's often used to create Common Gateway Interface (CGI) scripts for Web servers.

There's definitely an air of Big Brother to the program. If you only want folks coming from a specific domain to see the contents of a page, you can cloak it from the rest of the world. Everyone else will see a page at the same URL, but they will see a page with different content. You can also provide the same function based on a username and password. NetCloak uses three basic commands—show, hide, and insert—to work its magic. By combining these commands with variable information, you're able to deliver a high level of customization without hacking a perl script. In addition to domain, referrer, client, username, and password data, the variable information includes:

- Time of day
- Day of week
- Date
- Access count
- Countdown
- Random number
- Redirect
- User-entered variables

The time, day, and date variables allow you to serve up different pages at different times, as well as on different days and dates. Your site might have a special page that only runs during business hours, or perhaps when your business is closed. This functionality allows you to set up special holiday or weekend greeting pages without worrying about being around at midnight to "turn on the page." You might even want to add a bit of eye-opening fun to your pages by delivering a one-liner (or two) based upon these variables, such as in Figure 7-7.

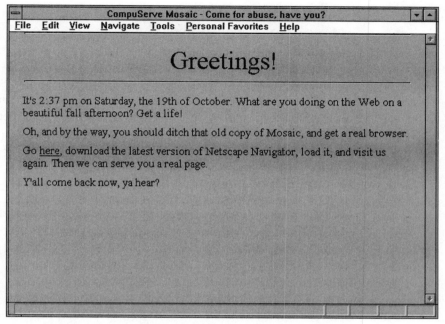

Figure 7-7: Now that should get their attention!

NetForms

Face it. The World Wide Web is a huge information appliance, constantly spewing out product data and sucking up prospect information. The faster your organization can inhale those leads, the faster they can go about the business of selling. NetForms will put a big, powerful engine behind the sleek and elegant forms you'll design in PageMill. The real beauty of a form only comes to light when it's fully functional. NetForms lets you design how a form *works,* not just how it *looks.* The program is based around four functions:

- **Createdoc**. Creates new HTML files on the fly by allowing users to simply fill out a form.
- **Insertfile**. Pops submitted data into an existing HTML file. Great for building guest books.
- **Textstore**. Stores submitted data in an ASCII text file for inclusion in a database.
- **Sendmail**. Provides e-mail autoreply.

Each of these four functions fulfills crucial Web site needs. The createdoc function lets nontechnical users create their own Web pages without requiring any knowledge of HTML, whatsoever. All users have to do is fill out a form and press the Submit button. This function is ideal for creating applications such as online classified ads or even for fun projects, like online recipe books (as shown in Figures 7-8 and 7-9). Textstore is the marketeer's dream, putting 500 horsepower under the lead-generating hood. Once a visitor submits the information, it's quickly whooshed off to an ASCII file without requiring any manual data entry.

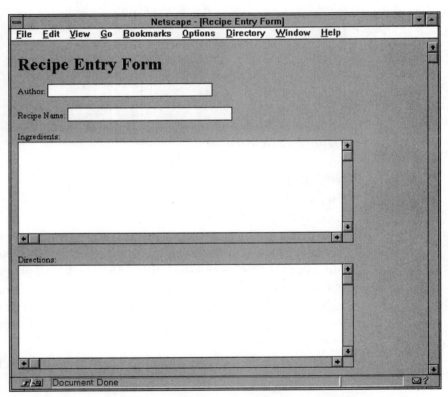

Figure 7-8: With createdoc, visitors need only know how to fill in the blanks.

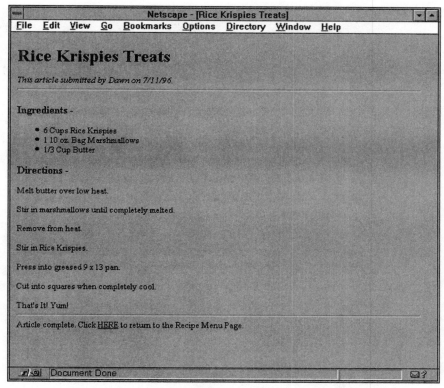

Figure 7-9: Dawn submitted her favorite recipe without a lick of HTML.

And have you ever looked twice down the snail mail chute, just to make sure your letters haven't gotten snagged on the way down to the mailbox? Although HTML's built-in mailto command provides a fast way to encourage visitors to drop you a line, it's lacking in one respect. When someone sends e-mail via a mailto link, they don't get any type of warm and fuzzy response telling them that the mail's been sent. Using NetForms' Sendmail function with a Response directive allows you to set up an autoreply function to immediately thank visitors for their valuable input.

TagBuilder

Adobe is bundling Maxum's new little utility, TagBuilder, with PageMill 2, free of charge. The program allows you to conveniently drag and drop all the features available in both NetCloak and NetForms into PageMill (as shown by Figure 7-10). TagBuilder saves time by automating the HTML code-generation process, allowing you to focus on the specific parameters of each code rather than worrying about keying in the beginning and ending tags. Including TagBuilder in the PageMill 2 box is a shrewd move on the part of Maxum, as it's bound to greatly increase the demand for their server products.

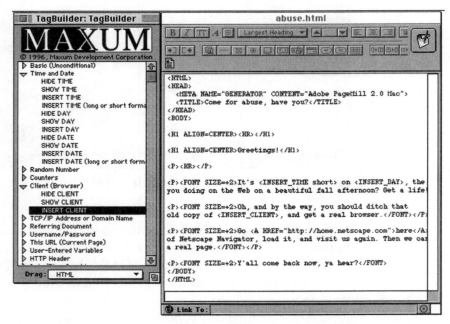

Figure 7-10: It's easy to drag and drop tags from TagBuilder into PageMill 2.

O'Reilly & Associates' PolyForm

http://polyform.ora.com/index.html

O'Reilly's Windows-based PolyForm is a "Web Form Construction Kit," designed for use with Windows 95 and NT servers that are Windows CGI 1.1 compliant, such as: O'Reilly's WebSite, Microsoft ISS, Netscape's Communications and Commerce servers, and Quarterdeck's WebSTAR. The package consists of both server software (the CGI) and the PolyForm application (which allows you to create the forms themselves).

PolyForm's ScriptWizard allows novices to quickly build custom forms by starting with prebuilt forms for information requests, feedback, order forms, and time sheets. The output from the forms can be saved on the server as text or data files, or they can be sent as e-mail. A thank-you confirmation can be sent to the visitor, through either a simple prebuilt page or by vectoring them to a specific URL. You can choose to have a copy of the information sent as e-mail. The Wizard-built forms may be used as is or they may be highly customized, depending on the application at hand.

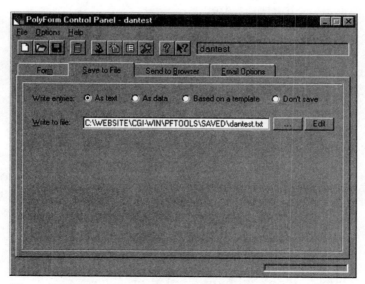

Figure 7-11: Forms can be tweaked in PolyForm's Control Panel.

Once a form is built, you can open it up in the PolyForm Control Panel to double-check the settings. The Control Panel centers around four function tabs: Form, Save to File, Send to Browser, and Email Options (as shown by Figure 7-11). You can customize their forms by entering their specific information in the fields before generating the forms (after which, you can hack the HTML to your heart's content). While PolyForm is a quick departure from the PageMill environment, it offers powerful capabilities that go far beyond what you can do with PageMill alone.

Tracking Your Visitors

As you've read elsewhere in this book, keeping track of your visitors is an important part of running a dynamic Web site. A number of commercial applications will help make that task easier, if you happen to be running your own Web server. If your site is sitting on a server at a commercial Web site hosting service, however, you may be at the mercy of their webmasters when it comes to the availability of site-tracking information and tools to analyze the traffic trends.

Looking for a Web Page Counter?
Net Digits' Web-Counter
http://www.digits.com/

As a Web server goes through its merry day, it is constantly updating its *log file*. These ASCII files contain a time-sorted list of site activity (file requests). Site-tracking tools work by sifting this information into a manageable state. In general, the information contained in each line of the server log includes time, client name, referring page, and requested page. We'll take a look at two site-tracking tools with different approaches.

O'Reilly & Associates' Statisphere

http://statisphere.ora.com/index.html

O'Reilly's Statisphere is a Windows Web site tweaker's dream come true. The 32-bit program, which runs on Windows 95 or NT, allows users to analyze the ASCII log file data from Windows, Macintosh, and UNIX Web servers. It provides real-time reporting and graphical charting. Statisphere is a stand-alone application with built-in graphing and HTML reports. Once the program has analyzed a log file, it automatically builds a Web page report that displays page activity, traffic by domain, and access by time/date. Figure 7-12 shows a sample Statisphere chart that displays a four-week daily traffic comparison. Charts such as these are valuable for watching the trends related to a Site's weekly traffic cycle (which can commonly drop off on the weekend).

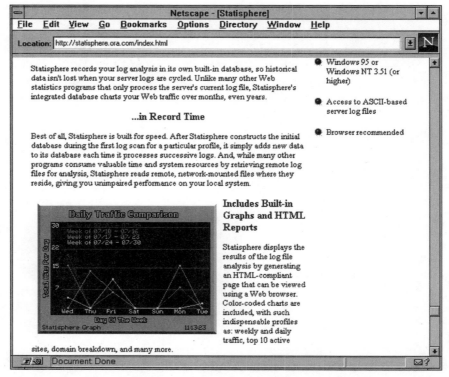

Figure 7-12: Statisphere delivers fast, graphical Web site traffic reports.

Statisphere can provide current and long-term reports for up to 16 different log files at one time, making it a wise choice for Web administrators who are responsible for multiple sites, as well as for folks who don't have the time (or expertise) to hack it out with database tools. It supports Apache, Microsoft IIS, NCSA/CERN, Netscape, and O'Reilly's own WebSite and WebSite Professional servers, as well as any other server that creates ASCII log files.

Everyware's Bolero

http://www.everyware.com/products/bolero/bolero.html
Bolero takes a slightly different approach to Web site traffic analysis, one that will appeal to the hard-core number-crunching crowd. Instead of providing an all-in-one approach, as with O'Reilly's Statisphere, the Macintosh-based Bolero takes log file data and stores it in an SQL database. If your shop is already using an ODBC-compliant database, such as Oracle, Informix, Sybase, Microsoft SQL, or Everyware's own Butler SQL, you'll probably want to take a close look at Bolero. Experienced database tweakers will be able to put that data to great use. While Bolero comes with a number of predefined Tango reports (more on Tango in a moment) to provide the most frequently requested statistics, you can use any SQL reporting and analysis tool to create your own custom reports. Figure 7-13 displays charts generated from Voyant.

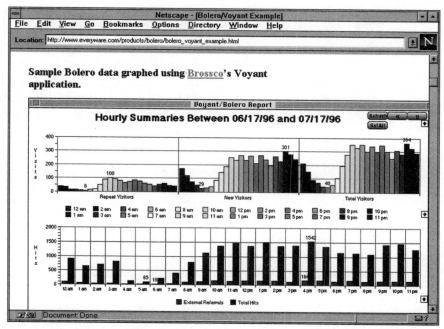

Figure 7-13: Bolero requires additional SQL tools to deliver graphical reports.

While the first version of Bolero was intended to support Quarterdeck's WebSTAR server, future versions should support Netscape NT and UNIX servers, as well as Microsoft's NT Internet Information Server.

Database Web Publishing

When you first start out to build a little Web site, it may be hard to imagine why you might ever need to integrate a database into your future plans. As your site grows, however, things can quickly get to the point where database Web publishing will be the only way to go. If you have a lot of information to present, and that information already resides in a database of one form or another, you should look into how you can use the existing database to fuel your site. There are a range of database Web publishing tools available today. The following programs represent only the first wave.

Everyware's Tango

http://www.everyware.com/products/tango/tango.html
Mississauga, Ontario-based Everyware stands at the forefront of Macintosh Web database development. Their popular Tango application development tool allows users to integrate ODBC-compliant databases into dynamic Web sites. (There's also a $349 upgradeable version designed specifically for use with Claris FileMaker Pro 3.0.) Tango consists of two parts, the Tango Editor and the Tango Application Server. The Tango Editor's visual development environment uses a drag-and-drop interface that enables the rapid creation of intricate applications by not requiring the developer to write HTML, SQL, or CGI code. The Tango Application Server is available as both a CGI application and as a WebSTAR Server plug-in. While the Tango Editor is Mac-based, the Tango Application Server runs on UNIX, Windows NT, and Macintosh servers.

What Are SQL & ODBC?
SQL stands for *Structured Query Language* (or "sequel"). It's a database query language that's prevalent in most client–server situations. ODBC is the acronym for *Open Database Connectivity,* which describes various high-end (i.e., big, powerful, and expensive) cross-platform databases, such as Oracle, Sybase, and Informix.

Everyware's Web site features some fun demonstrations of Tango technology. Figure 7-14 displays a sample form for an automotive wholesaler. We wanted to browse the sports cars available for over $40,000. (It's nice to dream, isn't it?) Pressing the Search button yielded the search results page, as shown by Figure 7-15. Tango retrieved the seven cars available in the price range, and automatically formatted them as a table, sorted alphabetically by manufacturer.

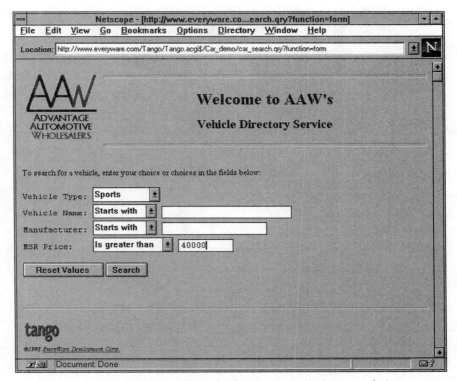

Figure 7-14: Visitors to the AAW Web (demonstration) site enter their automotive criteria.

Check the PageMill 2 CD-ROM!

Adobe has included demos of Everyware's Tango, Bolero, and Butler SQL on the CD-ROM, in addition to more goodies from Digital Comet, Pacific Coast, and WEB FM.

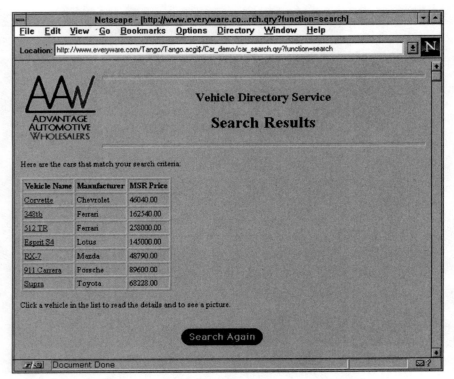

Figure 7-15: The Tango CGI returns all the sports cars available for over $40,000.

One of the most exciting aspects of Web database publishing is the ability to generate pages that allow the visitor to quickly "drill down" to get the full details on the information they are seeking. While the Mazda RX-7 and Lotus Esprit S4 both hold a special place in our heart, what we really wanted to see was the details on the Ferrari Testarossa. Clicking on the 512 TR link brought up a nifty little specifications page on the Italian racing red rocketship (as shown by Figure 7-16). After we took a look at those great horsepower and city gas mileage numbers, we were ready to pull out the checkbook!

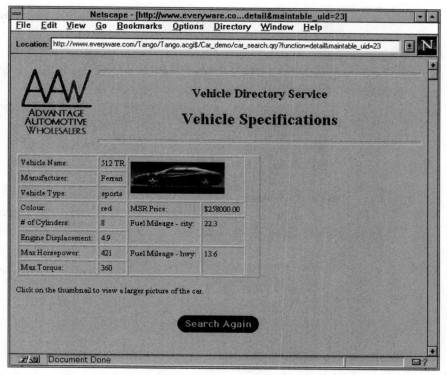

Figure 7-16: Visitors can drill down to get at the Testarossa's specifications and can even go one link further for the big picture.

Blue World's Lasso

http://www.blueworld.com/lasso/
Blue World Communications' Lasso is a Macintosh-based CGI application that allows Web site developers to build upon FileMaker Pro 3.0 databases. Lasso can be used with Macintosh WebSTAR servers as well as other Web servers that support the WebSTAR CGI specification. The program ships with prebuilt templates for some of the most common applications, including response forms, guest books, and online catalogs.

The employee search demo on Blue World's Web site provides a good demonstration of Lasso's capabilities. A human resources employee database is a common application for many companies and is an application that is likely to migrate to the intranet. We wanted to look for all the nice, helpful, energetic team players hired between 1/1/90 and 10/1/96 (as shown in Figure 7-17). It seems that great employees are hard to find, however. Figure 7-18 shows that only one employee, Pamela Day of the Marketing department, met our stringent criteria.

Netscape - [Lasso - Search Sample Employees Database]
File   Edit   View   Go   Bookmarks   Options   Directory   Window   Help
Location: http://www.blueworld.com/Lasso.acgi?[database]=Employees&[layout]=Detail&[format]=Example/Search.html&[show

Lasso: Search the Sample Employees Database

This is an example of how to use Lasso to search a FileMaker Pro database. The name of this file is **Search.html**; you'll find useful comments in it. All fields can be left blank (or given the value "All") to select all records in the database.

First Name   equals
Last Name   contains
Employee Number   equals
Email   equals
Comments   equals
Date Last Modified   >
Group   All   Shift ⦿ All ○ 1 ○ 2 ○ 3
Favorite Colored Dot   ⦿ All ○ ●Green ○ ●Purple ○ ●Red
Nice Traits   ☒ Nice ☒ Energetic ☒ Helpful ☒ Team Player
Hire Date   from   1/1/90   to   10/1/96
Logical Operator   ⦿ AND ○ OR
Sort By   Last Name   ascending

Document: Done

Figure 7-17: We're out to Lasso only the best employees!

Figure 7-18: The search results page provides the scoop on Pamela Day.

Corel's WEB.DATA

http:/www.corel.com/
If you're a Windows-based Web developer on a tight budget,
you'll want to check into Corel's new WEB.DATA program. Corel
has a long history of delivering powerful graphics and publishing
programs at groundbreaking low prices. With a street price of
$100, CorelWEB.DATA continues that tradition. The program can
be used as a CGI server application to provide live links between
your databases and Web pages. What's even more inspiring is the
company's commitment to the Java programming language

through their Barista technology. WEB.DATA holds the promise of publishing database information as graphical Java charts. Like all the other database Web publishing applications, however, WEB.DATA is strong on HTML table support. Figures 7-19 and 7-20 show two pages generated on the fly by WEB.DATA.

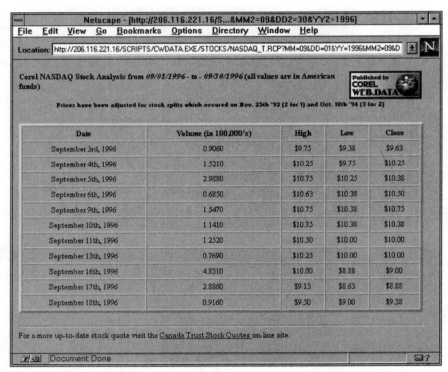

Figure 7-19: Stock charting is an ideal subject for database Web publishing.

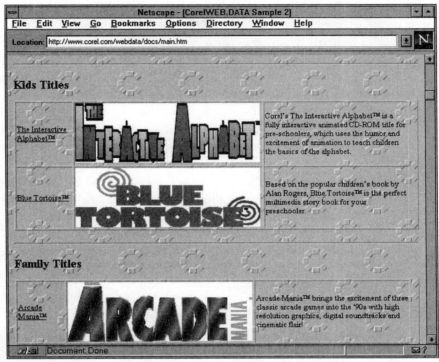

Figure 7-20: In this example, CorelWEB.DATA integrates images into tables.

WEB.DATA runs on Windows 95 or NT. It interfaces with desktop databases such as Microsoft Access, Microsoft Excel, Microsoft Foxpro, Borland dBASE, Borland Paradox, Lotus 123, Oracle, and any ODBC-compliant SQL database, as well as fixed-width and delimited ASCII text files.

Macromedia's Backstage Studios

http://www.macromedia.com/software/backstage/index.html
Last but certainly not least, Macromedia's Backstage Studios is
worth a look. This WYSIWYG Web page creation tool is also
marketed as Corel.WEB.DESIGNER. Macromedia packages
Backstage in four different ways, as shown by Figure 7-21. If
you're considering a complete Web database publishing solution,
the Macromedia Backstage Studios are the two packages that will
most interest you. The Desktop Studio is designed to hook to
desktop databases, while the Enterprise Studio is designed to
work with the big client/server databases, such as Oracle, Sybase,
and Informix.

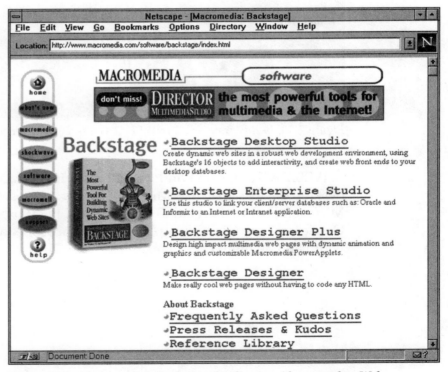

*Figure 7-21: Macromedia's Backstage Studios provide a complete Web
authoring/database solution.*

The package uses "Backstage Objects" to provide a fast, programming-free solution for the creation of dynamic applications. Web designers can use Backstage Objects to painlessly provide the functionality that is commonly associated with CGI scripting, without writing any code. While Macromedia initially shipped only a Windows version of Backstage, a Mac version is under development.

A Special Helping Hand

No matter who you are or what you do, there will come a time when you'll have to reach out for a little extra help with your PageMill questions. On occasion, everyone runs into a snag of one type or another. While CompuServe subscribers can check the PageMill section in the ADOBEFORUM—which is always staffed with competent Adobe support people, as well as truly helpful volunteers—there's a far more universal source for the rest of us.

The PageMill-Talk E-mail List

http://www.blueworld.com/lists/pagemill-talk/
How would you like to have a world full of folks ready to help you out with pressing PageMill questions? The online PageMill community is a friendly lot, quick to offer a suggestion or provide a potential fix. To subscribe to the PageMill-Talk e-mail list, hop on over to the Blue World Communications Web site (as shown in Figure 7-22). You have the option of subscribing either to the list itself (whereby you will receive list messages all day long as they are sent) or to the list digest (which compiles a day's worth of messages in one file and is sent out on a nightly basis). The method that works best for you will depend on your needs and the manner in which you access your e-mail. If you want instantaneous response (and a busy e-mailbox), the list may work for you. If you hate to sift through a zillion messages a day, however, the digest is ideal.

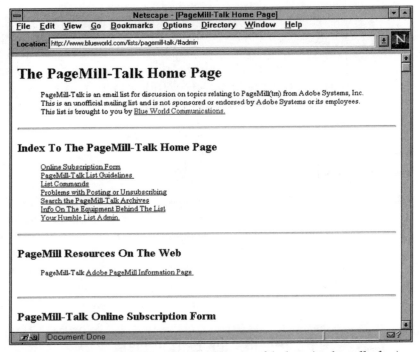

Figure 7-22: The PageMill-Talk e-mail list is a fabulous (and totally free) resource.

A Word to the Wise Regarding E-mail Lists...
No matter how you subscribe to an e-mail list, make sure you save the message that explains how to unsubscribe!

Moving On

This chapter focused on ways to make your Web site development life easier. By using the right programs to move files, create scripts, and track your visitors, you can become far more effective. These tools allow you to spend more time in the creative process, rather than being tied down by administrative duties. But it doesn't end there. The next chapter provides an overview of Web site management with Adobe SiteMill. You'll learn how SiteMill can help you to quickly clean up your act and banish those bad links.

chapter 8

Managing Your Web Site

Web sites are dynamic creatures. They live, breathe, and grow. As your site matures from a seedling into a sapling, you need to plan for its expansion. As its branches grow, you have to decide which to encourage and which to prune. A well-organized site will make your life easier and just takes a little thoughtful planning. You don't even have to be insanely compulsive to do a good job! With the right tools, organizing your Web site can be as easy as trimming the hedges.

Adobe SiteMill is one of the most highly regarded site management tools available today. The program offers an elegant, off-the-shelf solution to many common problems encountered by Web site builders. As this book was being written, SiteMill 1.0 was available only for the Macintosh platform. Rumor had it, however, that an updated version for both Mac and Windows platforms would be available shortly.

Site Management Issues

While Web site management is not a trivial matter, it does not have to become an all-consuming task. A sensible layout will enable you to create a site that allows for easy expansion. As you plan your site, you'll have to make some important decisions. The key is to conceptualize and implement an effective file hierarchy.

Some of the primary issues in site management are:

- How is the site organized?
- Where are the images stored?
- How are the links maintained?
- How are orphan files found and eliminated?

This chapter will help you to understand the issues that face a growing Web site. You will see how a typical site evolves while discovering how tedious it is to implement change in a manual scenario. After learning how bad it can be, you'll truly appreciate what Adobe SiteMill can do for you.

How Is the Site Organized?

In Chapter 5, you learned how to plan the navigational structure of your Web site. In addition to considering how your Web site is organized from a navigational perspective, you must think about how to organize its file structure. The former will often dictate the latter.

When a site is small, all the pages can happily coexist in one directory. As it grows however, things can quickly get out of hand. Your site may evolve to contain many *subsites*, or "sites within a site." When the level of complexity reaches a certain point, it will make good sense to reorganize your file structure so that each of the subsites has its own directory within the main site directory. Once the number of HTML and graphic files in one directory exceeds what you're comfortable wading through, this will rapidly become apparent.

If you carefully plan your site from the start, you can avoid much of the gut wrenching that accompanies rearranging your site on the fly. It can take eons to manually change all the internal URLs on a good-sized site. An automated method can save your sanity and untold time.

Where Do the Images Go?

In the simplest Web sites, you can toss all of your image files in the same directory with your HTML pages. This methodology only goes so far, however. Once your site has grown past two dozen files or so, things can quickly get out of hand. You don't want to have to wade through long lists of intermingled files. That's why it's a good idea to keep a separate directory (or directories) solely for images.

You may be able to get away with having one big image directory, or you may decide to break it up into smaller directories. These might be based on subject matter or perhaps by subsite. It's up to you to decide the criteria. You also have complete control over what you name the directories. PageMill, by default, names the directory Images, but that doesn't mean that you have to follow its lead. You are free to name the directory Graphics, Photos, Pix, or whatever suits your fancy.

One large (and not-so-large) site scenario might have you create a directory for common site graphics, along with separate directories contained in each of the subsite directories. This keeps the images with their subject matter and helps to trim down the size of the individual image directories. It also makes it easier to move complete directories around should the need come to pass.

Maintaining Links

You can think of links as the chains that hold your unruly Web site together. Break a link and all hell will bust loose. As shown in Figure 8-1, a site will "go 404," and return a "file not found" message when someone chooses a nonexistent file. While this isn't a life-threatening event, it's an unpleasant experience for the visitor, at best. Good webmasters strive to eliminate 404s from their site.

Don't Go 404!
When a visitor has requested a nonexistent file, 404 errors are returned by the Web server. These errors are often due to lackadaisical site maintenance. Some servers will include the actual error message number, while others will not.

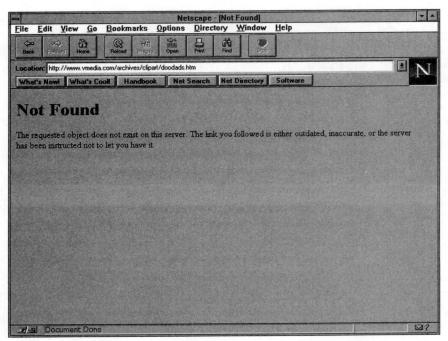

Figure 8-1: Where did the page go? If the Web server can't find a file, it will return a message like this.

A Web server will send back a 404 any time it can't find a specified file at a specific location. When a file actually is on the server, but is not where it's supposed to be, 404s will happen. The server will only look in the location where the URL asks it to look. And 404s frequently happen when you've moved a file, but haven't updated all of its incoming links. Anytime you move a file (or group of files) from one directory to another, you will have to update every occurrence of its URL within your site. Doing this task manually brings a whole new definition to the word tedious. Thankfully, there are automated methods to turn link maintenance into a simple task.

Be Careful When Deleting Pages

If you delete a Web page that's been cataloged by the search engines, visitors will continue to come to your site looking for a page that's long gone. If you must delete a popular page, create a forwarding page to explain where the page went, while suggesting a new link, as well.

Eliminating Orphan Files

Orphan files are Web site jetsam. These pages or graphics float unseen, just below the surface of your site and are not referenced by any other pages. Without any incoming links, there's no way for a browser to find an orphan file because it doesn't know its URL.

Orphan files are created as your site evolves. You might have used a background GIF in an earlier version of a page, only to replace it with a different GIF later on. Or perhaps you eliminated all links to a page, although you left the page untouched. Orphan files can be any type of unreferenced file, including:

- HTML pages
- GIF or JPEG graphics
- Sounds
- Movies
- Animations
- Image maps

In most cases, you'll want to eliminate orphan files. While they don't threaten the stability or navigational flow of your site, they take up unnecessary server space. Isolating orphan files without an automated site management application is a frustrating experience, however. It's no fun sitting down with a lengthy list of files on your site, trying to discern which files are live and which are not.

A Case for Select Orphans

There is one good use for orphan files, however. You might want to have a "semi-secret" page, accessible only by typing in its specific address. You might distribute this URL to a select group of people only and for a particular reason, such as to distribute confidential information. This is not a secure method, however, as a dedicated individual may be able to find the hidden files as easily as typing in obvious URL combinations. If you want your information to stay hidden, you should use password protection. Even though passwords *can* be hacked, for the most part, they're secure.

Adobe SiteMill to the Rescue!

Managing a good-sized Web site without SiteMill is like trying to till the south forty with an ox-drawn plow. Sure, you can get it done, but you (and your ox) will have to spend a lot of time and an inordinate amount of energy. As the farmer quickly supplanted the ox with the tractor, so too will you choose the ease and elegance of SiteMill.

SiteMill combines elegant Web site management features with the Web page building prowess of PageMill. If you've built your site with PageMill (or any other HTML tool), you can open it up with SiteMill and quickly whip your site into shape. Since all of PageMill's tools are contained within SiteMill, you can build your site from scratch as well. This allows you to receive the benefit of creating a well-organized and solidly linked site right from the start.

What SiteMill does is sheer genius, although it's not quite rocket science. The program simply looks at all the files (HTML ASCII files, graphics, sound clips, movies, and so on) within your site. It then catalogs and presents them in a graphic form, showing file structure and indicating links, both incoming and outgoing. Broken links have their own special view window, which allows you to quickly identify and fix problem files.

SiteMill works its magic on disks that are connected to your computer, either locally or across a network. You cannot directly work on directories that are reachable only via FTP. You can get around this limitation by keeping a duplicate (testing) Web site on your local drive or on a network server. Once you make the necessary changes to the testing site, you'll move all the files over en masse using FTP.

Using SiteMill for Web Site Management

In practice, SiteMill turns site management chores into a big drag-and-drop video game. The following section illustrates how we took a typical small site—a classic auto establishment—and rearranged it with SiteMill, in just a few minutes. This site started out as a cluttered, one-folder affair. Follow along as we whip it into shape by organizing the pages and graphics into specific folders. Figure 8-2 shows a typical page on the Classic Auto Web site. This is a "base" page for the 1934 Duesenberg, with links to engine, front, and back views of the car.

Figure 8-2: Now that's a Duesie!

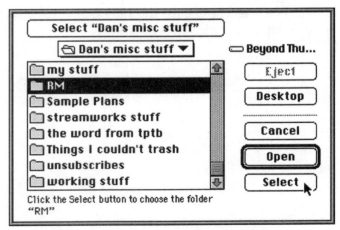

Figure 8-3: Selecting the RM root Web site folder.

Opening a Web Site in SiteMill

A site is opened by selecting the root folder of the Web site, as shown in Figure 8-3. The "root" folder is the one that ultimately holds everything for the site. Once you select the folder, SiteMill goes to work cataloging your entire site. The program looks only at files and folders (as well as nested files and folders) contained within the specified root folder. As you might surmise, the larger your site is and the more links you have, the longer the cataloging process will take. Once SiteMill has investigated all of your links, it will display the Site window (Figure 8-4) and Errors window.

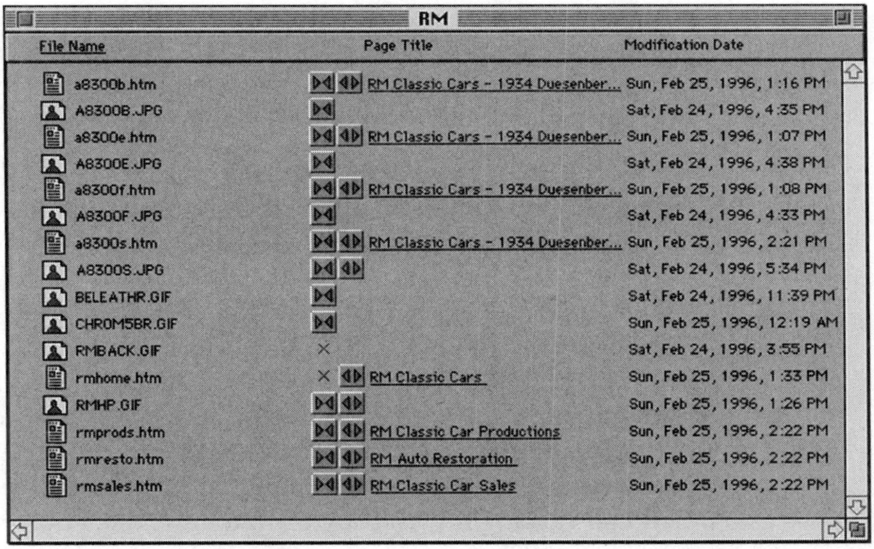

Figure 8-4: The original Site window shows filenames, page titles, link information, and dates.

The Site window uses a handful of icons to describe each file. SiteMill displays either a page or a graphic icon next to each file name. The arrows-in and arrows-out buttons tell you whether the page has incoming and outgoing links, respectively. Clicking on these buttons displays all of the linked pages for each. An X in either column indicates that the page has no links of that type.

The rmhome.htm page has links out, but no links in. This is an introductory home page and does not call for any links back. On the other hand, RMBACK.GIF is an orphan file, since it has no links in or out. This file was an extra background texture that was eliminated in the site design process. SiteMill does not allow users to delete files from within the application; instead, it requires that you jump out to the Finder to trash the file or to move it to a folder outside your site root folder.

After taking a look at how the site was shaping up, a decision was made to create three new folders within the root folder. This methodology was implemented to keep the root folder from getting cluttered as the site grows. It's important to note that these shots were taken with only the first car loaded in. The site will ultimately contain over a hundred cars. For each subsequent car, there were plans for as many as four pages and associated photographs. The three new folders were described as:

- carpages: to contain all the individual car pages.
- carpix: to contain all the individual car photographs.
- graphics: to contain all other site graphics.

Rearranging Files in SiteMill

Moving pages or graphics in SiteMill is a drag-and-drop procedure. After creating the carpix folder in the Finder, the file A8300F.JPG was dragged to the new folder (Figure 8-5). SiteMill responds to the action by asking if you really want to rewrite all the links to that file. Since A8300F.JPG is a front view photograph of the 1934 Duesenberg, it is only referenced by the a8300f.htm page.

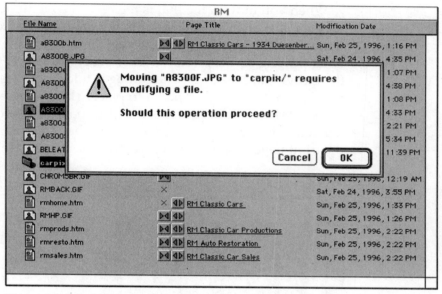

Figure 8-5: SiteMill has wonderful manners (asking you if it's OK to change the links)...

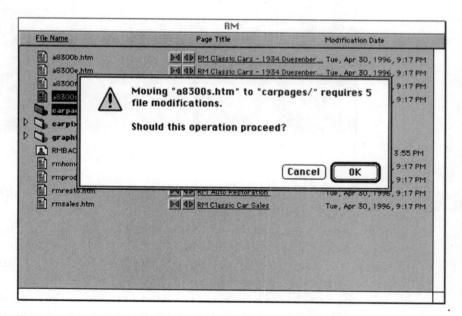

Figure 8-6: ...and it is extremely thorough (as it changes the URL in multiple locations)!

When you move a file that is referenced by a number of pages on your site, SiteMill will tell you how many URL occurrences there are and will update every single link, as shown in Figure 8-6. After putting all the photos in their proper place, we cleaned up the individual car pages. The carpages folder was created, and the a8300s.htm file was dropped into place. This file is the side view of the 1934 Duesenberg and is the main page for the car. As such, it is referenced by the front, engine, and back view, as well as from the front page of the Sales section (rmsales.htm) of the site.

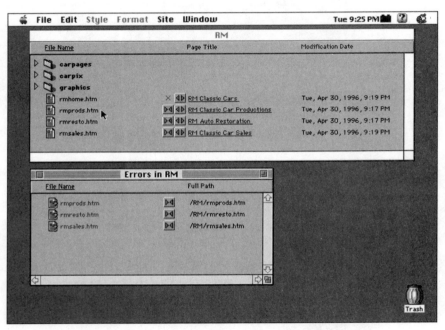

Figure 8-7: That's a nice-looking site, but there are a few things to fix.

After a fast round of drag and drop, the site was whipped into shape. Figure 8-7 displays the entire site, with all of the folders closed (compare that to the unorganized site, back in Figure 8-4). SiteMill's Errors window is open to check for any additional broken links. The trio of errors was quickly fixed by dragging and dropping the correct URLs from the rearranged Site window onto the pages in the Errors window. SiteMill instantly mended the links without fanfare. Figure 8-8 displays an exploded view of the cleaned-up site.

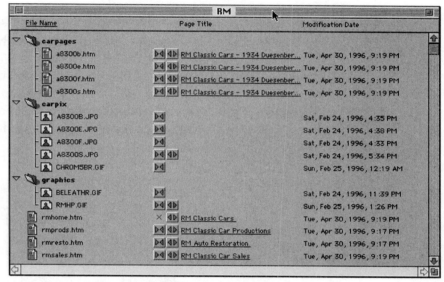

Figure 8-8: All your ducks (pages and graphics) in a row.

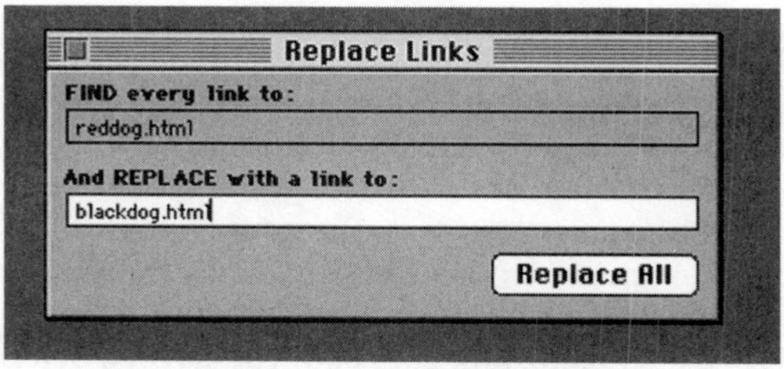

Figure 8-9: Instant link swapping with the Replace Links window.

SiteMill also allows you to update links through the Replace Links window. As shown in Figure 8-9, the Replace Links window lets you find and replace every instance of a specific link with lightning speed. Although the changes you make might not be as simple as changing all the reddog.html links to blackdog.html links, you'll find that this window comes in handy when you know the exact filename/URL of the links in question. After all, everything doesn't have to be drag and drop, now does it?

Monitoring External Links

External links can be monitored and updated through the External URLs window, as shown in Figure 8-10. This convenient window grows in usefulness as your list of external links expands. Most importantly, if you have an external URL linked in more than one location on your site, you can update it once, thus avoiding a painstaking search through every one of your pages for duplicate entries.

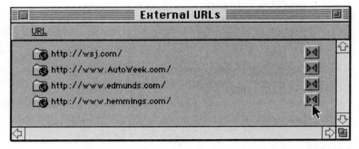

Figure 8-10: Watch those outgoing links with the External URLs window.

Monitoring external links can be a time-consuming task, best left to those days when you have "downtime" with nothing better to do. Unfortunately, SiteMill 1.0 doesn't have the ability to check to see that external links are in working order. There's little doubt that Adobe's engineers are looking for features to add to the next version. A scheme to check external links should be near the top of their list.

When an outside link goes bad, you have to determine whether it's a temporary or permanent situation. There can be any one of a number of reasons why a particular URL will "go off the scope." The server may have crashed, there might be line problems, or the site may be down for routine maintenance. It could even be too busy to accept connections. It's best to check the URL a few times over the course of the day before you consider pulling the outgoing link off your pages.

Other Site Management Tools

If you are partaking of heavy-duty Web site management tasks, SiteMill 1.0 does not do it all. The maiden version of the program is focused primarily on URL management. While that's what most site management entails, there will be cases where you'll need to make repetitive text changes to a large number of pages. Two common examples of this are when you reword a text navigation bar or update a copyright notice. In these situations, a batch-driven search-and-replace utility is in order.

The next chapter, "Text Editing Tools," includes information on a number of heavy-duty HTML/ASCII editors that allow you to make massive text changes to your Web site in one fell swoop.

Rearranging Your Site: A Caveat

Once your site is live, you run a major risk by rearranging your file structure. If your site has been around for a while, its layout has been stored, analyzed, and disseminated in a number of ways. This process will take place outside your realm of control. These "runaway librarians" include:

- Search engines
- Print media citations
- Incoming links from other sites
- Individual (personal) browser bookmarks

Before you implement any site structure changes, you should consider how it will affect the ways that visitors are referred to the various URLs within your site. If you move a page from the URL where any of these sources expect to find the page, visitors will receive a 404-File Not Found error when they try to access the URL. This is not a good thing! Let's take a look at how to deal with these important outside referrals.

How to Stay Out of Trouble

When you move an important page—especially the front page of a subsite—create a new page to leave in its old place. The new page should include some text to the tune of, "We've Moved..." along with a hotlink to the new location, as shown in Figure 8-11.

Figure 8-11: Don't forget to let them know where you moved!

What Happens With the Search Engines?

Left to their own devices, the search engines will find and catalog each and every public page on your Web site. If you have pages that are under password protection, the spiders won't catalog them, so you needn't worry about breaking those links. The only pages the spiders will catalog will be the pages that are open to all.

The search engines will actually help you in your efforts to rearrange your site. As the spiders revisit and recatalog your site, time will heal any wounds. They'll hit your pages, follow the new links, and do their job (hopefully) without a hiccup. Some search engines may appreciate notification when you make major changes. In any case, be sure to drop in linking pages in your key locations. Chapter 6 includes information on how to stay on top of the search engines.

How Should Print Media Citations Be Dealt With?

Everyone loves a mention in print. When a big magazine or book publishes your URL, you're likely to experience an increased hit rate. But when a publication prints a URL within your site, rather than your "front door," the results can be indelible. Once it's in print, it has been set in stone. If you move a page that's been cited in print, you'll infuriate your potential visitors if they can't get to the page.

It's impossible to control the media. Instead, you have to keep a diligent watch on the pages that are drawing attention to your site. If you move a page, be sure to leave a linking page in its place for a certain period of time. If a publication prints the wrong URL (within your site), put a linking page (sending visitors to the correct page) at that address as soon as possible. And consider it to be an opportunity to contact the publication so they can run a correction.

Incoming Links From Other Sites

If you've done your job well, pages within your Web site will make their way onto countless hot (and cool!) lists. While each and every one of these lists might not be huge and powerful, they're important to your Web site's success. You'll want to keep track of the referring URLs through some type of tracking program. The preceding chapter covered this topic with a discussion of Everyware's Bolero and O'Reilly's Statisphere, two popular desktop Web server tracking packages.

Once you've identified which Web sites have set up hotlinks to your pages, you can notify them if you make any changes to your site, such as the locations or names of your pages. This is more than common courtesy. It's karma. The webmasters should be grateful for your diligence in helping them avoid broken outgoing links. If you're linked back to them, they'll be more likely to return the favor when it's time for them to rearrange their Web sites.

Individual Browser Bookmarks

Your visitors are likely to bookmark individual pages within your site, rather than your front door. When you move or rename a page, and it just goes 404 on them, you're bound to tick them off. Unfortunately, you can't send e-mail to everyone that's bookmarked your pages, unless you've collected their e-mail addresses. Even so, sending out a note announcing a URL change might be considered bad Netiquette. Once again, the best solution is to drop in some linking pages in key locations.

Moving On

Web site management does not have to be a painstaking, manual affair. With Adobe SiteMill, you can keep your site neat and tidy without losing your mind. SiteMill keeps track of every link on your site without creating reams of paperwork or complicated schematics. If you manage a site consisting of more than just a few pages, you should seriously consider the upgrade. The peace of mind is well worth the cost of admission. Rearranging a Web site is not without its pitfalls. With due diligence, you can assure that your visitors find your site where they expect it to be.

In the next section we'll look at a wide range of Web page design resources, as we learn about the coolest tools, including powerful text editors, slick fonts, and awesome graphics programs.

part 4

Resources for Web Page Builders

This section of the book is intended to help you begin exploring the vast opportunities of Web page design. We'll look at how various tools can be used together with PageMill 2 to create awesome and effective designs. Starting with the admittedly less-than-exciting (though crucial) topic of text editing and file conversion, we'll quickly delve into the sum and substance of typefaces, design tools, and animation.

chapter 9

Cool Tools: Text Editing & File Conversion

No matter what the task at hand, your job will run far more smoothly if you have the proper tools at your disposal. In this chapter, we'll look at PageMill 2's new ASCII text editor, in addition to its other built-in text-handling features. These new properties were gladly received by the PageMill crowd, as PageMill 1.0 was sorely lacking with regard to text handling. Little things like a search and replace function, a spelling checker, and text import capabilities are features that we just take for granted. In the mad rush to get the first version out, however, Adobe had to omit these crucial features. With PageMill 2, Adobe has brought the program up to speed by adding these goodies, along with an integrated ASCII text editor.

This chapter will also focus on ways to increase your productivity by using a variety of text-conversion and editing utilities. While PageMill 2 is a vast improvement over the first version, there are a number of ways that you can ease the flow of existing documents into HTML pages. A few carefully chosen power tools can help to supercharge your productivity.

WordPerfect Packs a Wallop!

While PageMill 2 has its own find/replace and spell checking functions, it's always a good idea to use a competent word processing program to create content when you need access to other niceties such as a thesaurus or grammar checker. You can further streamline your work flow by using a word processor that performs reliable HTML exports. Corel's WordPerfect (WP) was one of the first word processors to perform acceptable HTML coding (back when it was still Novell WordPerfect, in late 1995), including table export. Figures 9-1 and 9-2 show a simple table as it appears in WordPerfect 3.5 for Macintosh and in Netscape Navigator.

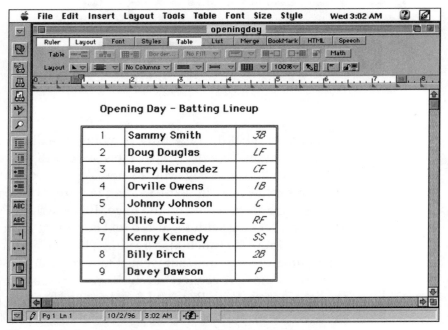

Figure 9-1: Creating tables in WordPerfect is a simple task.

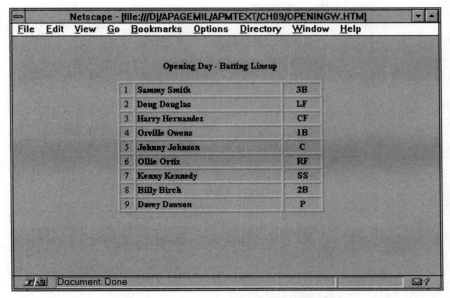

Figure 9-2: Tables export smoothly from WordPerfect into HTML, but what happened to the italics?

WordPerfect makes it easy to work with tables, and the program's HTML export is quite clean. There's no need to jump through any hoops to convert a WP file to HTML. All you need to do is choose the HTML format option when you save the file. Let's take a quick peek at how the program created this simple table. Here's the WordPerfect-generated HTML code for the Opening Day lineup:

```
<HTML>
<HEAD>
<TITLE></TITLE>
</HEAD>
<BODY>
<CENTER><B><BR>
Opening Day - Batting Lineup<BR>
</B><BR>
```

```
<TABLE BORDER WIDTH=293>
<TR VALIGN=top><TD ALIGN=center>1</TD><TD ALIGN=left><B>Sammy
Smith</B></TD><TD
ALIGN=center><B><I></B>3B</I></TD></TR>
<TR VALIGN=top><TD ALIGN=center><I></I>2</TD><TD
ALIGN=left><B>Doug
Douglas</B></TD><TD ALIGN=center><B><I></B>LF</I></TD></TR>
<TR VALIGN=top><TD ALIGN=center><I></I>3</TD><TD
ALIGN=left><B>Harry
Hernandez</B></TD><TD ALIGN=center><B><I></B>CF</I></TD></TR>
<TR VALIGN=top><TD ALIGN=center><I></I>4</TD><TD
ALIGN=left><B>Orville
Owens</B></TD><TD ALIGN=center><B><I></B>1B</I></TD></TR>
<TR VALIGN=top><TD ALIGN=center><I></I>5</TD><TD
ALIGN=left><B>Johnny
Johnson</B></TD><TD ALIGN=center><B><I></B>C</I></TD></TR>
<TR VALIGN=top><TD ALIGN=center><I></I>6</TD><TD
ALIGN=left><B>Ollie
Ortiz</B></TD><TD ALIGN=center><B><I></B>RF</I></TD></TR>
<TR VALIGN=top><TD ALIGN=center><I></I>7</TD><TD
ALIGN=left><B>Kenny
Kennedy</B></TD><TD ALIGN=center><B><I></B>SS</I></TD></TR>
<TR VALIGN=top><TD ALIGN=center><I></I>8</TD><TD
ALIGN=left><B>Billy
Birch</B></TD><TD ALIGN=center><B><I></B>2B</I></TD></TR>
<TR VALIGN=top><TD ALIGN=center><I></I>9</TD><TD
ALIGN=left><B>Davey
Dawson</B></TD><TD ALIGN=center><B><I></B>P</I></TD></TR>
</TABLE>
<I></I>

</BODY>
</HTML>
```

That looks pretty straightforward, doesn't it? We did encounter an anomaly or two upon opening up the file in PageMill, however. Figure 9-3 shows how the Opening Day lineup code looked after PageMill 2 ran through it. Notice that the program lost all the italic coding and added its defaults for the table border, cellspacing, and cellpadding. The loss of the italic coding was due to the manner in which the italics were assigned in WordPerfect. The syntax threw both Navigator and PageMill for a loop. When Navigator displayed the table, it ignored the italic commands and used boldface instead. When PageMill opened the file, it just chucked out the italic commands entirely! Even though this was a slight nuisance, changing the errant text back to italic didn't take much time.

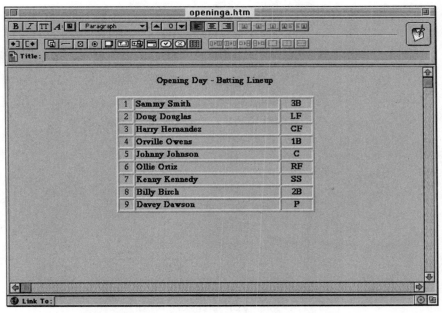

Figure 9-3: PageMill didn't like the way WordPerfect used the italic commands, so the program decided to nix them all.

Take a look at how the code appears after PageMill's interpretation:

```
<HTML>
<HEAD>
  <META NAME="GENERATOR" CONTENT="Adobe PageMill 2.0 Mac">
  <TITLE></TITLE>
</HEAD>
<BODY>

<P ALIGN=CENTER><B><BR>
Opening Day - Batting Lineup<BR>
</B><BR>
<TABLE BORDER="1" WIDTH="293" CELLSPACING="2"
CELLPADDING="0">
<TR VALIGN="TOP">
<TD ALIGN="CENTER">1</TD>
<TD><B>Sammy Smith</B></TD>
<TD ALIGN="CENTER"><B>3B</B></TD></TR>
<TR VALIGN="TOP">
<TD ALIGN="CENTER">2</TD>
<TD><B>Doug Douglas</B></TD>
<TD ALIGN="CENTER"><B>LF</B></TD></TR>
<TR VALIGN="TOP">
<TD ALIGN="CENTER">3</TD>
<TD><B>Harry Hernandez</B></TD>
<TD ALIGN="CENTER"><B>CF</B></TD></TR>
<TR VALIGN="TOP">
<TD ALIGN="CENTER">4</TD>
<TD><B>Orville Owens</B></TD>
<TD ALIGN="CENTER"><B>1B</B></TD></TR>
<TR VALIGN="TOP">
<TD ALIGN="CENTER">5</TD>
<TD><B>Johnny Johnson</B></TD>
<TD ALIGN="CENTER"><B>C</B></TD></TR>
<TR VALIGN="TOP">
<TD ALIGN="CENTER">6</TD>
<TD><B>Ollie Ortiz</B></TD>
<TD ALIGN="CENTER"><B>RF</B></TD></TR>
<TR VALIGN="TOP">
```

```
<TD ALIGN="CENTER">7</TD>
<TD><B>Kenny Kennedy</B></TD>
<TD ALIGN="CENTER"><B>SS</B></TD></TR>
<TR VALIGN="TOP">
<TD ALIGN="CENTER">8</TD>
<TD><B>Billy Birch</B></TD>
<TD ALIGN="CENTER"><B>2B</B></TD></TR>
<TR VALIGN="TOP">
<TD ALIGN="CENTER">9</TD>
<TD><B>Davey Dawson</B></TD>
<TD ALIGN="CENTER"><B>P</B></TD></TR>
</TABLE>
<BR>
<BR>
</P>

<P ALIGN=CENTER>
</BODY>
</HTML>
```

WordPerfect is a Web-savvy program, allowing you to breeze through most HTML coding chores without ever having to touch any HTML (of course, you'll still have to deal with URLs and the like). There are provisions for assigning headings and other styles, as well as for hyperlinking and placing images (complete with alternate text and scaling). The program provides control over document colors (background, text, hyperlink, active link, and visited link) and background textures.

The engineers at WordPerfect were keen on the Internet—back when the company was still held by Novell—while Microsoft was still fumbling around with the Microsoft Network. They took a leap ahead with the release of WordPerfect 3.5 for Macintosh, and now that the group is part of Corel, appear ready to take a quantum leap. The release of Corel's new Barista Java technology—in various application suites—should make quite a splash. Barista allows users of Corel products such as Ventura Publisher and CorelDRAW! to publish their Web pages as Java applets, opening up a whole new range of design possibilities.

Hold the Line With Placeholders!
To prevent PageMill from messing with HTML coding that you've created with another program, you can protect the coding by encasing it within a Placeholder. (Note: you should always do this before you bring the file into PageMill.) In an ASCII editor, type **<!—NOEDIT—>** before the coding you wish to protect, and type **<!—/NOEDIT—>** immediately after the text. Once the file has been opened in PageMill, a little Placeholder pylon (road hazard cone) will display in both Edit and Preview mode. A quick check in HTML Source mode will show that the code is, in fact, untouched. The Placeholder tags are really just HTML comment tags, and are ignored by all the browsers.

HTML Conversion From Native Files

Want to save a ton of time producing text-laden Web pages? Get in gear with a program or two that support automated HTML conversion. While HTML export features have crept into most of the mainstream applications—including word processors, spreadsheets, and page layout packages—you may often have to work with original source files from programs that do not support HTML export.

The release version of PageMill 2 should include file conversion utilities, although the public beta versions did not. Since we were not able to work with Adobe's file conversion utilities before the release of the program, we'll cover a pair of third-party applications. Watch for updated information on file conversion on this book's Online Updates on the Ventana Web site.

Terry Morse Software's Myrmidon

http://www.terrymorse.com/

Macintosh users have access to a wonderful HTML conversion resource in Terry Morse's Myrmidon. The program, which is available from the company's Web site (see Figure 9-4), takes a unique approach to the creation of HTML files. Myrmidon opens up huge possibilities by allowing you to create Web pages from any Macintosh program that can print text or graphics. Myrmidon is simply installed as a printer. Consequently, when you're ready to print, the (formerly Web-clueless) application thinks that it's sending a file to a printer. Myrmidon then gobbles up the stream of printer code that's sent down, chews on it for a while, and spits it back out as a Web page, complete with tables and inline images.

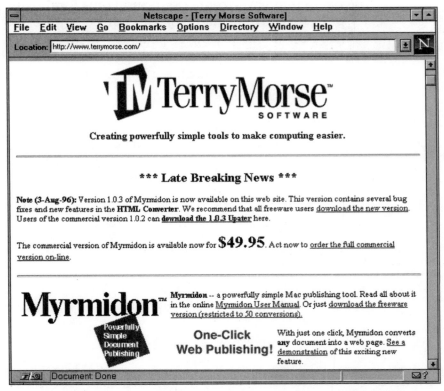

Figure 9-4: Myrmidon creates HTML documents with push-button ease.

This is a very cool thing, indeed. With Myrmidon, you can quickly format tables coming from most any application. The program promises to greatly speed up the process of converting legacy documents into Web pages, especially when working with files from older and custom Mac applications that lack HTML export capabilities. Myrmidon offers a world of utility for a modest fee (and just think what you can bill your clients!).

InfoAccess HTML Transit

http://www.infoaccess.com/
Windows-based Web publishers, fear not! There's a great HTML conversion utility for you, too. InfoAccess HTML Transit is a high-powered HTML production tool that allows you to batch process WordPerfect, Microsoft Word, and Lotus AmiPro format files. The program converts placed images into GIF or JPEG format files and features automatic table of contents and index generation. Large files can even be automatically segmented into individually linked Web pages. A trial version is available on the company's Web site (as shown in Figure 9-5).

InfoAccess has received much acclaim for HTML Transit from the PC press. The company has struck a string of deals with a variety of software developers to bundle their technology. One example is Corel's new WEB.GRAPHIC Suite, which includes a subset of HTML Transit, under the name CorelWEB.Transit.

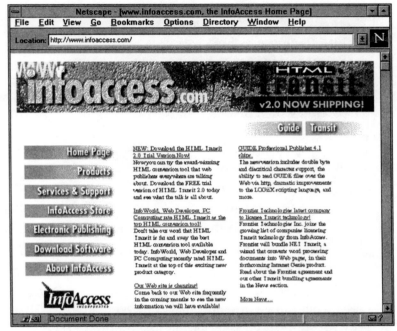

Figure 9-5: InfoAccess HTML Transit offers powerful file conversion utilities.

Converting QuarkXPress Pages

QuarkXPress is the most popular page layout package in the professional graphic arts community. As such, a staggeringly large number of printed pages are created with the program. When the Web revolution began, Quark-based desktop publishers soon realized that they needed a convenient way to convert their existing print-oriented pages into Web pages. While Quark itself floundered around getting its Immedia multimedia/Web publishing program out the door, QuarkXTension developers quickly moved in to fill the void. As of this writing, there are three Quark-to-HTML products of note. While the first two have been created for designers that do much of their Web page authoring in Quark itself, the third is intended to be used closely with Adobe PageMill 2.

Astrobyte BeyondPress

http://www.astrobyte.com

Promising to "reinvent your content," Denver-based Astrobyte was the first company to release a Web publishing QuarkX Tension, back in 1995. BeyondPress 2.0.4 uses a document content palette, which displays all the text and graphic elements contained within a document. You can pick and choose the elements and order in which you export to HTML. Text export functions offer a high level of versatility:

- Special text characters (such as ampersands and copyright symbols) are converted to their HTML equivalents.
- Quark style sheets can be mapped to HTML styles.
- Tables and lists can be preserved, as can text color and alignment.

BeyondPress offers a high degree of control over image export as well. Images are automatically converted to GIF or JPEG files, with support for interlaced GIF and progressive JPEG formats. Most importantly, the program will allow you to export any element (or group of elements), including text, as an anti-aliased image, with control over cropping, scaling, transparency, border width, and alternative text. All with the ability to index to either an optimal or custom palette!

The XTension offers more than just conversion capabilities, however. BeyondPress allows you to assign background textures, as well as background, text, and link colors. Both client- and server-side image maps are supported as is Apple Events scripting. Although BeyondPress 2.0.4 is Mac-only, it is multilingual (French, German, Dutch, and English). A demo version is available on Astrobyte's Web site (as shown in Figure 9-6).

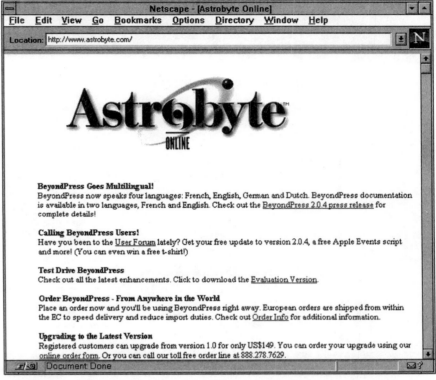

Figure 9-6: Don't just read about it. Go get the demo!

HexMac HexWeb XT

http://www.hexmac.com

HexMac's HexWeb XT 2.2, released in October 1996, offers some interesting new features. HexWeb provides the highest degree of flexibility for QuarkXPress-centric Web page designers. HexScape XT, which is bundled with HexWeb XT 2.2, allows designers to integrate Shockwave, QuickTime, Live Audio, and other Netscape plug-in elements from within QuarkXPress. While the company is based in Europe, their .com Web site, as shown in Figure 9-7, offers their products for sale to their American user base (the company has generated great interest in their support for the online newspaper market).

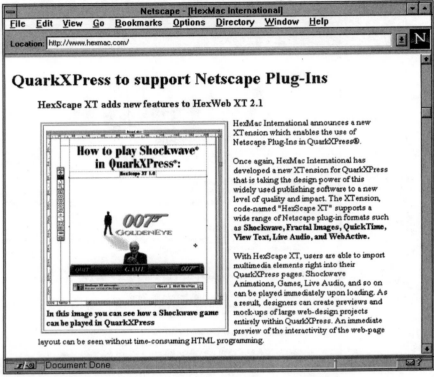

Figure 9-7: HexMac's HexWeb XT includes cutting-edge features.

While some features, such as support for Netscape Navigator 3.0's multicolumns, may be a bit too cutting edge for everyday Web play (until enough browsers provide support), other features, such as integrated FTP and link checking, make HexWeb XT worth looking into. The price of the software should fall somewhere between the other two offerings covered here.

Extensis CyberPress

http://www.extensis.com

Portland, Oregon-based Extensis is the latest addition to the Quark-to-HTML crowd, having announced CyberPress for QuarkXPress at Macworld Boston in August 1996. Extensis has upped the ante by slashing the price point. At press time, the company was selling CyberPress bundled with a copy of Adobe PageMill 2 for only $149, or one-fourth of what Astrobyte had been charging for BeyondPress. Like BeyondPress, CyberPress also uses a document control palette to manage exportable page elements (see Figure 9-8). The palette can also be used to assign URLs to individual elements.

Figure 9-8: Rearrange page elements in the CyberPress palette.

CyberPress provides control over text alignment and basic character formatting (bold, italic, superscript, and subscript), as well as text-to-HTML list and table functions. The package conveniently removes hard-coded bullets to avoid double bulleting. Tables can be exported with specified border widths and alignment. Images (as well as text boxes) can be exported as either GIF or JPEG files. While CyberPress does not offer the same extent of functionality as Astrobyte's BeyondPress, its low price tag makes it undeniably attractive. Interestingly enough, CyberPress was actually developed by Astrobyte as an entry-level product, and is being marketed solely by Extensis.

Do You Really Want to Hack Out HTML?

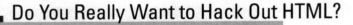

This is where we separate the wheat from the chaff, the men from the boys, and P.T. Barnum's proverbial suckers from their wallets. If you want to hack out HTML, you'd better be committed to the task, lest you end up committed to someplace less comfortable. You've probably heard the warnings: HTML editing is not for the meek and timid. But you know what? If you really want to hack it out, you can do it! It's really not rocket science.

One of the side benefits of PageMill is that it eases you into learning HTML. While you might not want to get involved with the code, if you spend any significant amount of time creating pages, eventually you'll learn a good bit of HTML, if only through osmosis. Like it or not, HTML will creep into your consciousness. But don't worry, we're not going to get into any HTML specifics here. The bookshelves are stuffed with a wide range of books for that (you might want to check out Ventana's excellent *HTML Publishing on the Internet*, which is available in both Macintosh and Windows versions). Instead, we'll recommend one power ASCII text tool in particular; one that has received universal praise for its high performance and good manners.

Bare Bones BBEdit

http://www.barebones.com/

Bare Bones Software has been riding a wave of popularity, thanks to its hot-rod ASCII text editor, BBEdit. The stripped-down program has gained quite a high degree of regard in the Macintosh Web publishing community and can help you to reach new levels of Web developer's nirvana. Although PageMill 2 includes an integrated text editor, it falls short of what's capable with a serious power tool. When used in combination with Adobe PageMill, BBEdit provides the extra punch that PageMill's text editor is lacking. Macintosh Web publishers, rejoice! There's a freeware copy of BBEdit Lite (as shown in Figure 9-9) on this book's CD-ROM.

Figure 9-9: BBEdit Lite provides a clean, fast ASCII text processing interface, which shows its code-editing roots. Features such as tab stops, line numbers, and invisibles can be toggled on or off.

BBEdit's dexterity is most evident when performing intricate search-and-replace routines. The program allows you to perform multiple (batch) file search and replaces, which saves insane amounts of time when you're changing repetitive Web page text such as copyright notices (as shown in Figure 9-10). With BBEdit's supercharged search-and-replace engine, you can target a directory full of files and swap a new chunk of text into every file that includes the matching pattern.

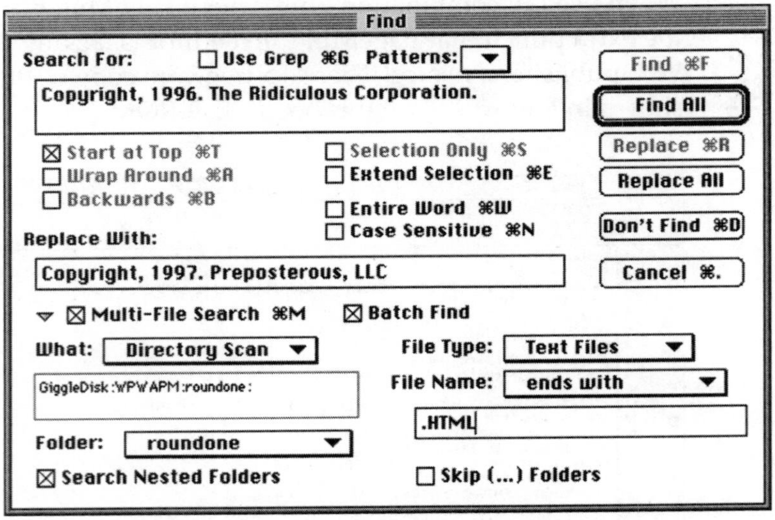

Figure 9-10: Using BBEdit's powerful search-and-replace engine, it was a breeze to change from the ridiculous to the preposterous!

The search-and-replace engine provides the capability to save frequently performed searches as patterns, allowing you to recall the search terms with just a click. You can also use BBEdit's Grep function (named after a UNIX utility, familiar only to serious geeks) to perform pattern matching, which further extends your search-and-replace possibilities by allowing you to swap out nonliteral text strings. Grep provides the ability to search for wildcard characters (such as any digit or line ending), as well as character strings.

In addition to serious search-and-replace functions (which are included in BBEdit Lite) the full version of BBEdit (available for just $79 to registered PageMill users) provides a host of other robust features, including support for scripting, drag and drop, FTP integration, spell checking, integrated HTML editing tools, and single-keystroke insertion of glossary text. BBEdit also uses Power Macintosh-native code for enhanced performance.

Moving On

Text-conversion and editing utilities are power tools that can help you get your job done faster and with less heartache. Choosing the appropriate tools means taking a close look at how your work flows now and how you plan on fine-tuning the flow in the future. The proper apparatus will enable you to produce pages in a highly automated manner, saving time and manpower. But enough of that techie stuff!

Sit back and strap in; we're about to take a wild ride. In the following chapters, you'll learn how you can expand your Web page design horizons through the use of cool fonts, powerful image-creation tools, and wicked animation tools.

chapter 10

Cool Tools & Typefaces

Typefaces set the tone for your Web page designs as much as any other graphical element, be it a subtle background texture or snazzy illustration. While you are currently not able to affect how the browser sees a particular style of type in your HTML text, you can use any one of zillions of typefaces in your GIF and JPEG graphics. Although Microsoft's Internet Explorer 3.0 introduced support for HTML 3.2—which includes Cascading Style Sheets (CSS) and the ability to specify typefaces—PageMill 2 does not support this level of HTML, and it will be some time until this technology is widely implemented in other Web page creation tools, as well.

The nomenclature of the type world can be a bit bewildering for both graphics greenhorns and journeymen alike. People have taken to referring to specific typefaces, such as Garamond Bold Italic, as either a typeface or a font. The two terms are now pretty much interchangeable, although this wasn't always the case. In the old days, a *font* used to refer to a group of associated typefaces. For example, the Garamond font would have been considered to include Garamond (roman), Garamond Bold, Garamond Italic, and Garamond Bold Italic. Consequently, Roman, Bold, Italic, and Bold Italic are *styles*, while Garamond Bold Italic is a *typeface*. Nowadays, folks refer to a specific typeface as a font. Is this something we should lose sleep over? Hardly.

There are a number of different type classes. One of the most distinct differences is between the serif and sans serif faces. *Serifs* are the fancy doodads and little feet that adorn faces such as Garamond and Times Roman. A *sans serif* face such as Helvetica or Futura, is without (sans) serifs. There are many types of *decorative* and *display* faces, including fancy *scripts* and way-cool (and some not-so-cool) trendy designs.

There is an incredible array of type available on the World Wide Web, with many free samples just for the asking (or is that downloading?). Scores of servers deliver scads of choices for every taste and budget. As you troll for type in this chapter, it will become apparent how vast (and immediate) your online typographic resources truly are. You're bound to pick up some great ideas and a few gratis typefaces, as well.

Let the truth be told, this author is a typophile, who'd rather spend his hard-earned pay on a good typeface than an expensive bottle of wine. After spending many years in the craft of setting type, it was inevitable that a deep admiration would ensue. One develops a certain fondness for the intricacies of type, for the subtle (and not-so-subtle) changes that the right choice of font will impart upon a piece. Typeface selection is a crucial decision in any serious graphic design, and is not to be taken lightly. This is not to say that the act of choosing a typeface is a tense and stuffy affair. On the contrary, it can be a wonderfully creative experience! Finding the right font for a design after an exhaustive search is akin to finding a long-lost piece to a puzzle.

PostScript or TrueType? Web Font Détente!

Most professional-quality fonts are available in PostScript format. Many of these are also available in TrueType format. The format you use is dictated by the environment you work in. The good news is that for the purposes of building Web pages, font format doesn't matter whatsoever! Regardless of whether you're a graphic designer or publisher using PostScript fonts, or whether you're an at-home hobbyist or in a normal office environment using TrueType fonts, you're going to be rasterizing those fonts into bitmap graphics.

If you're not familiar with how the two competing font formats came to be, here's a bit of background information to fill you in. PostScript is the horse that Adobe Systems rode to fame and fortune in the mid-1980s. PostScript broke new ground, and paved the way for the desktop publishing revolution. The format changed the game by defining characters with mathematical vector descriptions, rather then fixed bitmaps, which allowed for printer and resolution independence. For the very first time, people could purchase typefaces that would print on everything from a desktop laser printer through a $100,000 imagesetting system. PostScript created a huge market, and has become ubiquitous in the graphics, printing, and publishing world. Over the years, Adobe made generous profits by licensing its technology to printer manufacturers and font foundries.

The TrueType format was created by the unlikely alliance of Apple and Microsoft, in a backlash against Adobe. Apple, as the legend goes, had grown weary of lining Adobe's pockets with royalty dollars for the privilege of licensing PostScript for its popular LaserWriter. Apple licensed technology it had been developing to Microsoft to create a cross-platform font and imaging standard that would challenge Adobe PostScript. In retrospect, the move may have been one of Apple's most crucial blunders (or maybe not...it's had plenty over the years).

While TrueType is the most prevalent font format in the world today, it is frowned upon by the design and publishing community. TrueType has earned its bad rap for two primary reasons: an abundance of cheap, knockoff font collections and problems associated with high-end printing. With respect to the first beef, it's a prime example of caveat emptor. If you buy a package of 100 fonts for 10 bucks, you can expect dime-a-font quality.

PostScript & TrueType Merge Into OpenType

In May 1996, Adobe and Microsoft delivered a shocker and announced that the PostScript and TrueType formats would be merged into a new format, to be known as OpenType. One of the most profound benefits of this merging of technologies will be found on the World Wide Web. The two companies have proposed to use OpenType as the means to finally bring real typefaces (rather than browser default faces) to Web page text. OpenType will allow actual typefaces to hook onto specific pages and travel over the Internet.

At the present, the most commonly accepted way to present text in a specific typeface on a Web page is by rasterizing the text into a GIF or JPEG graphic. Rasterization takes the mathematical vector information that defines a character and turns it into a pixel-by-pixel description. While this might sound complicated for the end user, it's as easy as opening (or saving) a file. Rasterization can be accomplished in any one of a number of programs, ranging from CorelDRAW!, through Adobe Photoshop, and Fractal Design Painter. We'll cover those programs in Chapter 11.

So You Really Want Vectors, Eh?

Macromedia, Corel, and Micrografx all provide a means to deliver Web pages with vector art and type through the use of Netscape plug-ins.

Downloading Fonts From the Net

On the following pages, you'll be presented with dozens of Web sites where you can browse and, in certain cases, download fonts for your Mac or PC. Downloading fonts is no different from downloading any other type of file from the Internet. Just click on the link, assign a name, and wait for the file to download. Once the file has made its way to your hard drive, you'll probably need to decompress it before you load it into your system.

PC fonts are commonly zipped together with PKZIP. If the file was saved as a self-extracting archive file, it will have an .EXE extension, and all you'll have to do is double-click on it to extract the files. If the file has a .ZIP extension, you'll have to use a de-compression utility, such as PKUNZIP, WinZIP, or Drag and Zip to extract the font files.

Macintosh fonts are handled a little differently. They'll almost always be BinHexed and will probably be compressed with StuffIt, as well. If the file you download ends with .HQX, you'll know it's been BinHexed. BinHexing takes the Macintosh file's data and resource forks and packs them together into one bundle for transmission over the Net. DeBinHexing performs the opposite maneuver. (It helps to think of the Transporter Room on the Starship Enterprise.) Like the PC's ZIP files, the Macintosh's StuffIt files can either be self-extracting (.SEA) or not (.SIT). The freeware StuffIt Expander automatically deBinHexes and UnStuffs Mac files with aplomb.

If you don't have any decompression utilities on your computer, be sure to check this book's CD-ROM!

Trolling for Commercial Type

The first group of World Wide Web sites we'll visit are operated by typical commercial vendors. Later in this chapter, we'll stop by some sites that specialize in shareware typefaces where you can actually download and try out a font before paying the developer. Often shareware fonts cost less than regular commercial products, and while a serious typophile might think that shareware typefaces found on the Web would be of lesser quality, this is definitely not the case. In addition to the lower-priced shareware, there are even some freebies to be had! Many of the commercial font foundries offer free samples, there for the mere price of filling out a form. Ah, the joys and benefits of direct marketing on the Internet!

Note: Why are they called font foundries? It's a holdover from the old days of hot metal type when individual characters were cast in lead.

Each foundry treats its online type specimens differently. Some provide larger and more complete previews than others. And some sites are so cool they even allow you to interactively preview typestyles with your own headlines. We'll cruise through these sites (the addresses, or URLs, are included with the descriptions) and take in the sites, in alphabetical order starting with Adobe, the company that started the digital type revolution. Load up your gear, 'cause we're going fishing for type!

Adobe Systems

http://www.adobe.com
The Adobe Type Browser (http://www.adobe.com/type/ browser/main.html) is a handy little tool. It allows you to view font lists on the Adobe Web site by family, designer, class, and package. Figure 10-1 illustrates the detail provided about each font. In this case, we're able to learn that Hiroshige was designed by Cynthia Hollandsworth, who we're told was commissioned to create the font in 1986 for a book of woodblock prints by noted Japanese artist Ando Hiroshige. Now that's the type of information that's bound to impress your clients (or at least make them question your billable hours)!

Figure 10-1: Adobe's Type Browser provides historical details.

Adobe's site provides good-sized previews. As you can see in Figure 10-2, each individual typeface is displayed with a handful of lowercase characters in a large point size, followed by two lines of upper and lowercase characters. An earlier version of the site had provided full-page examples that featured accent and special characters. These older samples even included ligatures (combined characters, such as fi and fl). Although we appreciate the new large preview, we miss the more complete character sets of the previous pages.

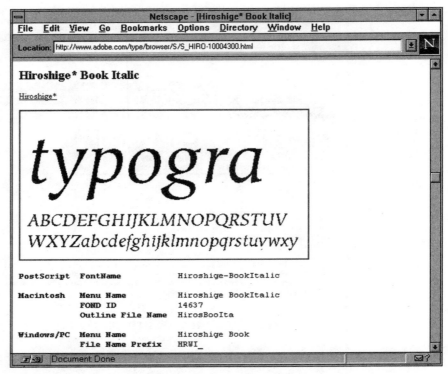

Figure 10-2: Adobe does not use anti-aliasing on its type specimen pages.

Agfa

http://www.agfahome.com

AgfaType offers a growing index of typographical specimens from an array of international type designers. The Agfa Creative Alliance was formed to encourage the creation of new and exciting typefaces. The online type specimens on Agfa's Web site are anti-aliased, and of good size, although they feature only abbreviated character sets. Figure 10-3 illustrates the handsome Citadel Line and Citadel Solid typefaces from Creative Alliance type designer Tobias Frere-Jones. Notable type designers in the alliance include such industry veterans as Matthew Carter and Sumner Stone.

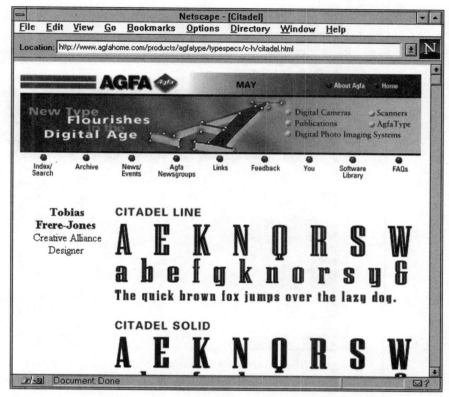

Figure 10-3: Tobias Frere-Jones' Citadel is an interesting slab serif family.

Bitstream

http://www.bitstream.com/
Bitstream's fonts are among the most popular in the world. The company came to be in the early 1980s at the dawn of the digital type revolution. Bitstream sells a number of CD-ROM font collections, in both TrueType and PostScript formats. When we visited their site (see Figure 10-4), we found solid information on Bitstream's emerging type technologies, TrueDoc and Cyberbit.

Figure 10-4: Bitstream's Web site offers information on emerging type technologies, such as TrueDoc and Cyberbit.

TrueDoc is Bitstream's strategy for font fidelity, which promises to give us the ability to dictate how the browser sees a particular style of type within HTML text. With TrueDoc, font information will travel along with the page. A Web page designer can design a page to use a specific typeface, and have that typeface download to the client's browser, along with the page. This ensures that the client will view the page with the fonts it was designed with, rather than the browser's default font.

Cyberbit is Bitstream's international font, designed for people who work with multilingual documents. To deal with the many variations and requirements of the world's languages, Cyberbit fonts include a whopping 8,500 characters.

Whither TrueDoc?

It's unclear how Bitstream's TrueDoc will hold up to the upcoming barrage of Microsoft and Adobe's new OpenType format. Stay tuned.

designOnline

http://www.dol.com/

The Web site of Alphabets, a small Chicago-based foundry, is known as designOnline. The company is a digital type pioneer, having entered the PostScript font arena back in 1987. It sells fonts developed in-house, as well as from a select number of independent type designers. The designOnline Web site offers a number of different design-oriented boutiques, including fontsOnline (Figure 10-5), and some wacky rubber stamp collections. You'll find the impressive International Type Founders CD-ROM featured in the fontsOnline section. The volume features the typographical talents of Alphabets, along with Emigre, House Industries, T-26, and a host of other small foundries.

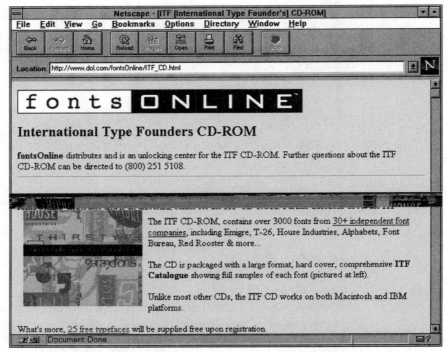

Figure 10-5: A variety of small foundries are featured on the ITF CD-ROM.

Alphabets' Web site promises an interactive font rasterizer/
previewer, similar in nature to Letraset's Ripper (which will be
reviewed in the Letraset section later on in this chapter). This will
be a most welcome addition. As you can see from Figure 10-6,
Alphabets' font specimens are limited to anti-aliased one liners.
The picture fonts, however, hold up well.

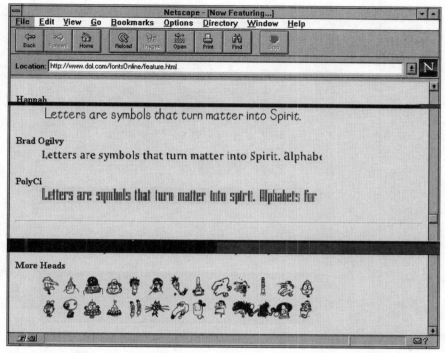

Figure 10-6: Picture fonts at the Alphabets Web site are worth the trip.

Digiteyes Multimedia TypeArt Library

http://www.typeart.com/

Digiteyes is a fun little foundry with a lively Web site exhibiting original designs. Their home page, as shown in Figure 10-7, provides links to their type-related amusements and quirky catalog. You'll find typesetting and design tips, as well as the Name That Font game. Digiteyes' type specimens are large, anti-aliased, and more like design experiments, in some cases, than traditional spec pages.

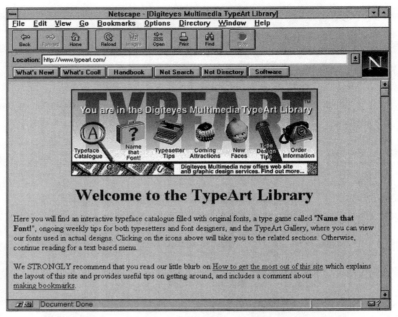

Figure 10-7: The Digiteyes Multimedia TypeArt home page is a typographical ride down the midway.

Into those oh-so-trendy, oh-so-hard-to-read grunge fonts? Then you'll be happy to learn about the Digiteyes Multimedia TypeArt Library. You'll find nasty little nuggets like Disorder, Mean Streak, and What the Hell?, as shown in Figure 10-8. Digiteyes provides historical context on its fonts, allowing us to learn the who, how, and why leading up to the creation of a particular font. Just the ticket for your favorite grunge historian (flannel shirt not included).

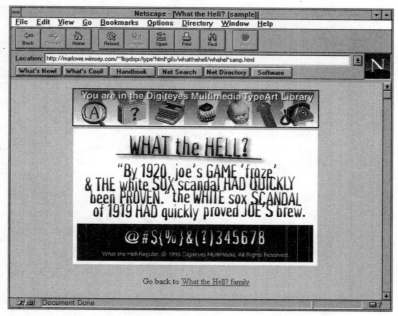

Figure 10-8: What the Hell?, indeed.

Emigre

http://www.emigre.com/

Since the mid-1980s, no other single small foundry has had the profound effect that Emigre has had upon the design world. The company began by selling bitmapped type designs that cofounder Zuzana Licko designed specifically for the (then) brand new Apple Macintosh. Those early experiments with bitmap type offer an interesting alternative today, for low resolution use in Web page graphics.

Emigre's Web site offers excellent non-aliased type specimens. Base-12, the font used in the copyright line at the bottom of the Remedy type specimen page shown in Figure 10-9 is part of a new family of Emigre fonts optimized for online viewing. Each of the families is displayed on a font-by-font basis. A brief history of each family is included, as well. Figure 10-10 details some of the typographical progression that led to Frank Heine's creation of the font Remedy.

Figure 10-9: If you haven't seen Emigre's Remedy before, you've seen three typefaces that echo its style.

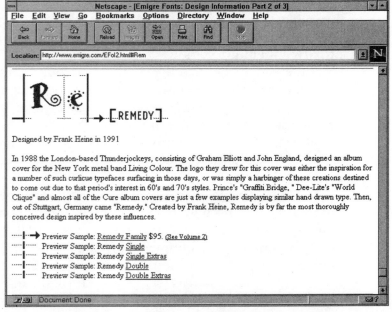

Figure 10-10: This page provides some history behind the creation of Remedy.

Image Club

http://www.imageclub.com/

Image Club has long been a trend setter. It offered the first serious library of PostScript fonts, and was a forerunner of the PostScript clip art field as well. The company began by selling its own fonts and soon added fonts from ITC, Letraset, ATF, and other foundries. Image Club is currently owned by Adobe (it was acquired and owned—ever so briefly—by Aldus, just before Adobe acquired Aldus). Image Club has always specialized in trendy display faces, and its home page (see Figure 10-11) makes it easy to stay up on the trends with hotlinks to their top 10 lists.

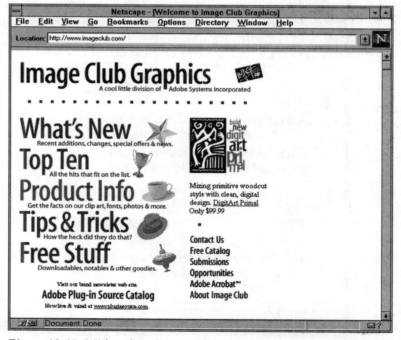

Figure 10-11: With a clean layout, it's easy to keep up with what's hot on Image Club's Web site.

As shown in Figure 10-12, the Image Club Web site provides a proper online type specimen for each font, along with some descriptive text. The type specimens are of sufficient size and are anti-aliased. The Web site contains a range of excellent content, in addition to font-related information. The online Tips & Tricks section, one of the nicest features of the site, shows how to create scores of cool effects with step-by-step instructions. The Tips & Tricks are mostly designed around Adobe products, such as Photoshop, but the techniques can be used with other applications as well.

Figure 10-12: Improv is an Image Club exclusive, designed by Noel Rubin.

International Typeface Corporation (ITC)

http://www.esselte.com/itc/

The International Typeface Corporation is one of the world's most respected type foundries and has published more than 800 high-quality typefaces. The company's offerings range from elegant text faces to whimsical display faces. ITC's fonts are widely licensed and are found in the collections of Adobe, Image Club, and Monotype, among others. The ITC Web site (see Figure 10-13) was in its formative state when we first stopped in. By the time you get the chance to cruise their way, you're bound to enjoy their online catalogs and designer profiles. The company has announced that it will offer one free font per month as an added incentive to visit their site.

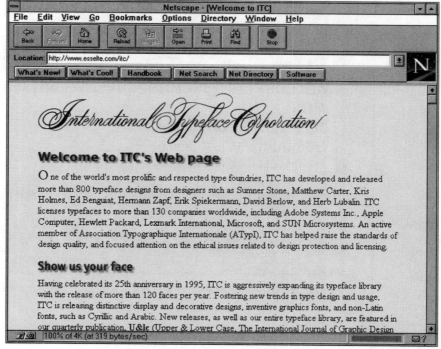

Figure 10-13: ITC has announced that it will provide a free font each month.

Letraset

http://www.letraset.com
Letraset specializes in cool and trendy display fonts, and I found their Web site to be one of the most engaging of all the type foundries. Font specimens—in this case, Buzzer 3 (see Figure 10-14)—are shown as anti-aliased character sets and in a sufficiently large point size. Letraset also gives away one free font per month. But instead of filling out a registration form, you'll have to go on a fact-finding Easter egg hunt.

Figure 10-14: The Letraset Web site offers excellent font specimen previews.

The greatest thing about Letraset's Web site, hands down, is a nifty device known as The Ripper. As you can see in Figure 10-15, The Ripper allows you to preview your headline text in any of Letraset's typefaces. It does this by rasterizing the outline font into a bitmapped screen representation (RIPping is the act of Raster Image Processing). In addition, The Ripper lets you choose the type size and gives you the choice of whether or not to anti-alias the preview.

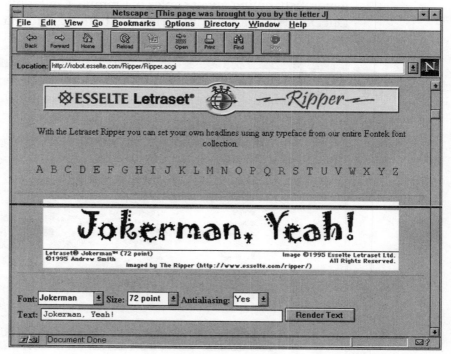

Figure 10-15: Letraset's awesome feature, The Ripper, lets you preview your headline text in any of their typefaces.

Linotype

http://www.linotype.com
Linotype is a classic old type foundry that helped lead the way in the transition to the electronic age of design. Its roots date back to the original Linotype Machine, which was invented by Ottmar Mergenthaler, way back in the 1880s. The Linotype Web site (see Figure 10-16) rewards you with a handful of free fonts in return for filling out a registration form. On our last visit, they were generously giving away copies of Optima, Centennial-Roman, and DucDeberry in PostScript format for both PC and Macintosh.

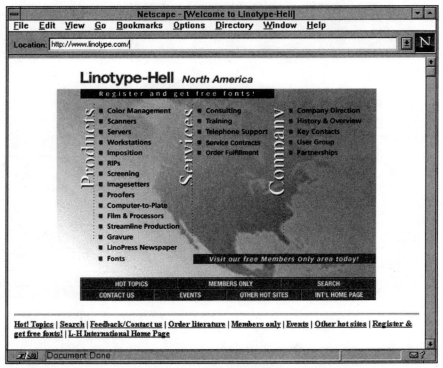

Figure 10-16: Register with Linotype's Web site and you'll be rewarded with free fonts!

Monotype

http://www.monotype.com
Monotype is another classic type foundry that's made the jump into the new world (see Figure 10-17). The company has focused much of its energies on screen font technology in recent years and has even provided OEM fonts for the likes of Microsoft. When we visited the Monotype Web site, it was very much a work in progress. Eventually, their Web site is scheduled to offer online demos and samples.

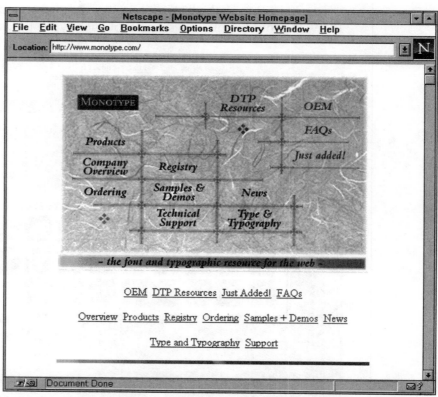

Figure 10-17: Monotype's Web site offers visitors classic type.

OptiFont

http://www.castcraft-software.com/

The folks at Castcraft Software have been in the type business for 60 years. They offer hundreds of typestyles—both TrueType and PostScript—in their OptiFont collections, at reasonable prices. The company takes great pride in their finely tuned "Kustom Kerned" typefaces, which feature between 1200 and 2500 kerning pairs per font. Their Web site has an interface that is reminiscent of an interactive CD-ROM, as shown in Figure 10-18. Most of the screens we encountered on the OptiFont site included text navigation, in addition to the big image maps. As illustrated in Figure 10-19, the font list offers a snippet of each type specimen.

Figure 10-18: The OptiFont Web site allows you to browse fonts alphabetically or by volume.

Figure 10-19: Economical OptiFont collections offer wide variety and good value for the dollar.

Publishers Depot

http://www.publishersdepot.com/

Publishers Depot (Figure 10-20) is an online department store for multimedia, Web, and print designers. Like a department store, you'll have tons of choices and will be able to wander the aisles for hours. And you can expect to pay department store prices for the pleasure and convenience of one-stop shopping. The Web site is the product of Picture Network International. In addition to fonts from Alphabets and Monotype, it features a staggering array of stock photography, illustrations, clip art, maps, and audio clips... just about any type of imagery that a designer might need at a moment's notice. The site requires membership, for which it charges a fee. To browse in depth, you'll be asked to set up an account.

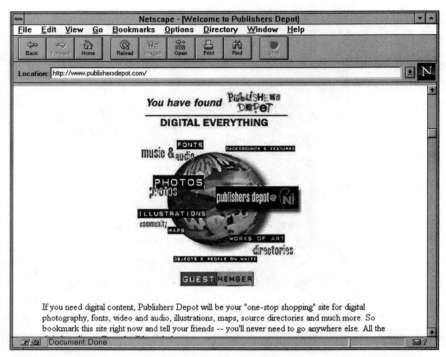

Figure 10-20: Stopping by Publishers Depot is like going on a trip to Bloomies. You'll have a great time...just remember to bring your gold cards.

Publish

http://www.publish.com/treasury/directories/foundry/
OK, so this isn't a foundry. But *Publish Magazine*'s Web site, Publish RGB, is truly a typographical treasure trove. Their online Directory to Type Foundries (See Figure 10-21) lists more than three dozen different foundries, from the smallest to the largest, with e-mail and hotlinks. This site is peppered with a number of downloadable sample fonts, which are available for those who register. Don't worry, you don't have to subscribe to get the fonts!

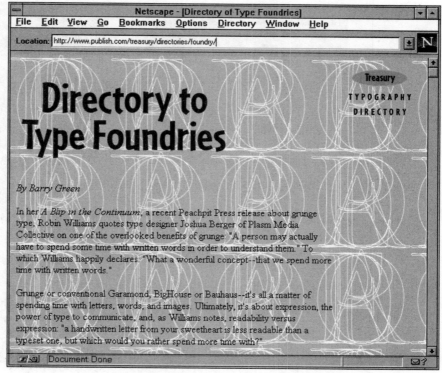

Figure 10-21: The Publish RGB online Directory to Type Foundries.

Each individual foundry is listed on its own page, as illustrated by the Thirstype page shown in Figure 10-22. Each directory page includes information on the computer platforms and type formats supported by each foundry as well as delivery and general pricing information. A small graphic on each page makes use of the foundry's pertinent typefaces.

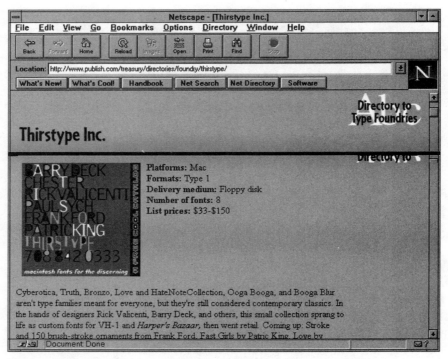

Figure 10-22: The Thirstype page in Publish RGB's Foundry Directory gives a taste of the foundry's wares.

Tiro Typeworks

http://www.portal.ca/~tiro/

Tiro is a small independent type foundry whose original fonts include a number of classical serif faces. Their target audience is the discriminating typographer. Floriana Italic, the typeface shown in Figure 10-23, is indicative of their high degree of craftsmanship. Tiro's online type specimens are large, crisp, and well presented, with the characters openly spaced and anti-aliased onto a pleasant beige parchment texture. The Web site is also home to Tiro's online typographical journal, "an online anthology of essays and articles relating to type design, typography, lettering and calligraphy, and letterpress printing."

Figure 10-23: Tiro's Floriana Italic.

We Saved the Grungiest for Last!

In doing the online research for this chapter, we came across some amazing font finds on the Internet. Our search turned up a number of funky little foundries that produce fun and edgy typefaces. These are the kinds of fonts that will have your pages bound for Net glory without maxing your Virtual Cash account.

There's been a lot said about *grunge fonts* recently. Grunge is a mid-90s font phenomenon, having its roots in rock and roll (where else?). Grunge fonts are twisted, tortured, faded, little critters that look as if they've been created through ninth-generation repro (a copy of a copy of a copy of a copy). Two of our favorite little foundries follow, with healthy heapings of grunge and other cool fonts.

Attention Earthling

http://www.attention-earthling.com
With a wild look torn from the pages of a science-fiction comic book, Attention Earthling offers a smattering of exciting new fonts on their Web site (Figure 10-24). You'll find a gaggle of grunge fonts, such as Flex 49, Dublux, and Fax-O-Matic, along with the scratchy Menace, aptly named Brillo, and other great designs. The Web site's fun animation and retro sci-fi graphic treatment makes searching for fonts an online experience.

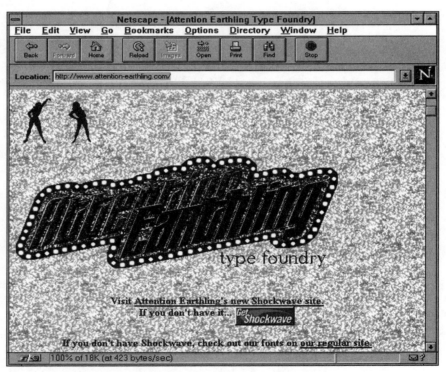

Figure 10-24: Attention Earthling! The fonts have landed!

Take a gander at Silverlux. It would look at home on a 1950s vacuum cleaner! An innovative use of frames allows font specimens to scroll across the bottom of the browser window (Figure 10-25). The Attention Earthling Web site features online ordering (and delivery), so you can pull out those credit cards and instantly charge up your designs. Their fonts are affordably priced in the $29 to $35 range.

Figure 10-25: Attention Earthling's creative use of frames allows font specimens to scroll along the bottom of the window.

Fonthead

http://www.fonthead.com/

Fonthead is a precedent-setting online foundry with infectious fonts, incredible prices, and cool freebies. Their Web site uses a clean, uncluttered design (Figure 10-26) that downloads quickly and displays their whimsical handiwork to its best advantage. Fonthead's fonts have a lively, upbeat feel and would be a good choice to lighten up the design of a Web page.

Figure 10-26: The Fonthead Web site features a clean design and fast downloads.

Fonthead's Volume One collection is comprised of 19 fonts, while their Volume Two set contains 17 fonts. Each collection is available separately at a mere $25. And you can purchase all 36 fonts for only $45! In addition to being insanely inexpensive, Fonthead offers a healthy offering of free downloadable fonts in your choice of PostScript (Mac) and TrueType (Mac and PC) formats. On the day of our visit, they were offering the mildly grungy Holstein and skinny handlettered SpillMilk from Volumes 1 and 2, along with a trio of fatmarkered GoodDog fonts from their upcoming Volume 3. Fonthead clearly spells out that these are totally free fonts, without any restrictions.

Figure 10-27: Fonthead offers a generous selection of freebie fonts.

Shareware Fonts

There are tons and tons of shareware fonts available on the Internet. If you're looking for something special, there's a good chance that it's out there, somewhere. It's important to remember, however, that shareware fonts are not free. If you use shareware fonts, you should support the hard-working designers that created them by sending in the registration fee. Some type designers are so cool that they don't even ask that you send the money to them. Instead, they request that you send the money to a specific charity. Now that's good Net karma.

> **Yahoo Fonts!**
> If you're out looking for more shareware fonts on the Web, be sure to check out the Font section on Yahoo!

DTP Internet Jumplist

http://www.teleport.com/~eidos/dtpij/
One of the best places to start looking for additional font Web and FTP sites is the DTP Internet Jumplist (Figure 10-28). This invaluable resource includes pointers to many of the commercial foundries listed above, in addition to small foundries and sites that specialize in shareware fonts.

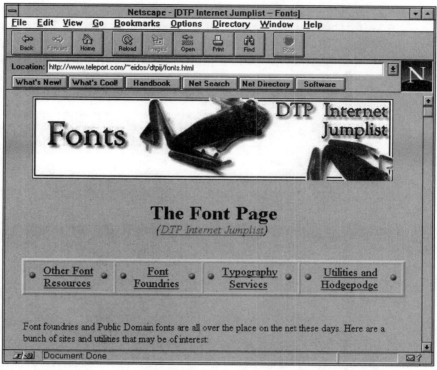

Figure 10-28: Hop on over to the DTP Internet Jumplist!

Into Railroad Memorabilia?
Get yourself to the station on time, and catch the very cool railroad-related fonts and icons at http://www.mcs.net/~dsdawdy/Fonts/products.html.

comp.fonts home page

http://jasper.ora.com:80/comp.fonts/index.html
This one is truly a labor of font love! The comp.fonts home page (Figure 10-29) includes a rapidly growing "Foundries on the Net" page and comp.fonts FAQ, along with the awesome Internet Font

Archives. The Archives provide previews of hundreds of fonts from a wide variety of sources. Fonts can be downloaded directly from the site, and you can even view fonts from CompuServe and America Online (although you can't download them from the Internet).

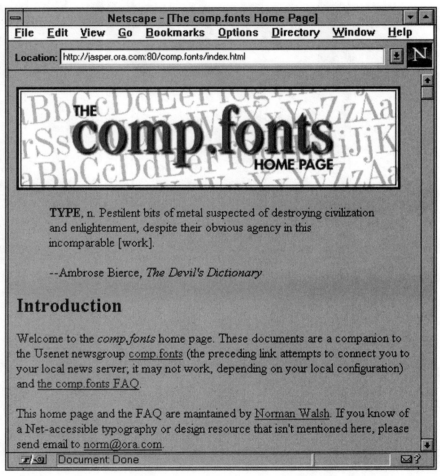

Figure 10-29: The comp.fonts home page is a terrific treasure trove of typographical treats.

If you're heavily into fonts, cruise the comp.fonts pages on a regular basis. Hot new foundries are added frequently, and the online previews, as shown in Figure 10-30, are invaluable. Don't forget to check out the comp.fonts newsgroup, as well, you'll get all the font news as it breaks.

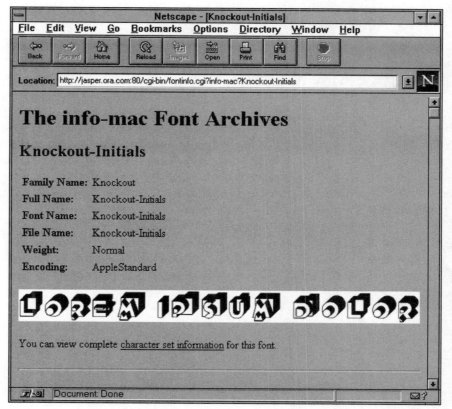

Figure 10-30: With online previews of fonts from the Internet, CompuServe, and America Online, comp.fonts is a comprehensive resource.

Check Out These FTP Font Sites!

For Windows: ftp://gatekeeper.dec.com/pub/micro/msdos/win3/ fonts/

For Macintosh: ftp://mac.archive.umich.edu/mac/ system.extensions/font/

 ## Moving On

In the preceding pages, you've learned where you can turn to on the Web for typographical information, as well as inspiration. A well-designed Web page combines great typography with compelling imagery. We've just got one more URL to drop here—http://www.philsfonts.com—the Web site of Phil's Fonts, a premiere purveyor of fine typefaces from more than 50 foundries. Be sure to check out Phil's wares!

In the next chapter, we'll take a look at some cool graphic tools that will help you to build the Taj Mahal of Web sites (even if you're not Donald Trump).

chapter 11

Cool Graphics Tools

There's far more to creating effective Web pages than just building the pages within PageMill. To create a really effective page, you need to start with really great graphics. And to build those great graphics, you must outfit your system with the proper programs. This chapter will focus on choosing the best graphics tools for Web design work. As such, this chapter is best thought of as an overview rather than a comprehensive dissertation on the subject. We'll see which programs are the coolest and quickly explain why they've earned our respect.

There are five basic categories for the graphics tools you'll need to build a Web site. Some programs, however, encompass many, or even all five, of the categories. Application suites, such as Macromedia's FreeHand Design Studio or CorelDRAW! include modules to handle almost any graphics task imaginable. The five most important categories of graphics tools for building Web pages are:

- Paint editors—for creating bitmap graphics with painterly tools.

- Plug-in filters—for tweaking, twisting, and twiddling bitmap graphics.

- Stand-alone texture generators—for creating cool bitmapped background images.
- Draw programs—for creating slick, hard-edged vector graphics that can be converted to GIF format.
- File conversion utilities—for conveniently moving files from one format to another.

Cutting-edge graphics tools represent an area where there is still a significant, though quickly closing, gap between the Macintosh and Windows platforms. As you read through this chapter, you'll notice that we've tagged each program with its availability status (as of this writing) for both platforms.

Paint Editors

Thankfully, the three most popular paint editors on the market—Adobe Photoshop, Fractal Design Painter, and Corel PHOTO-PAINT—are well suited for Web page work. And two of the three—Photoshop and Painter—operate on both Macintosh and Windows platforms. While it's highly likely that at least one of these three programs resides on your computer's hard disk, you'll soon learn some of the reasons why you might consider each program.

In addition to these three sales leaders, there are a number of other very capable paint editors on the market. The two high-end editors of choice (of late) have been Live Picture and Macromedia xRes. Both Live Picture and xRes were designed to deal with the huge files necessary for prepress work. While you probably wouldn't need to go out and purchase one of these two print production heavyweights just for doing Web page graphics, you should note that xRes is now included as part of the Macromedia FreeHand Design Studio (as well as the Macromedia Director Studio). That xRes provides the widest range of file format options is chief among its selling points as a Web page design tool.

Adobe Photoshop

Adobe Photoshop is the de facto cross-platform standard for image editing. It supports a wide range of file formats, including JPEG and GIF 89a. Photoshop's plug-in architecture (which has been adopted by every other image editor of note) ensures that the latest effects will always be just a purchase and a few clicks away. Photoshop offers some basic tools for creating seamless tiles. While the program's tiling features are not the most ornate, they get the job done without much fuss.

Mac vs. PC
Adobe Photoshop 3.0 is available for both Macintosh and Windows platforms. Photoshop 4.0 went into beta as this book went into production and may be available by the time you read this.

Creating Seamless Textures With Photoshop
The Offset filter is your primary means to a seamless end within Photoshop. It moves the edges of an image into the middle of the image, where you can easily discern and manually eliminate the seams. Once the seams are in the middle of the image, you'll use the Clone tool to obscure them. We'll illustrate the technique with just a few steps.

Figure 11-1: The original image before using Photoshop's Offset filter.

Figure 11-1 shows the original 200 X 200 pixel image in Photoshop. We'll use the Offset filter to move the edges of the image in by half the horizontal and vertical distance (100 pixels). The Wrap Around option must be selected from the Offset window in order for the image to wrap, and the Preview selection should be checked to preview the offset. When the filter is applied, it will cut the image into four distinct quarters, allowing the seams to be readily apparent. Once you can see them, as shown in Figure 11-2, you can eliminate them.

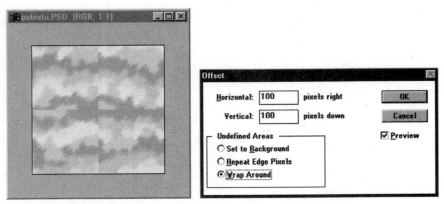

Figure 11-2: Applying the Offset filter…check out those seams!

Getting rid of the seams usually implies careful use of the Clone tool. You'll want to clone snippets of image over the seams, using a thoughtful blending technique and taking the time to zoom in and retouch with a variety of soft brushes. Applying the Offset filter a second time, with the same 100/100 pixel offset, lets you go in and catch things you may have missed or anomalies you may have created. It's a good idea to apply the Offset filter a few times, toggling between views, just to make sure that everything has been completely cleaned up. The finished image (Figure 11-3) should tile with nary a seam.

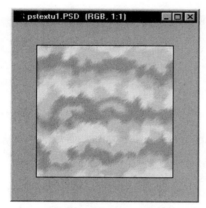

Figure 11-3: Nary a seam to be seen.

The other seamless tile-making option afforded by Photoshop is its impeccable import of Adobe Illustrator patterns. Photoshop ships with a rudimentary collection of patterns on its CD-ROM, but if you happen to have Illustrator, you can happily roll your own.

While you can complete many tiling tasks with just the Offset filter and a bit of hand work, Photoshop becomes a very competent seamless tile maker when you combine it with one of a number of third-party plug-in filters. And as you'll see in the next section, Photoshop's Offset filter is similar to Fractal Design Painter's Wrap-Around Seams feature.

Fractal Design Painter

From Fractal Design Painter's introduction in 1991 through its current version, it has maintained its place as the paint program of choice for electronic artists. The program's natural media punch and innovative interface combine to provide capabilities unmatched by any other paint application. While other programs, such as Corel PHOTO-PAINT and Fauve Matisse, have tried to duplicate Painter's features, none have come close to its implementation, or to its record of constant innovation.

Mac vs. PC
Fractal Design Painter 4.0 is available for both Macintosh and Windows platforms.

This program is deep. Really deep. There are many reasons to recommend it and many hours ahead to master it. Quite honestly, the subject of creating Web graphics with Painter is worthy of a book (or two) of its own. We're not going to go into all the details here, but should your interest be piqued, be sure to take a side trip to Fractal Design's Web site at http://www.fractal/com.

Why Painter 4.0 Is Cool for Web Pages

When Fractal Design Painter 4.0 was in development, hype over the World Wide Web was at a fever pitch. Fractal's engineers carefully considered how their flagship application fit into the big picture. What they came up with is very slick, indeed. The company built upon the program's strengths and added some killer features. At the core is the program's ability to rasterize vector artwork on the fly, by interpreting those hard-edged lines into something more appropriate for online imagery (where a little blur goes a long way). There are four additional reasons why Painter 4.0 is so cool for creating Web page graphics:

- Slick, seamless texture-creation tools.
- Image maps that can be easily created and quickly updated.
- Comprehensive file exports.
- Net Painter for collaborative artwork.

Creating Seamless Textures With Painter 4.0

Textures have long been one of Fractal Design Painter's strongest points, and consequently, seamless Web page background patterns are a snap. Painter 4.0 ships with over 130 paper textures and more than 300 seamless patterns on the CD-ROM. Custom seamless patterns can be quickly created with Painter's Wrap-Around Seams and Wrap-Around Colors features. Wrap-Around Seams performs a similar function to Photoshop's Offset filter by moving the edges of the image inward. Wrap-Around Colors takes you even further by carrying your brushstrokes off one edge of the image around onto the opposite side.

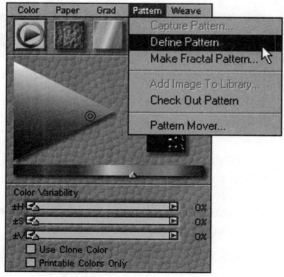

Figure 11-4: Defining a pattern in Painter 4.0.

Painter manages groups of patterns as palettes. To create a pattern, you must either define the entire image as a pattern (Figure 11-4) or capture a portion of an image as a pattern. Once an image has been converted into a pattern, you gain access to the Wrap-Around functions. To move the seams inward, simply hold down the shift key while you click and drag with the grabber hand. This method provides more feedback than Photoshop's method of specifying an offset in pixels. Figure 11-5 shows a clover pattern—which was created with Painter's Image Hose— before and after moving the seams inward.

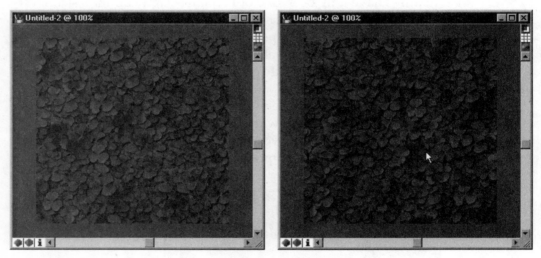

Figure 11-5: Moving in the pattern's seams, before and after.

The Image Hose can be an invaluable asset when creating seamless background textures. This nifty device allows you to spray out scads of images in a variety of random and ordered patterns. We used the Image Hose to spray more clover to obscure the seams in this tile (in Figure 11-5). You can use the Image Hoses that come with Painter, or you can create your own from any imagery that you have at hand.

Creating Image Maps With Painter 4.0

Painter's ability to create image maps provides the highest degree of flexibility, not only with the initial creation, but also with those all-important revisions. Painter creates image maps with hot spots linked to floaters (floating bitmap objects). After an illustration has been rearranged, the image is automatically remapped when the file is saved. Since moving a floater will cause its associated hotspot to move with it, building image maps in Painter, rather than PageMill, can be a tremendously convenient and wonderful time saver.

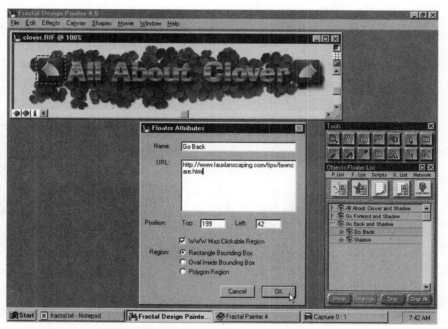

Figure 11-6: Assigning the URL to a Floater.

Figure 11-6 displays Painter's Floater Attributes dialog box. In this illustration you can see that the Go Back button is linked to the mythical lawncare page at http://www.fauxlandscaping.com/ tips/lawncare.html. Each Floater can be assigned a specific name, URL, position, and region. The position specifies the top left-hand corner of the hot spot. Once the WWW Map Clickable Region check box is selected, you have the choice of specifying a Rectangle Bounding Box, an Oval Inside Bounding Box, or a Polygon Region (for creating irregularly shaped hot spots).

Painter File Format Options

Fractal Design Painter saves its working files in RIFF format. This format preserves the image's full palette and floaters. When you're ready to create GIF or JPEG files for your Web pages, you have a number of file format options to choose from, as shown in Figure 11-7. The program allows you to perform GIF palette reduction at the time you save your file, as opposed to Photoshop, which indexes colors before the file is saved. Painter tells you exactly how many colors will be in the file's palette rather than telling you how many bits per pixel. Image colors can either be quantized—or "rounded"—to the nearest color or dithered.

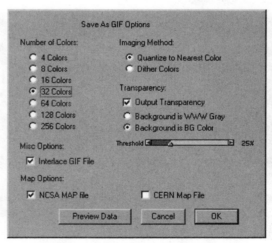

Figure 11-7: GIF and JPEG file options.

The Save As GIF Options dialog box allows you to save files in GIF 89a format, with or without interlacing (which provides that blurry fade-in effect) and transparency. You can choose between WWW Gray and BG color backgrounds with an adjustable threshold. A handy preview function lets you check out your images before you commit them to disk. This is an important feature, enabling you to make those critical palette reduction decisions. Finally, the dialog box allows you to choose between either NCSA or CERN Web server formats for your image maps.

The JPEG Encoding Quality dialog box offers just two choices; image quality and HTML Map format. You can choose between Excellent, High, Good, and Fair JPEG image quality. But as you probably know, the higher the image quality, the larger the file will be. When you're building Web graphics, it's easy to reach the overkill point. For most Web work, go for more compression. The Good option will usually do just fine.

Creating Collaborative Artwork With Net Painter

How many times have you wanted to work simultaneously with a colleague to develop a piece of artwork, but have been prevented from doing so because you were in different locales? Until now, the only solution was to run Farallon's Timbuktu to share screens. While Timbuktu is cool, it's a slow way to collaborate on artwork. The Net Painter feature, new in Painter 4.0, allows you to create artwork in a true interactive environment. You can work with one or a number of collaborators, whether they're in your office or halfway across the world.

In contrast to Timbuktu, Net Painter shares files, not screens. As you make alterations to your artwork, the changes are sent across the network as instructions, which are executed on the other machine(s). Control over the image is swapped back and forth via a traffic light metaphor. When you have the green light, you can make changes to the image. When you're finished with your edit, you pass control over to your colleague(s) by clicking on the red light.

You can use Net Painter within your organization on an intranet as well as over the Internet. The only restriction is that you must be running on a TCP/IP network (although corporate firewalls may need to be tweaked). Fractal recommends using a 28.8 modem if you're running over a dial-up account, but you can get by with a 14.4 modem. An ISDN connection would undoubtedly improve responsiveness. Net Painter is a cross-platform application, operating on Macintosh, Power Macintosh, and Windows 95 machines.

Corel PHOTO-PAINT

Any program that comes in a CorelDRAW! box has a huge advantage for the Windows user, in that it may already be sitting on your desktop. Corel's a huge seller and is an accepted standard at many PC-based organizations. Although Corel PHOTO-PAINT is filled with features, it has traditionally followed the pack, relying on me-too implementations. The latest incarnation, found in the CorelDRAW! 6 box, packs plenty of punch, however, with iterations of many features found in both Adobe Photoshop and Fractal Design Painter, along with some great filters licensed from plug-in developers, Xaos Tools and Alien Skin. The program also offers an impressive range of file conversion options.

Mac vs. PC
Corel PHOTO-PAINT is available only for the Windows platform. A paint editor will be packaged with the Macintosh version of CorelDRAW! 6.0, however.

Creating Seamless Textures With Corel PHOTO-PAINT

Corel has provided a huge variety of texture-making options. The program's CD-ROMs contain hundreds of premade textures in categories such as food, marble, paper, stone, textile, and wood. And Corel's fractal-based Texture Fill generator (Figure 11-8) can provide hours of fun as you explore its preset textures and create your own wild variations. The Texture Fill generator does not produce seamless textures, however. You'll have to do some tweaking with PHOTO-PAINT's Offset filter (which is functionally identical to its Photoshop namesake) to turn the textures into proper seamless tiles.

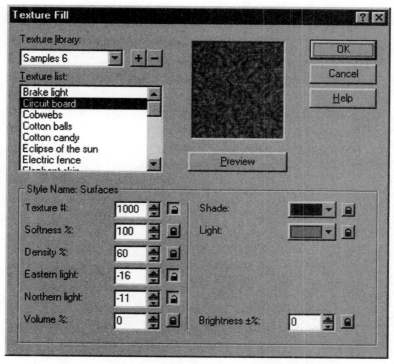

Figure 11-8: Corel PHOTO-PAINT's Texture Fill generator.

PHOTO-PAINT deserves the biggest pattern-making kudos for its licensing of Xaos Terrazzo seamless tiling plug-in, as well as its licensing of Paint Alchemy. We'll go into depth on Terrazzo in the next section on plug-ins.

Plug-in Punch!

Plug-in filters are little programs that work in conjunction with image editing packages—such as the aforementioned Adobe Photoshop, Fractal Design Painter, and Corel PHOTO-PAINT—that have been engineered to accept the Photoshop standard plug-in architecture. In addition to the big commercial applications, some shareware programs, such as Paint Shop Pro and NIH Image, can use the very same plug-in filters.

Plug-ins let you create impressive special effects with just a few clicks. In the following pages, we'll look at a number of plug-ins that can change the designs of your Web pages dramatically. Although there's a wide range of plug-ins on the market, we'll be focusing on those that apply most specifically to Web page projects.

Kai's Power Tools 3.0

Without question, there is no single plug-in package more popular than Kai's Power Tools (KPT). The attention is well deserved. The package is crammed full of awesome effects wrapped in an intriguing interface. While it's possible to experiment for hours at a time with KPT's many functions, Web page designers will be most interested in a handful of its powerful features:

- KPT Spheroid Designer
- KPT Gradient Designer
- KPT Texture Explorer
- KPT Seamless Welder

Mac vs. PC
Kai's Power Tools is available for both Macintosh and Windows platforms.

KPT Spheroid Designer: Bullet Factory
The Spheroid Designer is the spiritual cousin of the Orb in Woody Allen's *Sleeper*. It's round, it's cool, and it'll change your life (or at least your designs). New in KPT 3.0, this plug-in's sole purpose in life is to create delightfully textured 3D spheres. You can use these spheres as unique bullets in your Web pages.

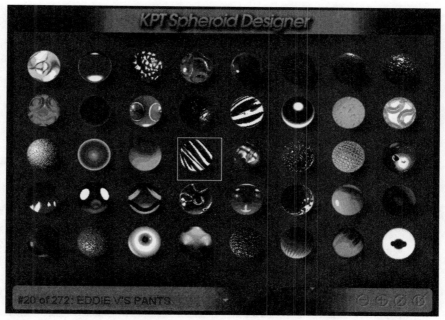

Figure 11-9: KPT Sphere presets—your marble collection was never this good!

If you're looking for inspiration, you can begin your spherical explorations by choosing from scores of preset spheres, as shown in Figure 11-9. There's little doubt that rock and roll was playing loudly in the studios when the presets were created. In typical Kai tradition, all of the presets have been meticulously named, with selections including Eddie V's Pants, Eighties Glob, Death Star, Sixties Housedress, Day Glo Curley Q, and Madonna's Favorite.

Once you've chosen the sphere preset, you can render it immediately, or you can tweak the many settings for hours on end. Figure 11-10 provides an annotated view of the KPT Spheroid Designer interface. There's a good deal to become accustomed to here. You may want to make a copy of this chart to help you locate all of the controls at a glance—even though the active control is always defined at the lower left hand corner of the control panel.

Figure 11-10: KPT Spheroid Designer.

At the center of the panel, the Big Ball provides an accurate preview of how the final rendered sphere will appear. The Big Ball is surrounded by four light sources, with individual settings for angle, polarity, highlight intensity, and color. To the upper left of the control panel, the Mutation Tree creates variations on the working sphere from similar to severe, depending on how high you click on the tree.

Looking down in a counterclockwise manner, you'll find the Global Controls at the bottom of the control panel. The three larger spheres influence sphere curvature, ambient lighting/ glossiness, and transparency. The four little dots regulate the light diffusion, diffuse hue, ambient intensity, and ambient hue. Looking across the interface, you'll see a stream of bubbles. These controls allow you to render from one to a zillion spheres at a clip. For the purposes of bullet creation though, you'll want to render individual spheres.

Just to the right of the bubble stream, you'll see the Bump Map controls. Bump maps are seamless grayscale images that allow you to impart a texture to a rendered sphere. The darker the gray, the deeper the shadow, and conversely, the lighter the gray, the higher the highlight. Bump maps can be repositioned by clicking and dragging in the bump map preview well. The four little dots to the right of the bump map preview well provide for control over the bump map's polarity, height, rotation, and zoom. Kai's Power Tools comes with a range of bump maps, and the program allows you to create your own, as well. The golf ball buttons used in Figure 11-11 are a good example of what's possible with a simple bump map.

Figure 11-11: A golf ball motif created with KPT Spheroid Designer.

KPT Gradient Designer: Smooth Sweeps

Sweeps, gradients, blends, fountain fills, vignettes, ramps, or color interpolations—call them what you will. In the not-so-distant past, it was only possible to blend between two different colors in one operation. Kai changed that, back in 1992, with the original Gradient Designer. Although it's now commonplace that illustration and paint programs allow for multicolored fills, KPT Gradient Designer 3.0 does an unparalleled job of creating dazzling custom fills between an unlimited number of colors with a comprehensive range of options. Figure 11-12 shows the Gradient Designer in action with a tasty sweep.

Figure 11-12: Ramp up to a virtual fountain of sweeping color interpolations and vibrant vignettes with the KPT Gradient Designer.

You can use the Gradient Designer to create distinctive background patterns for your Web pages. One of the most common background tricks is to create short-and-wide images that tile seamlessly. A short-and-wide image, by nature, should create a small file that downloads quickly. Since the pixels of a gradient fill should be similar top to bottom—in a horizontal sweep—the fill will tile with nary a seam.

Check the CD-ROM!
You'll find a nice selection of short-and-wide seamless textures on this book's CD-ROM.

Many of the variables in the Gradient Designer might seem to be over-the-top tweaky, but they provide for an incredible level of detail. The six basic controls are Mode, Loop, Repeat, Direction, Glue, and Opacity.

- Mode determines the shape of the gradient, allowing for common linear blends and sunbursts, as well as more exotic shapebursts, pathbursts, and gradients on paths.

- Loop assigns the direction of a gradient and the degree to which it is pinched to one end or the other.

- Repeat lets you "ping pong" a blend up from one to ten times within a selected area.

- Direction alters a gradient's angle of attack.

- Glue regulates how a gradient is applied to a selection, with options for Normal, Procedural (+ and -), Darken or Lighten Only, Multiply, Add, Subtract, Difference, and Screen modes.

- Opacity levels can be assigned by percentage or through predetermined settings, such as Checkerboards, Toned Grays, or Bright Hues.

Moving to the bottom of the KPT Gradient Designer window, you'll see that the controls never end. Settings for Hue, Saturation, Brightness, Contrast, Blur, Squeeze, and Cycle can be set for the overall gradient or for any portion within. For those who are gradientially challenged, Kai provides a good number of preset gradients to choose from should you not have the time to crank out your own custom designs.

KPT Texture Explorer: Fractal Finesse

The KPT Texture Explorer was one of the first filters responsible for setting Kai apart from all the other plug-in bundles. And yet, unrestrained use of the Texture Explorer can indelibly brand a piece of electronic art as being "overKaified." It's far too easy to be seduced by the Texture Explorer's fractal prowess. You should always avoid the electronic art equivalent of driving a car through Pep Boys with a magnet. A little restraint goes a long way. Having gotten that warning out of the way, let's take a gander at the Texture Explorer's interface.

Figure 11-13: Texture Presets are a great way to jump in.

Like other Kai filters, the KPT Texture Explorer comes equipped with a nice variety of preset effects, as shown in Figure 11-13. And once again, they're whimsically named, with selections such as Rasta UFOs, Aztec Shower Curtain, Trout on Tuesday, Frisbees in Space, and Grassy Knoll. You can start your textural explorations with an existing preset and quickly end up in texture la-la land.

Figure 11-14: The annotated KPT Texture Explorer 3.0 control panel.

The KPT Texture Explorer interface (Figure 11-14) continues the consistent Kai look and feel. On the left side of the control panel, you'll notice elements shared with the other plug-ins, such as Direction, Opacity, and Glue, as well as the fabled Mutation Tree. Looking downward, the gradient bar allows access to the gradient presets and controls. The sixteen smaller squares surrounding the selected texture display derivatives of the larger center texture and are triggered by the Mutation Tree. The rainbow marble between the Mutation Tree and the textures alters the derivative colors without affecting the textures.

Creating a cool texture is one thing, but making it a usable seamless texture is quite another, and that's where our next plug-in comes into play.

KPT Seamless Welder: Background Builder

Seams look good in one place: stockings. Creating quality seamless textures used to be an ordeal. While it's still not a trivial affair, at least it's relatively painless with the KPT Seamless Welder. Figure 11-15 shows a texture rendered with the Texture Explorer in Photoshop. We've selected a 216 X 216 pixel square, which will be converted into a usable background tile with the KPT Seamless Welder.

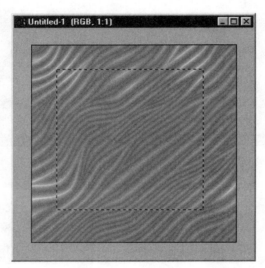

Figure 11-15: The original texture selected in Photoshop.

Figure 11-16: The KPT Seamless Welder makes it easy to create seamless tiles.

It's all done with mirrors, folks! When you use the Seamless Welder, you select an area within your original image, leaving an area surrounding the selection from which the filter will pull the image. The Seamless Welder mirrors and flips the image area from outside the active selection to the opposite side. There aren't a ton of controls to fiddle with. You can choose from either seamless or reflective modes, select the type of glue (to make it stick), and adjust the intensity of the effect. Figure 11-17 displays our frightening little texture as a background tile.

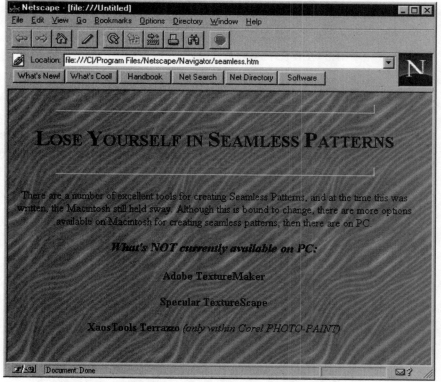

Figure 11-17: Here's our KPT-rendered tile on a Web page.

Although KPT's Flintstones-meet-the-Jetsons, consciousness-expanding interface may seem daunting at first, it will soon permeate your cerebral cortex. Take the time to perform a Vulcan mind meld with the program, and you will be amply rewarded.

But heed this warning: Kai's Power Tools is the black hole of time. Once you fire it up, don't expect to get up from your computer anytime soon. Have a nice trip!

Xaos Tools' Terrazzo—Tilemaker Supreme

When your seamless-texture-making needs aren't filled by the basic tiling functions provided by KPT, it's time to check out Xaos Tools's Terrazzo plug-in. Its sole purpose in life is to create scrumptious tiles with nary a seam. This little gem is a one-trick painted pony that you'll come back to ride happily again and again. Users of CorelDRAW! 6.0 will be happy to note that Xaos Tools's Terrazzo and Paint Alchemy plug-ins were bundled with the CorelDRAW! 6.0 package.

Mac vs. PC

Terrazzo has its roots on the Macintosh platform. The CorelDRAW! 6.0 bundle deal marked the plug-in's first appearance on the Windows platform.

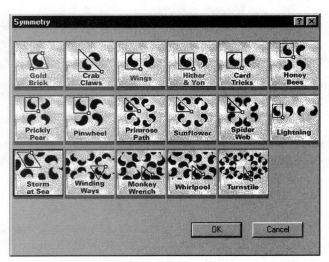

Figure 11-18: Terrazzo's 17 different symmetries allow for an infinite variety of seamless patterns.

Terrazzo provides far more powerful tile-creation options than the KPT Seamless Welder. Figure 11-18 displays the 17 different tiling symmetries that Terrazzo affords, in contrast to KPT's pair. Symmetries are the repeat patterns used to control the mirrors that create the seamless tiles. We created this original image in Photoshop, using the KPT Texture Explorer and Seamless Welder, but we were not satisfied with the tiling effect we'd obtained. Jumping to Corel PHOTO-PAINT, we opened the image and began experimenting with different symmetries and variations (Figure 11-19).

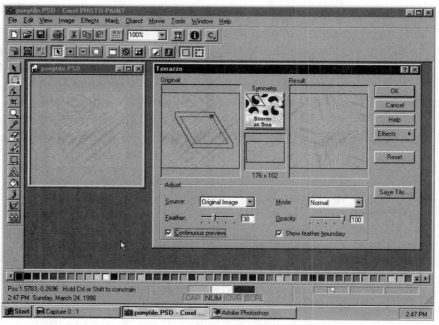

Figure 11-19: Tile tweaking with Xaos Tools' Terrazzo.

After choosing the Storm at Sea symmetry, we proceeded to tweak the feathering (the amount of "softness" around the edges of the tile, which help it blend seamlessly) to assure a smooth transition without getting too smudgy. Continuous preview mode allowed us to see how our finished tile would look as we moved the source area around the image well. Changing the size and shape of the image area affects the final size of the tile. You shouldn't think of seamless textures as always being square. In this case, our final texture measured 176 pixels across by 102 pixels tall.

Check the CD-ROM!

There are over 2,000 unique seamless textures created with Terrazzo on this book's CD-ROM.

Using the Terrazzo filter makes it easy to create groups of similar textures. These can be very useful when you want to vary backgrounds from Web page to Web page without having a wide variation in colors or patterns. By building your little collections of tiles from the same base image, you can help to ensure a consistent look and feel without imparting a stagnant background. It's a subtle trick, but one worth remembering.

Stand-alone Texture Generators

In the previous section, we focused on seamless-texture-generating Adobe Photoshop plug-ins. In this section, we will look at three stand-alone texture generators, Alien Skin Textureshop, Adobe TextureMaker, and Specular TextureScape. Each of these programs offers interesting and distinctive ways to create unique textures. Seamless texture generation has its roots in the world of 3D rendering and animation, and these three programs show their ties in varying degrees. With the use of background textures in Web page design being a far more recent phenomena, we can expect an increased development focus on features that support the environment, such as file formats and color muting.

Alien Skin Textureshop

Alien Skin Textureshop, from Virtus Corp., is unique in that it comes as both a stand-alone texture generator and as a Photoshop plug-in. Although it is marketed by Virtus, it was developed by Alien Skin software, the folks responsible for the Black Box plug-in set. The program generates seamless 2D and 3D textures with realistic lighting and shadows. The program goes about its work in an uncomplicated manner. You begin by choosing a master texture and then choose a mutation rate via a sliding control. Each time a master texture is mutated, it produces 15 different variations. The variations can be saved, previewed, and altered by means of lighting effects, scaling controls, and aspect ratio.

Mac vs. PC
Alien Skin 1.0 is available only for Macintosh.

While version 1.0 only had the ability to export files as PICT, BMP, or TIFF format, it's likely that an update will add GIF and JPEG formats. Fortunately, PageMill can convert PICT images on the fly, so you don't have to resort to a manual image conversion process (if you're working with the stand-alone version). Although the program was available initially only for Macintosh, the developer plans a Windows version.

Adobe TextureMaker

Adobe's TextureMaker, available initially only for Macintosh, takes an organic approach to texture building. The program comes with over 100 canned textures in categories that include clouds, fire, liquid, marble, and wood. The canned textures may be altered by changing lighting angles, color, and intensity. You can apply Photoshop plug-in filters, and it even allows you to emboss your own designs onto the textures. Much to its favor, TextureMaker will allow you to instantly create objects with a 3D look, including buttons and spheres. Like Alien Skin Textureshop, the first version of the TextureMaker is unfortunately limited in its file format export options. TextureMaker 1.0 only has the ability to create PICT and TIFF files. But once again, PageMill can handle the PICT-to-GIF conversion on the fly.

Mac vs. PC
Adobe's TextureMaker is available only for Macintosh.

Specular TextureScape

Specular TextureScape is the first of the stand-alone texture generators to go into a second version. The first version was no slouch, having received rave reviews from the press that included four stars from *Macworld*, *MacWEEK*, and *Publish*, as well as an Awesome rating from *New Media* and an Editor's Award (along with four mice) from *MacUser*. And as one might suspect, the extra release gives the program an added jump on the competition. With an interface that would be at home in the cockpit of a jet fighter, TextureScape affords a level of control that one would expect from a leading developer of three-dimensional rendering software.

Mac vs. PC
Specular's TextureScape 1.0 is currently available only for Macintosh. Word has it that version 2.0 will be released for Mac and Windows.

TextureScape 2.0 makes its magic by creating textures from PostScript outlines. The outlines are used to create patterns of objects that can be controlled by a number of means. The most intriguing textures are created by layering these patterns, one on top of another. The behavior the layers (and objects) display towards each other can be specified by blend, overlap, maximum, sum, difference, multiply, and divide. Object patterns can be altered by the grid origin, number of horizontal and vertical divisions, and variations.

Objects are assigned surface and shadow color, as well as shininess, transparency, bumpiness, convex/concave, and edge-softening characteristics. This provides total control of an object's appearance via slider controls or precise numeric input. Lighting is handled through four light sources, with variable angle, direction, intensity, and color. The program ships with more than 400 shapes and includes basic bezier drawing tools. Shapes in PostScript format can also be imported from any of the popular drawing programs, including Illustrator, FreeHand, and CorelDRAW!.

You'll find a demo version of TextureScape and Specular's awesome 3D Web Workshop on this book's CD-ROM.

Draw Programs

While the bitmap image editors that we discussed earlier have the distinct advantage of operating at the pixel level, it's safe to say that a good portion of Web graphics were created with one of the three most popular drawing packages. The latest versions of Adobe Illustrator, CorelDRAW!, and Macromedia FreeHand all have the ability to export bitmapped files from their vector artwork. The ease with which their vector illustrations may be rearranged is at the core of their popularity. While bitmap paint editors work strictly in pixels that are difficult to rework, vector-based drawing tools use mathematically derived objects that can be easily rearranged. Vector drawing programs can expedite the creation of both simple and complex graphic images.

These three programs are in a constant feature race as they try to outgun the competition. Each new version pushes one past the others in a certain feature set. Of the three, CorelDRAW! has grown to be the most feature laden, but recent versions of Illustrator and FreeHand have catapulted past DRAW in other respects. Unlike CorelDRAW!, both Illustrator and FreeHand are extensible through plug-in filters for both vectors and bitmaps. Instead of getting into a lengthy feature-by-feature comparison, we'll touch on the primary Web advantages of each program while avoiding a scorecard listing the number of fonts and amount of clip art.

Adobe Illustrator

Adobe Illustrator is the bezier drawing program that started it all. Over the past decade, the program has matured into a robust drawing environment that combines both vector drawing and bitmap images. Illustrator has grown slowly over the years, avoiding gimmickry while focusing on stability. Perhaps the biggest Web graphic advantage that Illustrator has over its competition is a simple one. You can drag and drop Adobe Illustrator images right into PageMill.

Illustrator is highly regarded for its reliability. Its files will rasterize cleanly into Photoshop with a minimum of surprises. Unfortunately, the Windows version of Adobe Illustrator has long lagged behind the Macintosh version. Hopefully, Illustrator 6.0 for Windows will appear by the time you read this, so that all the latest features, such as plug-ins, will be available on both platforms.

Mac vs. PC

Illustrator is available for both Macintosh and Windows platforms. The Windows version of Illustrator has lagged far behind the Macintosh version.

CorelDRAW!

What was once a compact, elegant drawing application has grown into the unwieldy behemoth of all graphic programs. The sheer volume of CorelDRAW! 6.0's feature set is unmatched by either Illustrator 6.0 or the stand-alone version of FreeHand 5.5. Its chief Web advantage is that it includes a full-featured drawing application (CorelDRAW!), a bitmap editor (Corel PHOTO-PAINT, see above), and a 3D modeling and rendering application (CorelDREAM 3D, a rebadged version of Ray Dream Designer).

Mac vs. PC

After a few false starts, CorelDRAW! finally arrived for the Macintosh platform in late summer 1996. The Mac version includes a powerful procedural texture generator not found in the corresponding Windows version. CorelDRAW! 7.0 for Windows is expected in the fall of 1996, with the Mac version to follow in the spring of 1997.

Corel has always allowed for the export and import of many different file formats. Corel's proprietary CMX format allows vector images to be placed on Web pages. These images can only be viewed by browsers, such as Netscape Navigator, that have been equipped with the CMX Viewer plug-in. Along more conventional Web image lines, CorelDRAW! has the ability to export files as both JPEG and GIF (including GIF 89a), GIF exports, as of build 169, were not rock solid , though. Rasterizing DRAW's native CDR files into Corel PHOTO-PAINT, however, provides acceptable results.

As experienced CorelDRAW! users know, the next version of the program is never more than a year away. Corel is unique among software developers in that it maintains a yearly development cycle. This corporate behavior can be considered either a negative or a positive, depending upon one's perspective.

Macromedia FreeHand

By itself, Macromedia FreeHand 5.5 is a formidable drawing program. But if there's a package that can go toe-to-toe with CorelDRAW! on a feature-by-feature basis, it's the Macromedia FreeHand Graphics Studio. The bundle combines the vector drawing acumen of FreeHand with 3D modeling and rendering (Extreme 3D), high-res bitmap editing (xRes), and font creation (Fontographer). FreeHand's biggest Web plus is the Shockwave plug-in, which allows browsers to access vector illustrations. This feature is most intriguing for sites that need to provide a high level of detail in their graphics, since the equation-based vectors will allow an almost infinite level of zooming in either direction.

Mac vs. PC
Macromedia FreeHand is available for both Macintosh and Windows platforms. The Windows version is incrementally behind the Mac version. FreeHand 7.0 should ship in the fall of 1996 for both platforms.

Macromedia established its Web presence early, and their Shockwave plug-in has gained an exponentially higher level of acceptance than Corel's CMX plug-in.

File Conversion Utilities

What's the big deal about file conversion? Well, if you have only a few files to convert, it isn't all that big a deal. Opening up a handful of images to resave in a specific format is a no-brainer once you've figured out which formats and flavor you're going to use, and you can probably handle most of your needs within your image editing application. The story changes when your volume goes up. File conversion utilities are called for when you have a large number of images to convert from one format to another. The power of batch file conversion allows your computer to automatically convert a list of images while you're off attending to more important matters—like lunch!

There are some great shareware programs out there, such as ThumbsPlus, Paint Shop Pro for Windows, and GIFConverter and GraphicConverter for Macintosh, but when the needs get extreme, the graphics professionals go looking for the power tools. And there's but one program that draws universal praise.

When the pros need industrial-strength batch conversions, they invariably turn to Equilibrium's Debabelizer. Although the interface can take a bit of getting used to, Debabelizer is one of those awesome programs that a Macintosh maven could always point to when a Windows zealot asked, "So what insanely great programs can't I get on the Windows platform?" The Macintosh maven needed only to reply, "Debabelizer."

Mac vs. PC

Debabelizer has traditionally been a Macintosh-only application. A Windows version should appear in 1996.

What makes Debabelizer so great? Simply put, the program affords the highest level of image conversion features, including:

- Highly scriptable batch processing.
- An unequaled selection of file formats.
- Unrivaled palette reduction options.

Moving On

It is a wise person who acknowledges that the only true constant is change. For nowhere is this more true than in the computer graphics world—it's the nature of the software beast. While this chapter reviewed some of the best programs available today for creating Web graphics on both Macintosh and Windows platforms, it's only a snapshot in history. In a constantly changing industry, it takes tons of time and devotion to stay on top of all the latest developments. You've got an advantage, however, in this book's Online Updates. We'll be keeping it updated with the latest changes as new versions and programs are released.

The next chapter pushes the graphics story one step further as we delve into the ultracool—Web page animation! We'll be looking at a number of ways to create animation on your Web page, including: animated GIFs, Java animations, and Macromedia's Shockwave.

chapter 12

Cool Animation Tools

It's safe to say that if you're reading this book, you're a child of the animated age. We've all grown up with the common experience of cartoons; we just had different reference points—Heckle and Jeckle, Tom and Jerry, or Itchy and Scratchy. This chapter will enable you to enter the world of animated Web pages. Together with the book's CD-ROM, it will provide the basic tools to create your own animations, whether you're working on a Macintosh or a PC.

Once you've seen your first animated Web page, you're bound to start dreaming about how you can bring that same excitement to your own designs. While animation might seem to be a daunting craft to master, rest assured, you can quickly learn how to add animation to your Web site. The trick is to determine which way to proceed. There are a number of methods to add animation to your Web site, from the easy to implement (and totally free) to the heavily technical (and consequently costly).

This chapter will demonstrate how easy it is to build GIF animations, and how you can use Java animation and Shockwave files to spice up your site. PageMill 2 makes it easy to just drag and drop these elements right into your Web page. We'll finish up with a little interview with the renowned Jaime Levy, who is among the vanguards of interactive design.

Animation Basics

You don't have to be the next Chuck Jones to successfully pull off an animated Web page. Just don't think of animation solely in the terms of your childhood cartoon heroes. There are different levels of animation—some achievable, some not. Although you won't create animations of a Loony Tunes caliber, you'll be able to create awesome sequences without having to enroll in art school.

Web page animations are created when the browser displays a series of frames (or cels) in sequence. Figure 12-1 shows the five different images used in a simple animation. The frames are sequenced (1, 2, 3, 4, 5, 4, 3, 2) and looped so that they appear to pulse in and out. As the browser displays the subsequent frames, the viewer gets the impression that the warning sign is flashing in a subtle manner.

Figure 12-1: These five frames are sequenced to create a pulsating warning sign.

The individual images were created with Fonthead's Holstein font and Adobe Photoshop's Gaussian Blur filter. The first image is unblurred, while the other four images have been blurred in increasing levels. You'll find a number of these pulsing signs in GIF89a format on this book's CD-ROM, as well as on the Online Updates.

While the types of animation you can create from scratch are only limited by your imagination, proper execution can take a good bit of time. The pulsing sign technique is easy to accomplish and can be delivered by any one of a number of methods. We'll begin by discussing server push.

Server Push (& Client Pull)

In the bad old days of Netscape Navigator 1.1, *server push* was the primary means to animate Web pages. This technique uses CGI scripts to push (send) a series of image files from the server to the client's browser. The image "moves" as each succeeding file is downloaded. Server push animations work best with tiny, limited palette animations. The smaller the individual files (animation frames) are, the faster the animation will download and play.

Server push is a technique that's fallen out of vogue, due to its propensity to "eat the pipe." With a server push, the connection between the server and the browser is open until either the server stops sending data (when an animation sequence ends) or when the Web surfer says, "Stop, I've had enough!" by hitting the Stop button. If the animation loops, or constantly cycles, it can consume bandwidth at a torrid pace.

Pushy, Pushy, Pushy

Two of the most notable sites to use server push in the early days were the Web zine *Word* (http://www.word.com) and the Web site developer, Razorfish (http://www.razorfish.com). Both endeavors are New York City-based, which brings some validity to the claim that New Yorkers are the pushiest people in the world (or at least on the World Wide Web). As of late May 1996, Razorfish continued to use a number of very cool pushes. You'll read more about *Word*, toward the end of this chapter.

Since server pushes can only be accomplished with CGI scripts, you should talk to your webmaster to see if any suitable scripts are available or if pushes are allowed at all. If your server's pipe is on its way to being maxed, there's a good chance that you'll be discouraged from using pushes.

Here are some fun places to see server push animations:

- The Langley Nite Owl Web Site
  http://yowl.library.pitt.edu/animate/
- Pix Technologies
  http://www.pix.com/www/index.html
- Levi's Jeans
  http://www.levi.com/menu
- The Debt Clock
  http://www.fusebox.com/debtclock/
- Xaos Tools
  http://www.xaostools.com/panfx/bubbles.html

Client pulls are similar to server pushes in that they are both schemes to download multiple files. The difference is as their names infer. While server pushes are fired from the server, client pulls are prompted from the browser. Client pulls are initiated by HTML coding, which forces the client to tell the sever, "Send me this particular file in X seconds." With server pushes, the pipe is open until broken. With client pulls, the pipe is reopened each time the client requests a new file. Server pushes can be faster, as you do not have to renegotiate a connection each time. The trade-off is made in the loss of pipe.

Of the two techniques, only client pulls remain in vogue. Server pushes have been outdated by new animation techniques. Client pulls, however, are fun little devices that allow the Web site designer to deliver a sequence of complete Web pages in a manner reminiscent of the old Burma Shave highway billboards (although you should use this procedure with artistic discretion). You can also use client pulls to create automatic "forwarding" pages when you move a page from one URL to another. When a browser hits the old URL, the forwarding page tells them to reset their book-mark, and (after a set amount of time) automatically sends the new page down to the browser.

More background information on both server push and client pulls is available on Netscape's Web site at http://search.netscape.com/assist/net_sites/pushpull.html. You'll even find a fun little server push animation of the Netscape mascot, Mozilla, at http://search.netscape.com/assist/net_sites/mozilla/index.html. While server push is reserved for those with a close relationship with their webmaster, (or with their own server), the following technique can be accomplished by anyone.

GIF Animation

If you're looking for an inexpensive, fast, and simple way to get your Web site hopping, look no further. Unlike techniques such as server push, GIF89a animations can bring movement to your site without costing much time, cash, or bandwidth. They're easy to implement in PageMill; just drag them and drop them into your pages as you would any other GIF image. You can use GIF89a animations for everything from bullets and buttons to imagemaps. PageMill 2's Preview mode allows you to see exactly how the animation will appear on the finished page.

Want to Animate Your Backgrounds?

You're out of luck. Animated GIF backgrounds are not supported in Netscape 2.x (and up). It's a true bummer of Web page design life ... a well-executed, morphing textured background would be too cool for words.

While the multipart GIF89a format has been in existence since the dark ages of 1989 (hence the name), GIF89a animations were only introduced to the World Wide Web community by Netscape Navigator 2.0 in late 1995. When Netscape took the wraps off GIF89a Web page animation, one of the first places it came into vogue was on advertising banners. Ad agency Web designers quickly discovered that they could use GIF animations to accomplish many of the design tricks that were previously possible only with server pushes.

The best way to learn about animated GIFs is to cruise the Web in search of some good examples. We've taken the time to scope out some of the best sites for you to take a gander at GIF89a, the poor Web designer's animation format of choice.

No Plug-ins Required!
Your visitors will not need any special plug-ins to view animated GIFs as long as they are using Microsoft's Internet Explorer or Netscape Navigator, versions 2.0 or better.

An Awesome Collection of Animated GIFs

http://trureality.com/
The Tru Realities GIF Animation Gallery is, perhaps, the foremost collection of GIF89a animations on the World Wide Web. Featuring a highly functional framed interface (there's a non-framed version, as well), Tru Realities shoehorns over 1400 GIF animations into a compact site (as shown by Figure 12-2). The selections range from scores of little rotating buttons and cute dancing rules to gorgeous three-dimensional animations.

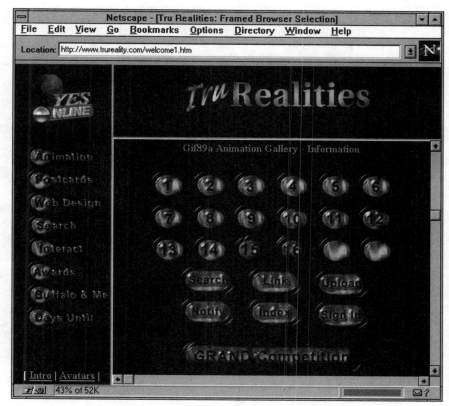

Figure 12-2: Tru Realities framed interface provides access to countless animated GIFs.

As this was being written, the Tru Realities animation site was in the process of expanding into its sixteenth gallery. The individual galleries are selectable through a client-side imagemap. They are then broken down into separate collections, which are accessible through drop-down lists. Individual animations are thoughtfully annotated with their creator's names (Figure 12-3). Tru Realities provides a unique showcase for the work of Web animation artists, beginner and expert alike.

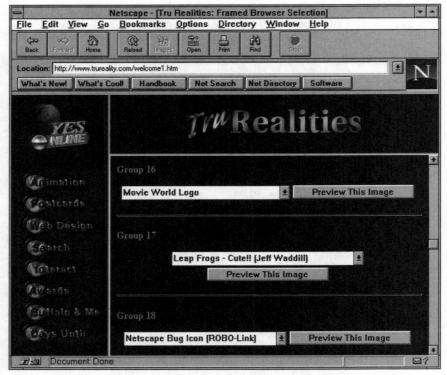

Figure 12-3: The Animation section is divided into galleries and drop-down lists.

Webmistress Marlina Mahoney has pulled off a number of neat tricks in implementing the site. When visitors choose an animation, and click on the Preview This Image button, the animation is played in a separate preview window. This is accomplished through the use of a neat little JavaScript hack, as shown by the cute dancing egg in Figure 12-4. Another JavaScript automatically keeps track of page revisions. The site features update notification, so you can register your e-mail address and get mail sent to you when the animation library gets updated.

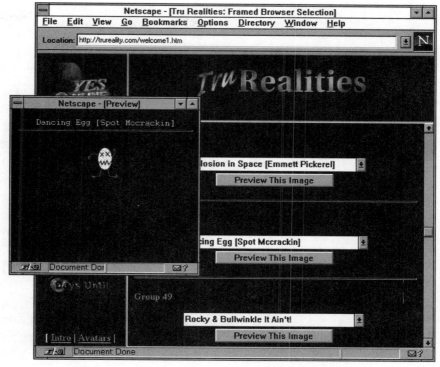

Figure 12-4: A slick little JavaScript routine pops up a preview window for each animation on the Tru Realities Web site.

Tru Realities is a wonderful resource for Web designers and lovers of spicy finger food, alike. In addition to its huge storehouse of animated GIFs, Tru Realities features a jumplist of other animation sites and seamless background texture sites. There's even a collection of links to Buffalo wings recipes and Buffalo, New York Web sites! (You guessed right—Tru Realities is based in Buffalo.)

Here's a handful of additional Web sites that feature GIF89a animations:

- Mikey's Collection of Animated GIFs
  http://www.geocities.com/SoHo/1085/

- The 1st Internet Gallery of GIF89a Animation
  http://members.aol.com/royalef/gallery.htm

- The GIF Animation Thrift Shop
  http://www.tiac.net/users/stacey/gifshop.html
- Rose's Animated GIFs
  http://www.wanderers.com/rose/animate.html

Once you've seen a few dozen animated GIFs, you'll begin to get the gist of it. Creating your own animations is not an insurmountable task, nor will you have to break the bank. The Macintosh freeware program, GifBuilder, included on this book's CD-ROM, is well implemented and easy to learn. Windows users will find the slightly more complicated "bookware" GIF Construction Set on the CD-ROM, as well.

Now, let's see how easy it is to create an animated GIF. We'll start by looking at Yves Piguet's elegant little Mac freeware program, GifBuilder.

GifBuilder

Yves Piguet's GifBuilder is a one-purpose tool that does exactly what it sets out to do. This tiny program's sole purpose in life is to create GIF89a animations. It does so through an uncluttered interface that lets you build animations with drag-and-drop ease. All you need to do to build your first animation is start the program, open up the folder containing the individual files, and start dragging the files into GifBuilder's Frames window (you can also import files through a dialogue box, if you wish). Once you drag a file into the Frames window, its specifications are displayed, as shown by Figure 12-5. The window shows you the size, position, disposal method, frame delay, and transparency of each individual frame.

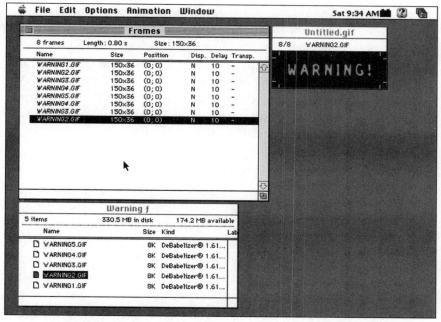

Figure 12-5: Drag and drop your individual images into GifBuilder's Frames window.

These specifications control how each frame is displayed and dealt with. The Options menu provides access to interlacing, color palette, color depth (1, 2, 4, or 8 bits per pixel), dithering, image size, background color, looping, transparency, frame position, interframe delay, and disposal method controls. You can use the position controls to reposition an image within the animation without creating a new file.

Rearranging Frames

Once you've got your images into the Frames window, they're easy to boss around. If you bring the individual frames into the Frames window in the wrong sequence, don't fret. You can change the sequence by dragging and dropping the frames within the window. In addition, the Edit menu gives you the ability to duplicate a frame, reverse the order of selected frames, or sort selected frames by alphanumeric sequence. If you need to remove a frame, all you have to do is select it, and press the Delete key. As you select individual frames, they'll be previewed in a separate window. You can preview the entire animation either by running it in its entirety or by stepping through the frames. The animation preview features are accessed either through the Animation menu or by keyboard shortcut (Command+R and Command+T, respectively). Double-clicking on a frame will open up the image file in your image editing application.

Creating a Scrolling Text Animation

Talk about your cheap tricks! Figure 12-6 shows how a single file was used to create a scrolling, ticker-like warning marquee. This was done by assigning a sequence of horizontal (x) coordinates, starting with a position that was far enough to move the first image to the left of the frame. The animation's background color was set to the same black as the image's background. The disposal method was set to the background color, as well; this prevents the marqueed text from leaving behind any not-so-happy trails (little chunks of each frame).

Once the settings are complete, all you have to do is save the file, and GifBuilder will do its thing and create a new animated GIF file. The sequence that started out as 15 frames of an 8K file will be converted into a single 8K animated file. GifBuilder is a beautiful thing, indeed. But don't worry, if you're not using a Macintosh, you haven't been left out in the cold. Next up on the slate is Steve Rimmer's Windows-based GIF Construction Set.

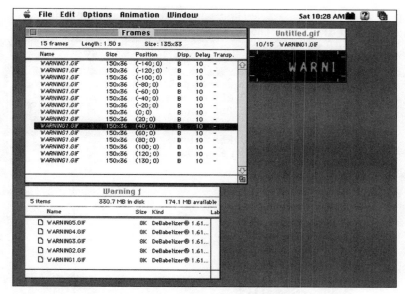

Figure 12-6: Creating a scrolling text animation is as easy as setting the position, background, and disposal methods.

GIF Construction Set

Steve Rimmer's GIF Construction Set has been the GIF animation tool of choice for many Windows-based Web designers. Although it takes a slightly different tack than the Mac-based GifBuilder (and lacks the latter's drag-and-drop ease), it offers powerful control over GIF animations. The program is bookware; if you like and use the program, Rimmer asks that you buy a copy of his novel, *The Order*. For only $6.99 (plus shipping, if you can't find the book locally), GIF Construction Set is an incredible bargain.

Like GifBuilder, GIF Construction Set is a one-trick pony. It exists primarily to build GIF animations (OK, so you can use it to just assign transparency to a single GIF image, but let's not nitpick). But instead of using drag and drop to build sequences, GIFCon uses its Insert Object palette (as shown in Figure 12-7) to add images. In addition to inserting images, the Insert Object palette is used to place control blocks, comments, text, and looping controls.

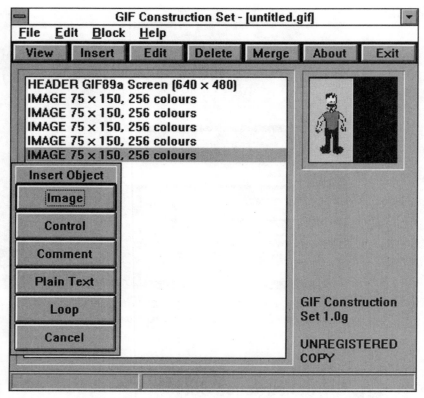

Figure 12-7: No drag and drop here. The Insert Object palette is used to place elements.

GIF Construction Set uses separate control blocks to handle transparency, user input, interframe delay, and disposal method. The Edit Control Block dialog box (Figure 12-8) provides convenient access to these characteristics. The program's eyedropper tool makes transparent color selection a snap. One control block can carry through an entire animation, unless you need to fiddle with things like XY-coordinates, as in the scrolling marquee example.

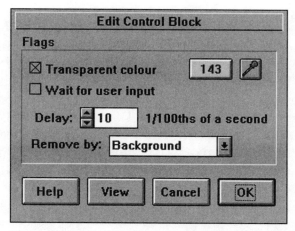

Figure 12-8: The Edit Control Block dialog box takes charge of individual frame options.

While GIFCon 1.0g lacks the sequence-shuffling (and frame-naming) savvy of GifBuilder, we hold hope that these features will be added in future versions. The program packs plenty of wallop, and who knows...if you aren't into reading Steve Rimmer's book, you can always give it away as a gift!

Here are some great places to learn more about animated GIFs:

■ Netscape—GIF Animations
http://home.netscape.com/comprod/products/navigator/version_2.0/gif_animation/index.html

■ GIF Animation on the WWW
http://www.reiworld.com/royalef/gifanim.htm

■ cnet features—techno—gif89a
http://www.cnet.com/Content/Features/Techno/Gif89/

Want to Turn a Video Into an Animated GIF?
Check out the Converting QuickTime to GIF Animation Tutorial at http://www.zone.org/foltz/qt-gif/.

What About the Commercial Apps?

While most of the early innovations in GIF89a animation have come from the shareware developers, the big commercial developers have been hard at work as well. Recognizing the need to integrate the technology into their existing applications, graphics software developers such as Corel and Macromedia have incorporated GIF89a animation into their graphics suites. As this book came screaming down to its deadline, we were able to take a quick look at Corel's WEB.MOVE from the Corel WEB.GRAPHICS Suite (as shown in Figure 12-9).

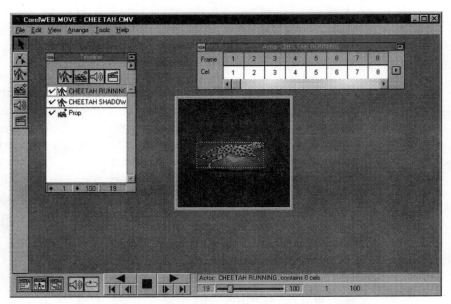

Figure 12-9: Corel.WEB.MOVE works with actors and timelines allowing export to GIF89a, Java, and QuickTime formats.

WEB.MOVE is a full-featured animation program that allows users to create intricate GIF89a animation files with object paths and complicated scoring. GIF animation is only a start, however. The program supports Java and QuickTime (Apple's cross-platform audio-video standard) formats, making it an attractive choice for Windows-based Web developers.

Some GIF89a Animation Pointers

Many of the things you've learned about creating great GIF files apply to animated GIFs as well. You want to ensure speed and stability while providing a pleasant experience for your visitors. Animation adds a new list of things to watch for:

- **Keep them small**. By now, this one should be obvious. The bigger the size of the image and the more frames, the longer it will take to download. Be realistic about what you can accomplish.

- **Don't interlace the images**. Interlacing is cool for static GIFs, but not for animated GIFs. The "underwater look" just doesn't cut it.

- **Watch your interframe delay times**. You can specify this time in increments of a hundredth of a second, or you can designate it to be "as fast as possible." Quite often, you'll need to slow things down a bit to make your animation run smoothly. Keep in mind that "as fast as possible" means different timing on different machines.

- **Use looped animations judiciously**. Hard drive racking can be irritating to your visitors, as the animations constantly play from their disk cache. Once the browsers fully support the loop command, we can all avoid using infinite loops.

- **Throw out the garbage.** Use the proper disposal method lest your animation be plagued with not-so-happy trails of digital litter.

- **Limit the number of animations on a page**. More than a few animations on a page can be overkill. Use your best judgment.

- **Above all: go wild!** If you have a killer idea for an animation, by all means, try it. If it doesn't work out on the first, second, or even third shot, keep plugging away until you make it work.

Next, we'll take a look at Macromedia's Shockwave, a technology that has combined slick animation techniques with sizzling soundtracks and scintillating scripting.

Shockwave Animation

Macromedia's Shockwave first rumbled through the Web in late 1996. The technology has raised quite a stir in the Web community by bringing the power of Macromedia Director and the creativity of its massive user base (well over 250,000 users) to the Internet. Director is the most prevalent tool in the multimedia industry, and Macromedia boasts some of the most talented third-party developers in the world.

Shockwave adds an enhanced level of interactivity to Web pages. While you can set up a standard GIF animation as a hot link or even an imagemap, once the visitor clicks on the image, the image (itself) doesn't do anything. It merely sends the visitor off to the linked Web page or anchor. The most basic Shockwave animations, however, can be programmed to do something when clicked on (other than simply jumping to another page). A button might beep, appear as if it were clicked, or an additional animation sequence may be triggered. And best of all, Shockwave animations can be added to Web pages created with PageMill 2 by simply dragging and dropping the file from the desktop into your page.

Need the Shockwave Plug-in?
We've saved you the time and trouble of downloading the Shockwave plug-in! You'll find it included on this book's CD-ROM, along with a host of other essential plug-ins.

Shockwave animations can deliver everything from arcade game action to interactive edutainment, via the Internet. Since Macromedia Director is the tool of choice for so many professional multimedia developers, it's a natural that these firms are flocking to the World Wide Web to hawk their skills. The high caliber of Shockwave animations available on the Web today is staggering. Acclaimed CD-ROM developers such as Pop Rocket and Mediaband are literally giving their Shockwave games away as an enticement to pull visitors into their Web sites.

In order for visitors to experience Shockwave animation, they must have the Shockwave plug-in installed in their browser. The plug-in has proven to be one of the most popular on the Internet; Macromedia claims that their site has served up million upon millions of copies of the installation files. Shockwave will be bundled with Netscape Navigator and Microsoft's Internet Explorer. Macromedia has also announced that it will be integrated with Apple's Cyberdog technology.

Want to Learn More?

Darrel Plant's *Shockwave! Breathe New Life into Your Web Pages* (Ventana), is a great resource for budding animators. As a special treat, you'll find sample Shockwave animations from Darrel's book on this book's CD-ROM.

To create your own Shockwave sequences from scratch, you'll have to get your hands on a copy of Macromedia Director 4 or 5. Director movie files need to be processed through Macromedia's Afterburner utility (which they provide free of charge to registered Director users, via their Web site) to create a Shockwave file. It doesn't matter what platform you create or play back on. Shockwave is a cross-platform technology, fully supported on both Macintosh and Windows.

You don't have to have Director to add Shockwave to your site, however. It's easy to incorporate existing Shockwave files from third-party sources. There's a vast array of ready-made Shockwave animations out on the Internet for the picking. Of course, you'll have to be respectful of the creator's copyrights, but that should go without saying. Copyright doesn't have to be a problem. In fact, many of the smaller Shockwave goodies are freeware!

Shock-Bauble!

http://207.69.132.225/abtboble.htm
You'll find Shockwave tidbits galore at the Shock-Bauble Web site
(see Figure 12-10). The site was created by @dver@ctive, an interactive media developer located in Chapel Hill, NC. Shock-Baubles
are compact animations, with most files weighing in at under 12K.
These tasty little tidbits are for the most part freeware. If you use
one of the more than one hundred Shock-Baubles on the site, in
most cases, you owe only a wink and a nod to the developer
(although a small credit on your Web page is a nice touch, as is an
e-mail message thanking the bauble's creator). The cool little
calculator, shown in Figure 12-11, is an excellent example of what
can be accomplished with Director's Lingo programming language. There's no need to study up on your code—just download
the file and drag it into PageMill!

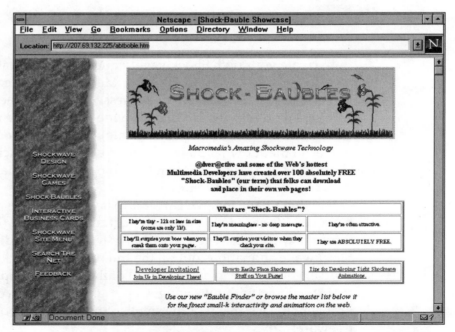

*Figure 12-10: The Shock-Bauble Web site is a great place to pick up some tight
Shockwave animations.*

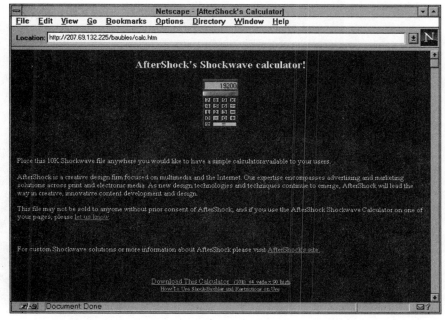

Figure 12-11: Add a cute interactive calculator to your Web site without hacking any code!

The Shock-Bauble site includes work from developers in the U.S., Europe, and Australia (among other locales). Shockwave is truly an international phenomenon, with "shocked" sites shaking to the surface around the globe. Here's a selection of some of the best we've found:

- Macromedia's Shockwave Epicenter
  http://www.macromedia.com/Tools/Shockwave/
  Gallery/Epicenter/index.html

- Marc's Shockwave Shop
  http://mediaband.com/shockwave/index.html

- Pop Rocket's Game Arena
  http://www.poprocket.com/shockwave/

- The ShockeR List
  http://www.shocker.com/shocker/

- Mama's Shockwave Salon
  http://www.eat.com/shockwave-salon/
- AfterShock
  http://www.ashock.com/html/main.html
- The Adrenaline Vault
  http://www.avault.com/shock.html
- Abstract Funhouse Shockwave Page
  http://starcreations.com/abstract/funhouse/ga-shock.htm

Some Shockwave History

If you're interested in learning more about the history of Shockwave and Director, check out what Marc Canter, cofounder of Macromedia has to say at http://mediaband.com/shockwave/shockstorymain.html.

 ## Java Animation

It's nearly impossible to escape all the hype that's been attached to Sun's Java programming language. Rest assured, we're not going to get into how to create full-blown Java apps—it's just not an easy hack for the average Web page designer and it's not within the scope of this humble book. However, there's one neat way that you can incorporate Java into your site without exploding your brain: Java animation. A number of applications have quickly come to market to deliver fast and easy Java animation. And once again, PageMill 2 makes adding animation a snap by allowing you to drag and drop Java applets straight from the desktop (although the Java animation programs can commonly create all the requisite HTML coding, if you so choose to use it).

Gamelan!
http://www.gamelan.com
The megasite of Java applets.

Egor Animator

http://www.sausage.com/
It's Alive! Egor Animator, from Australian developer, Sausage Software (the folks responsible for the HotDog HTML editor), was the first commercial Windows program to exploit the possibilities of Java animation. Sausage was quick to market and quick to come out with a second version, as well. The latest edition, version 2.0, sports a whimsical interface, as shown in Figure 12-12. It allows you to create simple animations from GIF or JPEG files created in other applications.

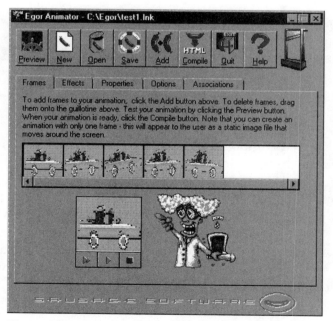

Figure 12-12: With a tip of the hat to Dr. Frankenstein, Egor Animator adds a jolt of Java animation.

Egor gives you the capability to add a soundtrack to an entire animation, as well as the ability to link a sound to a specific frame. Just the ticket for that smashing window or falling anvil! The program also lets you link a URL to an individual frame, which makes it simple to create rotating advertising banners for multiple URLs.

WebBurst

http://www.powerproduction.com/
Macintosh Web developers in search of serious Java animation will be wise to check out powerproduction's WebBurst. With great reviews from the press, including a "Freakin' Awesome" from Mac Addict and four stars from MacWEEK, the program comes highly recommended. WebBurst Java applets are more than simple animations. The program allows users to build truly interactive Java animation with support for conditions such as play, stop, show, and hide.

Check the CD-ROM!
Take a look on this book's CD-ROM. . . you'll find a demo version of powerproduction's WebBurst. Cool!

WebBurst imports AIFF and SND sounds, along with PICT images, through drag and drop. Since the program features an integrated set of drawing tools, users are not hamstrung by imported images. Objects are treated as animation sprites, allowing for precise positioning and movement along a path with control over speed. When an animation is complete, sounds are exported in AU format, images are exported as GIFs, and the Java applets and supporting HTML code are written. The code is then pasted into your HTML document.

QuickTime Movies

Want to put some real moving pictures on your Web site? QuickTime movies are the most popular way to deliver video clips via the Web. The medium allows you to show everything from your Frisbee-catching family dog to your latest whizzy invention in glorious full motion. Like the other forms of animation, it's easy to add QuickTime animation to Web pages in PageMill by simply dragging and dropping the files from the desktop (you can also use the place command or copy and paste).

QuickTime movies are typically very large, since they contain both sound and video. Adding a QuickTime clip to a Web page is a powerful way to convey information, but you should always make the QuickTime movie an optional choice for your visitors. Put the clip on a separate page, and make sure the link to that page includes a polite warning about the file size.

Unfortunately, creating QuickTime clips is a relatively hardware-intensive task. You'll need a video capture board in your PC or Mac (or an AV-Mac) and a VCR or camcorder in addition to a video-editing application such as Adobe Premiere. Of course, if you have a buddy that already has all of those goodies, you're probably in luck!

A Site Done Right: *Word*

http://www.WORD.com

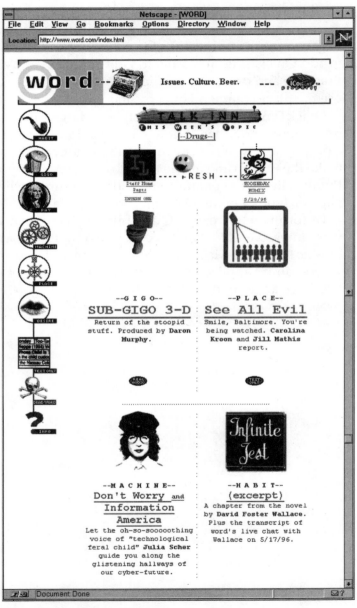

Figure 12-13: Get the WORD!

Jaime Levy defines the edge. As Creative Director for the WORD.com zine (Figure 12-13), Jaime is a catalyst in shredding perceptions of what great Web site design is all about. She began designing for the Web after five years of intense Director experience and a graduate degree from NYU. Her work with online animation has earned her great acclaim, and her speaking engagements are priceless. In addition to honing her craft until the wee hours, Jaime teaches at NYU's Interactive Telecommunications Program (ITP).

I hooked up with Jaime via e-mail (how else would you expect?), and the following serves as proof that clicking those Mailto links can get you in big trouble. Jaime pulls no punches.

What was your background before *Word*? How did it prepare you for the Web, design-wise?

I created the first electronic magazine in 1990, CyberRag, *as my graduate thesis at NYU ITP, the graduate Interactive Telecommunications Program in the film school at the Tisch School of Arts. My background was in film and video. I came to study this because I was a video artist who was interested in interactive TV.*

When did you first start using server push, GIF89a, Shockwave, and Java animations? Are you still doing pushes?

I did the first server push on WORD in March of '95 when it was the only way to do animation. I used Shockwave on WORD as soon as the plug-in was available cross-platform and the first GIF89a immediately, since they really required nothing on the client side. As of June 1, 1996, the real distinction for using the different types of animation is as follows:

The only reason to use CGI animation anymore is that they are the only form of cross-platform streaming animation that doesn't require a plug-in. I would use CGI pushes over GIFanimator, Java, and Shockwave when creating an animation that uses over 5 frames. Often, I push QuickTime videos which have been turned into animated GIFs, with many (sometimes up to 200) frames. CGI streaming is great because the user can just sit on a page and have the pictures pushed through as they come, without worrying about bandwidth. Whether the user is 14.4 or

T1, it will just push the frames through as fast as the client (user) can handle it. This is great, especially when accompanied by a Real Audio soundtrack. We used this in Roxanna's nails where you hear the ICon secretary blabbing about the Internet in relation to her nails and as she talks it just pushed images (Figure 12-14).

Figure 12-14: The "Roxanna's Nails" story features a Real Audio soundtrack running over a server-pushed animation of (what else) Roxanna's nails!

If this were Shockwave or a GIF animation, we could only have 3 to 6 frames since they are big and would require the user to download the file in its entirety before it played. With CGI I can just keep pushing them though without the wait period. If you aren't cycling through images, but want to push endless images, CGI is the only way to go. I would use Shockwave ONLY if the animation was interactive. Although some people say Shockwave cycles look better than GIF animator cycles, I still think GIF animations have the advantage over Shockwave, as they don't require the plug-in. Shockwave is great if you want to have it click to several other places or do more than one thing. I basically only use Shockwave if the animation is interactive. And Shockwave is still the only way to do synched sound.

GIFanimation is the way to go for doing short, tiny 2 to 6 cel animations. However, you only want a couple on a page at a time, as the program is weak for handling timing and looping. Its best point is that it requires no plug-ins, and is consistent from PC to Mac in terms of display and downloading.

How did your audience react to the *WORD* animations? What kind of feedback did you get?

We got great reactions because we made small and beautiful 3D animations that enhanced the content. As opposed to just using animation for the sake of animation. We used it for animated titles and every section in WORD has a different animation to go with the content. Most GIF animations on the Web suck, because they make the page look as if it's blinking, but if used correctly and subtly, they can be effective for a multimedia experience.

Has the Net eaten your life? Have you become a total/Web/slave, like the rest of us?

I am a slave to developing content for new media. The Web is just my distribution medium of choice for 95-96. As far as I am concerned now, the WEB is DEAD! I am now developing content for distribution on the TV set. The stuff I am making now is either demos for people to navigate through using their remote control on their TV using WebTV or creating real-time online virtual environments in the Palace.

Moving On

Adding just the right amount of animation can change your site from a collection of static pages into an action-packed fun ride. As a Web designer, it's your responsibility to determine what type of animation to add to your pages, if any. Whether you decide on adding server push, GIF 89a, Shockwave, or Java animations depends upon your competencies, resources, and circumstances. Poorly executed and gratuitous animations are a distraction at best. Well-executed animations, on the other hand, are an invaluable addition.

As with so many design decisions, less is more and more is less. True elegance in Web page design is a direct result of simplicity.

part 5

Appendices

appendix A

About the Companion CD-ROM

The CD-ROM included with your copy of *Web Publishing With Adobe PageMill 2* contains valuable software programs, texture, button, and background files, as well as examples files.

Navigating the CD-ROM

Your choices for navigating the CD-ROM appear on the opening screen. You can quit the CD, view the software, browse the Hot Picks, or learn more about Ventana.

The software is listed in the Install folder on the CD. You can install the items one at a time to your hard drive by dragging them from the folder onto your desktop.

To View the CD-ROM

Windows

Double click on the LAUNCHME.EXE file from your Windows Explorer or File Manager. For optimum WINDOWS performance:

1. Copy the LAUNCHME.EXE and LAUNCHME.INI files to the same directory on your hard drive.

2. Open the LAUNCHME.INI file in a text editor such as Notepad.

3. Find the section in the INI file that reads:
   ```
   [Memory]
   ;ExtraMemory=400
   ;Amount of kBytes over and above physical memory for
   use by a projector.
   ```

4. If your computer has enough memory to do so, delete the semicolon from the ExtraMemory line, and change the ExtraMemory setting to a higher number.

5. Save the changes to the LAUNCHME.INI File, and close the text editor.

6. With the CD-ROM still inserted, launch the viewer from the hard drive.

If the viewer still does not run properly on your machine, you can access the material on the CD-ROM directly through Windows Explorer.

Macintosh

Double click on the CD-ROM icon on your desktop. If the viewer does not run properly on your machine, follow the below instructions for optimum performance:

1. Copy the Launch Me file to your hard drive.

2. Click once on the Launch Me file.

3. Select Get Info from the File menu.

4. If your computer has enough memory to do so, change the amount in the Preferred size field to a higher number.

5. Close the info box.

6. With the CD-ROM still inserted, launch the viewer from the hard drive.

If the viewer still does not run properly on your machine, you can access the files on the CD-ROM directly by double-clicking on the CD icon on your desktop.

Software on the CD-ROM

Software	Descriptions
3-D Web Workshop demo	3-D Web Workshop provides a comprehensive set of tools and pre-rendered graphics for quickly and easily adding high-impact 3-D graphics and animations to Web pages. Visit Specular's Web site at: http:// www.specular.com.
Adobe Acrobat Reader 2.1	A portable document reader. To download the latest version, visit Adobe's Web site at: http:// www.adobe.com.
BACKGROUNDS	A number of seamless pattern GIF backgrounds created by Daniel Gray for use with Web site creation.
BBEdit Lite 3.5.1	BBEdit Lite is a freeware text editor, built on the same foundation technology as the commercial version.
BBEdit4.0 demo	BBEdit 4.0 is a high-performance text and HTML editor for Web page designers, programmers, and anyone else with a need to search, manipulate, and transform large amounts of textual data.

Software	Descriptions
BULLETS	Hundreds of bullets created by Daniel Gray for use in Web site design and creation.
BUTTONS	A wide variety of buttons created by Daniel Gray for use in Web site design and creation.
Crescendo 2.02	A MIDI plug-in for Netscape 2.0 browsers which lets users listen to MIDI files embedded in Web pages. Web Site developers can now add background music to their Web pages. To find out more about Live Update's Crescendo, visit their Web site at: http://www.liveupdate.com.
Envoy Plug-In	A plug-in for Netscape Navigator 2.0 that enables viewing of Envoy documents. Envoy is a rich document format that preserves any document's page layout, fonts, and graphics in a compact format ideal for Web publishing. Envoy is a product of Tumbleweed Software.
GIFANIMS	GIF animations created by Daniel Gray.
GIFBuilder	A utility for creating animated GIF files.
JPEGView	A graphics viewing and manipulation program.
Lightning Strike	Lightning Strike is an inline image decompressor for viewing images compressed using Lightning Strike, Infinet Op's wavelet-based compression technology. Images compressed using this technology vary from 10:1 to 150:1 and higher; compression varies without significant loss of quality. Ride the bolt....Check it out for yourself!
LView Pro	LView Pro is a shareware product that enables the Web page designer to view and manipulate images—continuous use requires payment of registration fees. More information about LView Pro can be found at: http://www.lview.com. LView Pro is Copyright (C) 1993-1996 by Leonardo Haddad Loureiro.

Software	Descriptions
Fractal Design Painter 4.0 demo	Fractal Design Painter is the world's leading paint program. Painter's astounding Natural-Media features simulate the tools and textures of traditional artists' materials. From crayons to calligraphy, oils to airbrushes, pencils to watercolor, Painter turns your computer into an artist's studio. To find out more about Fractal Design, visit their Web site at http://www.fractal.com.
PALETTES	The Netscape 216 color palette.
Macromedia Shockwave	Shockwave is the standard for viewing interactive multimedia and high-impact graphics on the Web. For more information about Shockwave, visit Macromedia's Web site at http://www.macromedia.com.
Shockwave Animations	A number of Shockwave animations created by Darrel Plant.
Sizzler	Sizzler plug-in is a stream-based multimedia software plug-in for Netscape Navigator that allows Web users to play live, with real-time interactive animation and multimedia. Sizzler converter allows creative Web page designers to convert files to the Sizzler format in order to incorporate animation and multimedia into their Web site. To learn more about Sizzler, visit Totally Hip Software's Web site at http://www.totallyhip.com.

Software	Descriptions
Talker 2.0	Talker is a Netscape plug-in that lets Web pages talk and sing to Macintosh users, using Apple computer's text-to-speech software. Users may download all the software they need, including Apple's text-to-speech software, at the Talker Web site: http://www.mvpsolutions.com/plug-in/talker.html.
TEXTURES	Textures created by Daniel Gray for use in Web page design.
TrueSpeech	The TrueSpeech Player is an application that lets you play any TrueSpeech encoded sound files (WAV files) in real time as you are downloading them from the World Wide Web. The sound is played within seconds from the moment you begin to download the speech files. The TrueSpeech Player allows you to hear the sound without having to wait for the entire sound file transfer to be completed. Download the latest version at: http://www.dspg.com/internet.htm.
VDOLive 1.0	The client application that lets you watch streaming video over the Internet. No more waiting for lengthy file downloads. Visit http://www.vdolive.com to find out more, and download the latest version.

Technical Support

Technical support is available for installation-related problems only. The technical support office is open from 8:00 A.M. to 6:00 P.M. Monday through Friday and can be reached via the following methods:

Phone: (919) 544-9404 extension 81
Faxback Answer System: (919) 544-9404 extension 85
E-mail: help@vmedia.com
FAX: (919) 544-9472
World Wide Web: http://www.vmedia.com/support
America Online: keyword *Ventana*

Limits of Liability & Disclaimer of Warranty

The authors and publisher of this book have used their best efforts in preparing the CD-ROM and the programs contained in it. These efforts include the development, research, and testing of the theories and programs to determine their effectiveness. The authors and publisher make no warranty of any kind expressed or implied with regard to these programs or the documentation contained in this book.

The authors and publisher shall not be liable in the event of incidental or consequential damages in connection with, or arising out of, the furnishing, performance, or use of the programs, associated instructions, and/or claims of productivity gains.

Some of the software on this CD-ROM is shareware; there may be additional charges (owed to the software authors/makers) incurred for their registration and continued use. See individual program's README or VREADME.TXT files for more information.

appendix B

PageMill 2 Installation

Installing the Macintosh version of PageMill 2 is much like installing any other Mac application. You've probably been through the drill a few dozen times by now, but if not, just follow these simple steps and you'll have the program up and running in a flash. Before you begin the installation process, Adobe recommends that you shut off all virus-protection software and restart with extensions off (by holding down the Shift key while restarting). After restarting:

What About Windows?

As we go to press, we were not able to provide installation procedures for the Windows version of Adobe PageMill 2, due to the timing of the product release. We are committed to providing support for both platforms; you will find a file on the *Web Publishing with Adobe PageMill 2* Web site that details the Windows installation procedures.

1. If you're installing from CD-ROM, insert the CD-ROM in the CD-ROM drive. If you're installing from floppy disks, insert the first floppy disk. The disk folder will open automatically.

2. Double-click on the Install Adobe PageMill icon. The Installer "splash" screen will display. Click on the Continue button.

3. The Electronic End User License Agreement screen will display. Take a quick read of the text (if you're so inclined), and click Accept when you're ready to proceed. The Install Adobe PageMill dialog box will appear, as shown in Figure B-1.

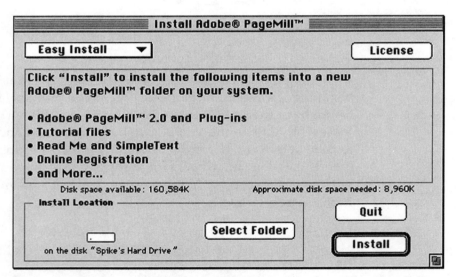

Figure B-1: If you're not sure what you need to load, go for an Easy Install. Just click the Install button, and the installation program will figure it out for you.

4. Easy Install is the no-brainer approach to installation. It will automatically figure out what to load, although it will gobble up some disk space. If your hard drive space is precious, and you want to pare things down, choose the Custom Installation option.

5. Select the folder that you want to place the PageMill files into, and click Install. The Installer will ask for your name, company, and serial number. You cannot install the program without entering a valid serial number. Click OK to proceed with installation.

6. If you're installing from floppy disks, you will be prompted to insert each subsequent disk. When the installation has run its course, you can click Quit.

7. Turn your virus protection software back on (if you turned it off), and restart your system.

Memory Requirements

By default, PageMill 2 will install itself with minimum memory requirements of 4,000K and a preferred size of 6,000K. If you have sufficient RAM, you'll probably want to raise these figures by a handful of megabytes. Most importantly, you should raise the memory settings each time you add a plug-in to PageMill, as you would with any browser. To change PageMill's memory settings, select the PageMill icon from the desktop (the program should not be running), and press Command+I to open the program's information window, as shown by Figure B-2. Enter the new memory settings, and close the window.

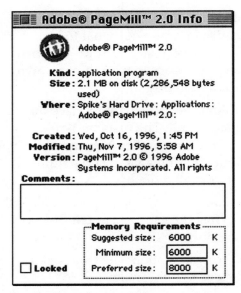

Figure B-2: It's a good idea to give your most important programs a little room to stretch their legs by raising their memory requirements.

Index

C

F

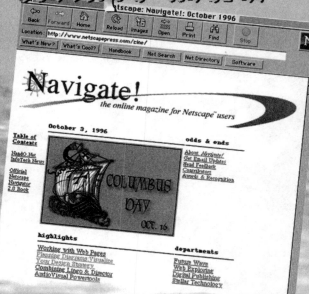

Design Online!

Interactive Web Publishing With Microsoft Tools

$49.99, 818 pages, illustrated, part #: 462-6

Take advantage of Microsoft's broad range of development tools to produce powerful web pages; program with VBScript; create virtual 3D worlds; and incorporate the functionality of Office applications with OLE. The CD-ROM features demos/lite versions of third party software, sample code.

Looking Good Online

$39.99, 450 pages, illustrated, part #: 469-3

Create well-designed, organized web sites—incorporating text, graphics, digital photos, backgrounds and forms. Features studies of successful sites and design tips from pros. The companion CD-ROM includes samples from online professionals; buttons, backgrounds, templates and graphics.

Internet Business 500

$39.95, 450 pages, illustrated, part #: 287-9

This authoritative list of the most useful, most valuable online resources for business is also the most current list, linked to a regularly updated *Online Companion* on the Internet. The companion CD-ROM features a hyperlinked version of the entire text of the book.

The Comprehensive Guide to VBScript

$39.99, 864 pages, illustrated, part #: 470-7

The only encyclopedic reference to VBScript and HTML commands and features. Complete with practical examples for plugging directly into programs. The companion CD-ROM features a hypertext version of the book, along with shareware, templates, utilities and more.

 Books marked with this logo include *Online Udates*™, which include free additional online resources, chapter updates and regularly updated links to related resources from Ventana.

Web Publishing With Adobe PageMill 2

$34.99, 450 pages, illustrated, part #: 458-2

Here's the ultimate guide to designing professional web pages. Now, creating and designing pages on the Web is a simple, drag-and-drop function. Learn to pump up PageMill with tips, tricks and troubleshooting strategies in this step-by-step tutorial for designing professional pages. The CD-ROM features Netscape plug-ins, original textures, graphical and text-editing tools, sample backgrounds, icons, buttons, bars, GIF and JPEG images, Shockwave animations.

Web Publishing With Macromedia Backstage 2

$49.99, 500 pages, illustrated, part #: 598-3

Farewell to HTML! This overview of all four tiers of Backstage lets users jump in at their own level. With the focus on processes as well as techniques, readers learn everything they need to create center-stage pages. The CD-ROM includes plug-ins, applets, animations, audio files, Director xTras and demos.

Web Publishing With QuarkImmedia

$39.99, 450 pages, illustrated, part #: 525-8

Use multimedia to learn multimedia, building on the power of QuarkXPress. Step-by-step instructions introduce basic features and techniques, moving quickly to delivering dynamic documents for the Web and other electronic media. The CD-ROM features an interactive manual and sample movie gallery with displays showing settings and steps. Both are written in QuarkImmedia.

Web Publishing With Microsoft FrontPage 97

$34.99, 500 pages, illustrated, part #: 478-2

Web page publishing for everyone! Streamline web-site creation and automate maintenance, all without programming! Covers introductory-to-advanced techniques, with hands-on examples. For Internet and intranet developers. The CD-ROM includes all web-site examples from the book, FrontPage add-ons, shareware, clip art and more.

Make it Multimedia

Microsoft SoftImage|3D Professional Techniques 🌐

$69.99, 524 pages, illustrated, part #: 499-5

Here's your comprehensive guide to modeling, animation &
rendering. Create intuitive, visually rich 3D images with this
award-winning technology. Follow the structured tutorial to
master modeling, animation and rendering, and to increase your
3D productivity. The CD-ROM features tutorials, sample scenes,
textures, scripts, shaders, images and animations.

LightWave 3D 5 Character Animation f/x 🌐

$69.99, 700 pages, illustrated, part #: 532-0

Master the fine—and lucrative—art of 3D character animation.
Traditional animators and computer graphic artists alike will
discover everything they need to know: lighting, motion,
caricature, composition, rendering ... right down to work-flow
strategies. The CD-ROM features a collection of the most popular
LightWave plug-ins, scripts, storyboards, finished animations,
models and much more.

3D Studio MAX f/x 🌐

$49.99, 552 pages, illustrated, part #: 427-8

Create Hollywood-style special effects! Plunge into 3D animation
with step-by-step instructions for lighting, camera movements,
optical effects, texture maps, storyboarding, cinematography,
editing and much more. The companion CD-ROM features free
plug-ins, all the tutorials from the book, 300+ original texture
maps and animations.

Looking Good in 3D 🌐

$39.99, 400 pages, illustrated, part #: 434-4

A guide to thinking, planning and designing in 3D. Become the
da Vinci of the 3D world! Learn the artistic elements involved in
3D design—light, motion, perspective, animation and more—to
create effective interactive projects. The CD-ROM includes
samples from the book, templates, fonts and graphics.

TO ORDER ANY VENTANA TITLE, COMPLETE THIS ORDER FORM AND MAIL OR FAX IT TO US, WITH PAYMENT, FOR QUICK SHIPMENT.

TITLE	PART #	QTY	PRICE	TOTAL

SHIPPING

For all standard orders, please ADD $4.50/first book, $1.35/each additional.
For "two-day air," ADD $8.25/first book, $2.25/each additional.
For orders to Canada, ADD $6.50/book.
For orders sent C.O.D., ADD $4.50 to your shipping rate.
North Carolina residents must ADD 6% sales tax.
International orders require additional shipping charges.

SUBTOTAL = $ _____

SHIPPING = $ _____

TAX = $ _____

TOTAL = $ _____

**Or, save 15%–order online.
http://www.vmedia.com**

Mail to: Ventana • PO Box 13964 • Research Triangle Park, NC 27709-3964 ☎ 800/743-5369 • Fax 919/544-9472

Name _____

E-mail _____   Daytime phone _____

Company _____

Address (No PO Box) _____

City _____   State _____   Zip _____

Payment enclosed ___VISA ___MC ___ Acc't # _____   Exp. date _____

Signature _____   Exact name on card _____

Check your local bookstore or software retailer for these and other bestselling titles, or call toll free: **800/743-5369**

MACROMEDIA

End-User License Agreement

PLEASE READ THIS DOCUMENT CAREFULLY BEFORE BREAKING THE SEAL ON THE MEDIA PACK-AGE. THIS AGREEMENT LICENSES THE ENCLOSED SOFTWARE TO YOU AND CONTAINS WARRANTY AND LIABILITY DISCLAIMERS. BY BREAKING THE SEAL ON THE MEDIA ENVELOPE, YOU ARE CONFIRMING YOUR ACCEPTANCE OF THE SOFTWARE AND AGREEING TO BECOME BOUND BY THE TERMS OF THIS AGREEMENT. IF YOU DO NOT WISH TO DO SO, DO NOT BREAK THE SEAL. INSTEAD, PROMPTLY RETURN THE ENTIRE PACKAGE, INCLUDING THE UNOPENED MEDIA PACKAGE, TO THE PLACE WHERE YOU OBTAINED IT, FOR A FULL REFUND.

1. Definitions

(a) "Macromedia« Software" means the software program included in the enclosed package, and all related updates supplied by Macromedia.

(b) "Macromedia Product" means the Macromedia Software and the related
documentation and models and multimedia content (such as animation, sound, and graphics), and all related updates supplied by Macromedia.

2. License. This Agreement allows you to:
(a) Use the Macromedia Software on a single computer.

(b) Make one copy of the Macromedia Software in machine-readable form solely for backup purposes. You must reproduce on any such copy all copyright
notices and any other proprietary legends on the original copy of the Macromedia Software.

(c) Certain Macromedia Software is licensed with additional rights as set forth in the Supplementary Rights Addendum that may be included in the package for this Macromedia Product.

3. Supplementary Licenses
Certain rights are not granted under this Agreement, but may be available under a separate agreement. If you would like to enter into a Site or Network License, please contact Macromedia.

4. Restrictions

You may not make or distribute copies of the Macromedia Product, or electronically transfer the Macromedia Software from one computer to another or over a network. You may not decompile, reverse engineer, disassemble, or otherwise reduce the Macromedia Software to a human-perceivable form. Youmay not modify, rent, resell for profit, distribute, or create derivativeworks based upon the Macromedia Software or any part thereof. You will notexport or reexport, directly or indirectly, the Macromedia Product into any country prohibited by the United States Export Administration Act and the regulations thereunder.

5. Ownership

The foregoing license gives you limited rights to use the Macromedia Software. Although you own the disk on which the Macromedia Software is recorded, you do not become the owner of, and Macromedia retains title to, the Macromedia Product, and all copies thereof. All rights not specifically granted in this Agreement, includin Federal and International Copyrights, are reserved by Macromedia.

6. Limited Warranties

(a) Macromedia warrants that, for a period of ninety (90) days from the date of delivery (as evidenced by a copy of your receipt): (i) when used with a recommended hardware configuration, the Macromedia Software will perform in substantial conformance with the documentation supplied as part of the Macromedia Product; and (ii) that the media on which the Macromedia Software is furnished will be free from defects in materials and workmanship under normal use. EXCEPT AS SET FORTH IN THE FOREGOING LIMITED WARRANTY, MACROMEDIA DISCLAIMS ALL OTHER WARRANTIES, EITHER EXPRESS OR IMPLIED, INCLUDING THE WARRANTIES OF MERCHANTABILITY, FITNESS FOR A PARTICULAR PURPOSE, AND NON-INFRINGEMENT. IF APPLICABLE LAW IMPLIES ANY WARRANTIES WITH RESPECT TO THE MACROMEDIA PRODUCT, ALL SUCH WARRANTIES ARE LIMITED IN DURATION TO NINETY (90)

DAYS FROM THE DATE OF DELIVERY. No oral or written information or advice given by Macromedia, its dealers, distributors, agents, or employees shall create a warranty or in any way increase the scope of this warranty.

(b) SOME STATES DO NOT ALLOW THE EXCLUSION OF IMPLIED WARRANTIES, SO THE ABOVE EXCLUSION MAY NOT APPLY TO YOU. THIS WARRANTY GIVES YOU SPECIFIC LEGAL RIGHTS AND YOU MAY ALSO HAVE OTHER LEGAL RIGHTS WHICH VARY FROM STATE TO STATE.

7. Exclusive Remedy Your exclusive remedy under Section 6 is to return the Macromedia Software to the place you acquired it, with a copy of your receipt and a description of the problem. Macromedia will use reasonable commercial efforts to supply you with a replacement copy of the Macromedia Software that substantially conforms to the documentation, provide a replacement for the defective media, or refund to you your purchase price for the Macromedia Software, at its option. Macromedia shall have no responsibility with respect to Macromedia Software that has been altered in any way, if the media has been damaged by accident, abuse, or misapplication, or if the non conformance arises out of use of the Macromedia Software in conjunction with software not supplied by Macromedia.

8. Limitations of Damages

(a) MACROMEDIA SHALL NOT BE LIABLE FOR ANY INDIRECT, SPECIAL, INCIDENTAL OR CONSEQUENTIAL DAMAGES (INCLUDING DAMAGES FOR LOSS OF BUSINESS, LOSS OF PROFITS, OR THE LIKE), WHETHER BASED ON BREACH OF CONTRACT, TORT (INCLUDING NEGLIGENCE), PRODUCT LIABILITY, OR OTHERWISE, EVEN IF MACROMEDIA OR ITS REPRESENTATIVES HAVE BEEN ADVISED OF THE POSSIBILITY OF SUCH DAMAGES AND EVEN IF A REMEDY SET FORTH HEREIN IS FOUND TO HAVE FAILED OF ITS ESSENTIAL PURPOSE.

(b) Macromedia's total liability to you for actual damages for any cause whatsoever will be limited to the greater of $500 or the amount paid by you for the Macromedia Software that caused such damages.

(c) SOME STATES DO NOT ALLOW THE LIMITATION OR EXCLUSION OF LIABILITY FOR INCIDENTAL OR CONSEQUENTIAL DAMAGES, SO THE ABOVE LIMITATION OR EXCLUSION MAY NOT APPLY TO YOU.

9. Basis of Bargain

The limited warranty, exclusive remedies, and limited liability set forth above are fundamental elements of the basis of the bargain between Macromedia and you. Macromedia would not be able to provide the MacromediaSoftware on an economic basis without such limitations.

10. Government End Users

The Macromedia Product is "Restricted Computer Software." RESTRICTED RIGHTS LEGEND Use, duplication, or disclosure by the Government is subject to restrictions as set forth in subparagraph (c)(1)(ii) of the Rights in Technical Data and Computer Software clause at DFARS 252.227-7013. Manufacturer: Macromedia, Inc., 600 Townsend, San Francisco, CA 94103

11. General

This Agreement shall be governed by the internal laws of the State of California. This Agreement contains the complete agreement between the parties with respect to the subject matter hereof, and supersedes all prior or contemporaneous agreements or understandings, whether oral or written. All questions concerning this Agreement shall be directed to: Macromedia, Inc., 600 Townsend, San Francisco, CA 94103, Attention: Chief Financial Officer.

Macromedia is a registered trademark of Macromedia, Inc.
Suzanne Porta
Publisher Programs Associate
Macromedia, Inc.
600 Townsend Street, Suite 310
San Francisco, CA, 94103 USA
e-mail: sporta@macromedia.com